ADVANCE PRAISE FOR

Black Outlaws

"Carlyle Van Thompson has done it again! An audacious literary and cultural critic willing to ask unflinching questions about the limits and liabilities of racialist logics, Thompson takes on four canonical African-American writers and their embattled Black male protagonists (Richard Wright's Cross Damon, Chester Himes' Charles Taylor, Walter Mosley's Ezekiel Rawlins, and Ernest Gaines' Jefferson) to thematize the traumatic implications of race-based marginalization. And he is the perfect guide for such an important journey through America's psycho-racial landscape—bold, iconoclastic, confrontational, and unapologetic. Thompson carefully demonstrates the extent to which race-based vulnerabilities are fundamentally constituted by the naturalized realities of gendered differences and the seemingly effortless reproduction of legal and class hierarchies. If Du Bois famously framed a version of the Black American experience as a question of always being made to feel one's status as a 'problem,' Thompson extends that insight by asking us to imagine such renderings of problematic blackness (of literally and figuratively 'outlawed' black masculinities) as institutionalizing a definition of racial criminality that includes African Americans into the narrative of American life as a kind of constitutive exclusion. You've probably read all four of these authors before—many times. But you haven't quite read them like this!"

John L. Jackson, Jr., Author of
Racial Paranoia: The Unintended Consequences of Political Correctness

Black Outlaws

AFRICAN AMERICAN LITERATURE AND CULTURE

Expanding and Exploding the Boundaries

Carlyle V. Thompson
General Editor

Vol. 13

PETER LANG
New York • Washington, D.C./Baltimore • Bern
Frankfurt • Berlin • Brussels • Vienna • Oxford

Carlyle Van Thompson

Black Outlaws

Race, Law, and Male Subjectivity in African American Literature and Culture

PETER LANG
New York • Washington, D.C./Baltimore • Bern
Frankfurt • Berlin • Brussels • Vienna • Oxford

Library of Congress Cataloging-in-Publication Data

Thompson, Carlyle Van.
Black outlaws: race, law, and male subjectivity
in African American literature and culture / Carlyle Van Thompson.
p. cm. —— (African American literature and culture: expanding
and exploding the boundaries; v. 13)
Includes bibliographical references and index.
1. American literature——African American authors——History and criticism.
2. African Americans——Legal status, laws, etc. 3. Outlaws in literature.
4. Masculinity in literature. 5. Subjectivity in literature.
6. African American men in literature. 7. Law and literature——
United States——History. I. Title.
PS153.N5T477   810.9'896073——dc22   2009043496
ISBN 978-0-8204-8637-6
ISSN 1528-3887

Bibliographic information published by **Die Deutsche Nationalbibliothek**.
Die Deutsche Nationalbibliothek lists this publication in the "Deutsche
Nationalbibliografie"; detailed bibliographic data is available
on the Internet at http://dnb.d-nb.de/.

The paper in this book meets the guidelines for permanence and durability
of the Committee on Production Guidelines for Book Longevity
of the Council of Library Resources.

© 2010 Peter Lang Publishing, Inc., New York
29 Broadway, 18th floor, New York, NY 10006
www.peterlang.com

Printed in the United States of America

Dedication

This book is proudly dedicated to Cynthia-Pullen Thompson and Jabari Joseph James Jawara Thompson along with my intellectually tenacious students at Medgar Evers College and the Center for Worker Education at City College both institutions in the City University of New York, especially the Black males who are writing themselves into existence.

Contents

Acknowledgments

This project, the last book in a trilogy on race and white supremacist culture in America, is directly related to my teaching of African American literature at Medgar Evers College, CUNY and at City College, Center for Worker Education especially that in my African American Literature II from the Harlem Renaissance to the Present class. Many of the students in these classes combine academic work and other responsibilities with a level of intellectual intensity that allows them to write themselves into existence in a manner that does not reinforce and reinscribe the dominant discourses of racial, class, color, ethnic, and gender hegemony. Here many students moved to sophisticated critical analysis, especially with regard to their high-stakes research papers. Accordingly, my sagacious and sanguine students at Medgar Evers College and City College infuse this project because it was in these classrooms that I began to raise the critical questions and test out the theories associated with Black male subjectivity and the issues of race, gender, and law within the context of America's white supremacist culture, a patriarchal culture that tends to especially marginalize and demonize Black males with legal and extralegal means. From the Fugitive Slaves Laws and the *Dred Scott* Supreme Court decision of 1857 to the death penalty, laws and extra-legal measures contextualize my discussion of Black male subjectivity.

Paradoxically, but not surprisingly, many of the students in these classes have not been introduced to African American literature in any extensive manner before coming to college, but they embrace these texts because they can see themselves and their issues being illustrated and examined in ways that convey the complexity of Black male life in American society and culture. That too many Black males are in a precarious economic and psychological state (I refer to the tens of thousands of Black males incarcerated in prisons or in detention centers, on probation, unemployed, underemployed, uneducated, and in foster care) speaks to the problematic notion of America being a democracy where all individuals regardless of race, ethnicity, class, gender, or color are viewed as full citizens and viable members of the society. In fact, in some tragic sense many Black males have become enemies of the state. Like the majestically democratic aspect of Black classical music called jazz, this issue of inclusion is central to the lives of many Medgar Evers College students and their families; thus it infuses my critical analysis of literature and culture. For me there is a symbiotic relationship between effective teaching and academic scholarship. Under President Edison O. Jackson's purposeful intervention the Black Male Empowerment Center has grown and developed its goal to support Black males in their intellectual pursuits; the many speakers and students involved in this program fuel this project. As with my first two projects, President Jackson has been a staunch supporter; Black male students at Medgar Evers College and indeed in the City University of New York could not have a stronger advocate.

I am also grateful for the enduring intellectual support and friendship of my colleague George P. Cunningham of Brooklyn College, CUNY; he was always available for me to work out both the major issues as well as the minor problems. Although we would often embark on different intellectual roads in our numerous discussions, we would often turn philosophical corners and come face to face on many of the contextual and theoretical issues in African American literature and culture. Again James de Jongh of City College, CUNY, and the Institute for Research on African Diaspora in the Americas and the Caribbean (IRADAC) have my sincere gratitude for their continuous support and appreciation of my literary projects. My previous two books have significantly benefited from the Works in Progress at CUNY on the African Diaspora, an Interdisciplinary Conferences, and this current project is no exception. Whether I presented a paper or just attended the panels at the conference, the benefits were enormous because of the intellectual intensity and the collegial atmosphere among the many CUNY professors working in similar and dissimilar areas. Of special note here must be Jon-Christian Suggs of John Jay College, CUNY, and the Graduate Center and his seminal work: *Whispered Consolations: Law and Narrative in African American Literature;* Suggs' text represents a definitive study on race and literature. Again Phyllis Korper at Peter Lang, here in New York, has been enormously supportive in advancing my intellectual work to the national and international levels of academia and beyond. Their enduring support for my projects and especially this innovative series *African American Literature and Culture: Expanding and Exploding the Boundaries* is much appreciated. To date the series has published some of the most important scholarship in African American literature and culture, especially by junior scholars.

And to Cynthia Pullen-Thompson, your enduring support makes these literary projects more rewarding, enjoyable, and productive, especially our in-depth discussions of African American literature and writers. Like me, you enjoy the written word with its power to transform and your feedback, questions, and intellectual intensity bring another level of sophistication to this project.

Foreword

In America's white supremacist society there remains the critical need for African American scholars to expose, denounce, and examine those thoughts that are contradictory to the notion of a democratic philosophy, epistemology, and cosmology. In my first extremely controversial book on race and Black male subjectivity, *The Tragic Black Buck: Racial Masquerading in the American Literary Imagination,* I critically examine the paradoxical theme of light-skinned Black male individuals passing for white in Charles Waddell Chesnutt's *The House Behind the Cedars,* James Weldon Johnson's *The Autobiography of an Ex-Coloured Man,* F. Scott Fitzgerald's *The Great Gatsby,* and William Faulkner's *Light in August.* And in my second provocative critical project, *Eating the Black Body: Miscegenation as Sexual Consumption in African American Literature and Culture,* I critically examine the issue of sexual violence (the mutilation, castration, and lynching of Black males and the whippings, molestation, and rape of Black females as acts of sexual consumption on the part of sadistic white males in the context of Black people's enduring resistance) in the works of Richard Wright, John Oliver Killens, Gayl Jones, and Octavia Butler in their works "Between the World and Me (1935)," *Youngblood* (1954), *Corregidora* (1979), and *Kindred* (1985). This seminal project, *Black Outlaws: Race, Law, and Male Subjectivity in African American Literature and Culture,* comes out of my ongoing questions, speculations, and concerns about race, Black male life, and legal matters in America's intrinsically white supremacist and patriarchal culture. For Black people, especially Black males, the quest for the American Dream represents the fundamental and pervasive paradox of their existence in a country that has too often denied their humanity and their desire for socioeconomic inclusion.

Black males in African American literature from the slave narratives to the present have always represented a powerful presence in their sanguine attempts to achieve socioeconomic subjectivity within the parameters of America's white supremacist culture. Beginning with the brutal and bloody enslavement and forced migration of Africans, Black males especially represent a paradox in that they have been viewed as a critical to the development of white wealth through forced breeding with Black women and through their labor as well as being viewed as a threat to white male domination. Like ghosts dragging their weighty chains through shadowy and mysterious caverns, Black people have endured lifetimes of deep psychological trauma with little or no systematic healing. In many ways Frederick Douglass' *Narrative of the Life of Frederick Douglass, An American Slave Written by Himself* (1845) and David Walker's *Appeal, in Four Articles; Together with a Preamble, to the Coloured Citizens of the World, but in Particular, and Very Expressly, to Those of the United States of America* (1829) represent the seminal call of Black male subjectivity that many other Black male writers have responded to in terms of the Black man's desire for agency within the oppressive conditions of white male supremacy and its ongoing legacy. The holocaust of the African slave experience in America along with the philosophy of white supremacy have characterized the Black man as a "buck," a derogatory and racist term that denotes the assumed sexual prowess and sexual threat to white women, in particular. Few scholars can argue against the concept that Black manhood in America is deeply rooted in the slave experience and the period of Jim Crow segregation. Douglass and Walker represent the steadfast determination for freedom as well as white people's anger and apprehension with regard to miscegenation between Black males and white females. To many racist whites, Douglass represents their worst nightmare: he obtained his freedom, he spoke out against white people's oppression of Blacks, and after his Black wife of forty-four years died, he married his white secretary, Helen Pitts. On the other hand, Walker who opposed miscegenation issued a clarion call to slave owners and enslaved Blacks about the horrors of America's slavery. Thomas Jefferson, with his racist views in *Notes on the State of Virginia* (1782), is fundamental to an understanding of whites' apprehensions of miscegenation and concerns of the unreadability of Black people. Further, the explosive and controversial film *The Birth of a Nation* (1915) by D. W. Griffith is critical for an understanding of both the ongoing racist construction of the Black male in some literary texts and the iconography associated with the Black male as dangerous and lecherous. From Charles Waddell Chesnutt to Walter Mosley, many Black male writers have taken on the challenge of depicting a true, however paradoxical it might seem, image of the Black man in his enduring quest for agency, to be part of America and the American Dream.

With the prophetic Frederick Douglass and David Walker in mind, this project will examine the Black man as a paradox in African American literature. That many Black males have been caught in the pernicious web of racial oppression and that their struggles have not always been successful are aspects of the tragic circumstances that many Black writers explicate.

In my view, many Black male figures in much of African American literature can be viewed as heroic figures; their struggles highlight the tremendous spirit and determination in the face of relentless racial and racial injustice. Indeed the snarling winds of white supremacy and white nationalism have created a perpetual hurricane in the socioeconomic lives of too many Black men. Too often, tragic circumstances are used by some writers to contextualize Black male representations in their attempt to achieve stable socioeconomic subjectivity. Beyond an analysis of the desperate conditions of these Black men, my enduring focus will be on the truly innovative and bodacious attempts to survive and thrive despite the challenges of white supremacy and white nationalism. Indeed these four African American literary texts challenge the too often stereotypical characterizations of Black males and represent them in the full complexity of their desires and subjectivities.

1. A Disturbing and Paradoxical Presence: Black Male Subjectivity, Legal Matters and Redemption in African American Literature and Culture

Negroes [Blacks] want to be treated like men [and women]: a perfectly straightforward statement, containing only seven words. People who have mastered Kant, Hegel, Shakespeare, Marx, Freud, and the Bible find this statement utterly impenetrable. The idea seems to threaten profound, barely conscious assumptions. A kind of panic paralyzes their features, as though they found themselves trapped at the edge of a steep place.

—*James Baldwin, "Fifth Avenue Uptown"*

In American film, we experience some of the most powerful representations of Black males and Black male subjectivity, especially with regard to the American legal system and issues involving criminality. *Training Day* (2001) and *American Gangster* (2007), both starring Denzel Washington, are extremely constructive in considering many Black males and their problematic relationships with America's legal system and the extra-legal rituals that have affected Black people since the days of enslavement and Jim Crow. From the slave patrollers to the police, white males with authority have sought to keep Blacks both in a state of enduring apprehension and in a marginal socioeconomic position.

Police corruption and malfeasance are always a provocative subject in fact and in cinematic fiction; we are drawn to these controversial narratives because they represent the fundamental antithesis of America's idyllic notion of justice, law, and order. Directed by Antoine Fuqua, *Training Day* presents us with one of the most disturbing representations in modern American society: the violent and fundamentally corrupt police officer, who also happens to be a Black male. Considering the period of enslavement, not surprisingly, Black males have an extremely long history of being victims of America's legal and extra-legal systems of justice; often times these systems were not easily distinguished. With numerous white judges, prosecutors, police officers, and correction officers being members of the Ku Klux Klan and other white supremacist groups, many Blacks have always looked askance at their roles in upholding justice in the society. Police misconduct and police brutality remain a constant plague in many Black communities because of their inherent power as articulated by Damu Smith:

> Police have unique and awesome power in that the government has placed authority at their disposal, and has delegated to them not only the right but the responsibility to exercise that authority to a degree that no other individual, official, or organization legally enjoys. Not only are the police expected to inquire, to observe, and to detain, but they are expected to use violence and force, even deadly force if deemed appropriate. No other occupation can legally claim this degree of official sanction. (45)

As Smith explicates, this amount of total power renders the possibility for official abuse. However, Smith's analysis is ripe with essentialism about the police; white male police officers have certain rights and privileges that many Black police officers do not, and Black officers are subjected to more disciplinary actions that their white counterparts.

In *Training Day*, Alonzo Harris (Denzel Washington) plays the role of a Black highly decorated, well-respected, and extraordinary evil sergeant in the narcotics division of the Los Angeles Police Department; we see an American tragedy encapsulated by power, greed, and deception. The true manifestation of Harris' extraordinary malevolence becomes evident in his tutelage of the white Jake Hoyt (Ethan Hawke), a new member of the narcotics squad who desires a quick promotion if he can cut the mustard with his new boss, Alonzo Harris. Unknown to Jake is the fact that from Alonzo's phone call to his home until the end of the day, he will be tested, tempted, and turned into the antithesis of a police officer who protects and serves his community. With a new wife and a nine-month-old baby girl at home, Jake Hoyt leaves for his new assignment in a pristine search of the American Dream (represented by the homes of his superiors on the police force); however, like the naïve Jay Gatsby in F. Scott Fitzgerald's *The Great Gatsby* (1925), he will find some insurmountable forces lying in wait for him during the next twenty-four hours. Additionally, with Jake's statement about the other police officers that he admires for their splendid homes we discover his fatal flaw—ambition and a desire to please those in power.

Like Clyde Griffiths in Theodore Dreiser's classic novel *American Tragedy* (1925), we are faced with desire, conflict, and a tragic resolution. Alonzo's phone call represents the first indication that things will not be standard operating procedure; Jake's wife answers the phone, and her facial expression conveys something is not right about the caller (we get the sense that the caller has said something somewhat inappropriate or disrespectful). Here, Jake, preparing to bring his newly pressed uniform and polished badge, is thrown off guard and receives explicit instructions from Alonzo on what to wear, what weapons to bring, and where to met Alonzo, emphasizing that only fairies [faggots] go to roll call. Later, he tells Jake that he has to unlearn everything he learned at the Police Academy because that stuff will get him killed; the power dynamic becomes established here and there is the sense that Jake's manhood is undermined in the presence of his wife, who listens to Jake's responses to Alonzo. When they first meet in the Quality Café diner, Alonzo is dressed in a black knit skullcap, a black leather jacket, a buttoned-up black shirt; here we understand that by Alonzo's flip ebullience he will be constantly throwing Jake off guard and Jake will have to learn to always be on guard; nothing will be normal. From the diner where they meet to Alonzo's car that he calls the office (beyond the obvious phallocentric connotation the black Monte Carlo muscle car signifies on both Alonzo's hyper-heterosexual masculinity as well as his problem in Las Vegas with the sadistically violent Russians, who are serious about collecting debts), Jake is psychologically challenged and physically tested as he is manipulated into smoking acid-laced marijuana and drinking beer and whiskey while on duty. Alonzo's rationalization is that narcotics undercover police officers have to behave like criminals in order to trap criminals. Early in the film, in one particularly disturbing scene in his car, Alonzo stops his "sexy" car in the middle of an intersection and points his 9mm gun in Jake's face when Jake refuses one of his many orders. At gunpoint, Jake realizes that his American Dream of a promotion and a big house is disappearing like an ice cube in the afternoon sun, so he decides go against what he knows is the right thing to do; he smokes the acid-laced marijuana.

Before this incident, Alonzo, with a demeanor of nihilism and narcissism, informs Jake that this is the only day and he has to prove himself and repeats his analogy of fairies being those officers in uniform. Jake, hearing his wife's cautionary words in his head and having no idea of the full significance, replies: "I will do anything you want me to do." Thus Jake's training has begun, but there is also insight and information rendered that lets Jake develop respect for Harris. Alonzo informs his mentee that he has 38 cases pending trial, 63 active investigations, 250 cases he cannot clear and that "judges gave over fifteen thousand man-years of incarceration time based on his investigation." Also, as the head of the team, he supervises five officers with different personalities and problems, and most importantly, he informs Jake that he could be number six if he acts right. The Hegelian master and slave dialectic comes to mind as the innocent and in some ways even angelic Jake will discover a demonic and fundamentally disingenuous training officer. Here Alonzo's seductive discourse presents himself as an aggressive detective who is not always successful with his cases. Jake asks him if he will be taught the "old school Rodney King shit," and Alonzo cruises into teacher role and tells him that they do not roll like that anymore; the criminals are too strong and that it is now about psychological warfare. Psychologically, what becomes apparent is that despite their obvious racial differences Alonzo and Jake are one and the same; Jake is a younger, more naïve, and more ethical version of Alonzo. This twenty-hour journey into police hell becomes a long Lacanian moment for Jake.

Training Day illustrates a gradual escalation of criminal activity in the guise of law enforcement, all designed to test Jake's limits of moral and ethical conduct. What also becomes clear from Alonzo's Machiavellian statements is his problematic moral and ethical conduct. When questioning Jake about his wife and daughter, Alonzo reveals he has four sons and is willing to help Jake's wife have a son because he cannot miss in that area; this remark recalls Alonzo's question about Jake "tapping the ass" of his first female supervisor. Alonzo's sexual crudeness and blatant disrespect here are unmistakable, but Jake, striving for a permanent assignment, is in no position to aggressively challenge his superior officer. Their first action involves a stop of three youthful college students (two white males and a white female) who bought drugs from one of Alonzo's seventeen-year-old Latino informants, Neto (Abel Soto). Here like a lion pouncing upon a young gazelle, Alonzo terrorizes the white college students by using profanity, putting his gun in their faces, and threatening to take their vehicle and have Neto and his friends "run a train" on the white girl. Alonzo takes their marijuana, their pipe, their cigarettes, and while pulling on the ear of the driver threatens to slap the white girl and knock the taste out of her mouth if she moves her hand from the glass. This "college lesson," where there is no arrest or citation will be mild in terms of the training lesson that Jake will experience; paradoxically, this is the marijuana mixed with PCP that Jake consumes. The importance of this scene resides in the fact that some whites come from their communities into Black and Latino urban communities to buy drugs, resulting in an escalation of crime in these neighborhoods. As Christian Parenti argues in *Lockdown America: Police and Prisons in the Age of Crisis* (2000), the growing importance of the city has led to a zero tolerance level for crime:

> In the last decade the pressure to police effectively and secure urban areas has become all the more important. For centuries 'the urban' has been synonymous with filth, lawlessness, and danger, but in recent years cities have taken on renewed economic and social importance as sites of accumulation, speculation, and innovative profit making. For cities to work as they must they must be, or appear and feel, safe . . . . This polarization of urban space and social relations has in turn required a new layer of regulation and exclusion, so as to protect the new hyper-aestheticized, playground quarters of the postmodern metropolis from their flip sides of misery. This contradiction, between the dangers of the cities and their

value, has spawned yet another revolution in American law enforcement: the rise of zero tolerance/quality of life policing. (70)

What is critical here is that Black and Latino police officers such as Alonzo Harris are playing a significant role in making the urban communities safer for whites, especially with gentrification on the rise. Providing another lesson (referred to as "manning up") to Jake, Alonzo states that "a good narcotics agent should have narcotics in his blood." Further rationalizing his point, Alonzo states that an undercover officer who refuses to consume drugs could be killed. What becomes clearer to viewers and to Jake is that the demarcation line between criminals and undercover officers is not finite; there is extreme slippage. This suggests the entrapment strategies that some police use to arrest criminals so that they can obtain information about higher-level criminals, especially drug dealers. Alonzo's "college lesson" is repeated when Jake jumps out of the car when he views a young Latina Catholic high school female being sexually assaulted by two degenerates. After watching Jake fight it out with the two men until he is able to handcuff them, Alonzo then proceeds to search them and terrorize them by taking their drugs and money. One of them calls Alonzo a bitch and tells him to "suck his dick." Alonzo hits the bloodied suspect in the throat and threatens to shoot him in his testicles, leaving only one nut. In language that recalls the beating and sodomy of Abner Louima in Brooklyn, New York, Alonzo hits him in the groin with one of two 9mm pistols and states: "I'd cut your fucking dick off and stick it up your funky ass. Bitch." Again these criminal rapists (one Black and the other Latino) are not arrested; however, back in the 'office" Alonzo and Jake eventually bond after Jake agrees with Alonzo that Jake did what he had do by using a choke hold on one of the rapists, which Alonzo reminds him is a direct violation of Los Angeles police department procedure. "To protect the sheep, you got to catch the wolf. It takes a wolf to catch a wolf...Protect the sheep by killing wolves," reiterates Alonzo in another of his pedagogical moments. Jake begins to realize the complexity of his role as an undercover officer: he attempts to imitate Alonzo by howling like a wolf although Alonzo says his first attempts sound more like a rooster. And despite his initial criticism, Alonzo with a modicum of sincerity compliments him and acknowledges that Jake did "the right thing" by fending off the rapists because it reminded him of his days as a inexperienced police officer.

On another misadventure in the Imperial Courts section of the hood that appears to the now-suspicious Jake to be an official undercover police action (Alonzo has Jake put on a windbreaker identifying himself as a police officer), he discovers the absolutely criminal and violently hazardous aspects of Alonzo's behavior. Information for this investigation is obtained by forcing a pen down the throat of a drug dealer named Blue

(Snoop Dog) until he vomits up three bags of drugs; like a vicious pit-bull running loose in the streets, Alonzo then sarcastically threatens him with arrest and ten to thirty years in prison if he does not come up with the name and address of a higher-level drug dealer, Sandman, a gang member currently incarcerated. With a Chinese restaurant menu passing as a warrant, Alonzo bangs on the door of Sandman's residence, announcing that he has a search warrant. Sandman's wife (Macy Gray) with her squeaky voice and ostentatious fingernails, sensing that Jake is a rookie and smelling the liquor on his breath, begins to challenge him: "Punk-ass, bitch-ass, crooked-ass cop" while Alonzo searches the bedroom for drugs and money. After Alonzo pockets Sandman's money, he arrogantly states that he did not find anything and announces to the woman that a mistake was made. This scene escalates to chaotic violence when the women discovers that the money was taken and screams out to the gangbangers across the street that Alonzo and Jake are not police officers and that she wants her money back. Like a violent scenes out of a Westerns like *High Noon* and *Gunsmoke* or gangster films like *Pulp Fiction, Scarface, The Godfather*, and *American Gangster,* Alonzo enrages in an full-fledge shootout with five gangbangers. With little or no respect for innocent bystanders or Black people in their homes, Alonzo and the tattooed gang-bangers exchange automatic gunfire until Jake is able to drive them away as bullets come crashing into the rear window of the car. What becomes truly interesting about this scene is that Alonzo and the gangbangers are holding and shooting their automatic pistols in the same manner; there is no distinction in their mannerisms. Alonzo's philosophy is clearly stated: "We the police we can do anything." Indeed, throughout the film Alonzo Harris dresses in all black with bling-bling jewelry (ironically, this includes a big platinum-and-diamond crucifix) and his badge (when needed) hanging from his neck; the ostentatious jewelry and the badge announce the central conflict, a gangster–detective.

This violent encounter causes Jake additional stress and frustration as he articulates fears of being handcuffed and placed in an prison orange jumpsuit. Then the film presents an Oedipal fork in the road as Alonzo orders Jake to stop the car. Here Alonzo tells Jake that if cannot handle the level of violence that they just experienced, he should go back to the precinct and "Get a nice job lighting flares or measuring car wrecks." With unmistakable intensity and defiance, Alonzo bluntly informs Jake that he has to decide if he is a wolf or a sheep. Showing his tattoo and foreshadowing the film's conclusion "Death is Certain, Life is Not" inked on his forearm with crossed swords below, Alonzo encourages Jake to get his ink. Tortured and conflicted, Jake decides to get back in the car with Alonzo and resume his training day. Jake has now faced unexpected violence and possibly deadly confrontations, but the most disturbing aspects have been the things that his training officer has seduced and forced him to do with his promotion to detective as the proverbial carrot constantly dangling before him. Like the strange sounds and strange animals dangling from the trees in Joseph Conrad's *The Heart of Darkness* (1899), this film becomes a model of how Black and Third World countries and neighborhoods are characterized in many Hollywood films. In the neighborhood or "The Jungle" where Alonzo's El Salvadorian mistress or "dime" Sara (Eva Mendez) lives, Alonzo informs Jake that he has all of these niggers under his thumb. Here Alonzo's professional police corruption becomes mirrored by his personal/pleasurable corruption as Jake becomes aware of Alonzo and Sara's son (Kyiel N. Jolly); after eating, Jake babysits and falls asleep while Alonzo and Sara have sexual relations. Alonzo's narcissism and emotional detachment are clearly evident in his relationship with his young son; his only action of affection is to kiss his hand and place it on his son's forehead.

Not surprisingly, Jake's make-the-grade-or-fail test continues, but there is the sense that more portentous experiences are ahead as he is caught in a paradox of promotion or demotion. Just as there exists a hierarchy of criminals (Blue and Sandman), the film illustrates a hierarchy of corruption within the Los Angeles Police Department. The Three Wise Men: Captain Lou Jacobs, Stan Gursky who runs the D. A. shooting team (Tom Berenger), and Detective Doug Rosselli are the white men who call the shots for Alonzo and his criminal crew of police officers. The critical issue here is that despite Alonzo's superior status over Jake, white male supremacy remains the order of the day. As Norm Stamper argues in *Breaking Rank* (2005): "Clean or dirty cops in America have always served the elites: white, moneyed, propertied, the politically entrenched. It is not hard to understand why people of color, the poor, and younger Americans did not and do not, look upon the police as 'theirs'" (362). At an upscale restaurant (an obvious contrast to the Quality Cafe), Alonzo introduces Jake to his white handlers, and it is here that we hear for the second time that Alonzo had an expensive weekend in Las Vegas involving the Russian mafia. Although Alonzo attempts to shrug off the precarious and potentially lethal situation, Captain Jacobs informs him that the "Russians don't care if you're a cop. They'll wack you. You ought to get on a plane." Alonzo's haughty response is that he has a plan to come up with the money by "taxing' one of his first informants. Obtaining his white masters' approval to take money (tax) from one of his informants, Alonzo receives the ominous warning: "I do not want to see you on the front page like the others" [corrupt police officers]. Jake's training day is now at a high level upon meeting the Three Wise Men and upon seeing Alonzo opening Stan Gursky's car and placing a bundle of money in the trunk (which we later learns is $40,000) to pay the Three Wise Men for arrest warrants, for knowledge of when drug tests will be schedule, and basic protection for his criminal activities while on duty. In terms of analogies Alonzo represents the American Dream to Jake, and the Three Wise Men represent the American Dream to Alonzo.

Jake's test and final examination occur at the home of Alonzo's "friend" Roger (Scott Glenn), a retired big-time drug dealer who plans to go to the Philippines. They have already been here in order for Alonzo to ascertain if Roger would be home later in the day. It was here that Jake met Roger, drank liquor, and was told that he was just like Alonzo when Alonzo was a rookie detective. Now that he has the "green light" from the Three Wise Men, Alonzo begins to put things in motion to "tax" Roger. For this investigation Alonzo and his crew of five other corrupt police officers need a legitimate warrant, tools for digging, a power saw, protective armor, and shotguns; however, Jake remains clueless to what this operation is about and what critical role Alonzo will require him to play until is too late. With shotguns and automatic weapons pointed at him, Alonzo informs Roger that the Three Wise Men require that he be taxed and that he "gotta render unto Caesar." Alonzo further explains that they [the Three Wise Men] have "their boats, and mistresses, house payments" and that he is just a lowly civil servant doing what he is told. Knowing that Roger's stash is underneath the kitchen floor, they dig and come up with a trunk with $4 million, but the official story will be that there was only $3 million. When Alonzo reveals that each officer will receive $250,000, Jake refuses stating that the only checks he receives have "L.A.P.D." on them. Alonzo and the other officers realize that Jake represents a serious threat if he does not take his part of the money, so Alonzo creates a final test for Jake. Alonzo orders Jake to shoot Roger in cold blood. This represents the supreme test, and the critical question here is: How far will Jake go for success, for a promotion? Because Jake refuses to shoot Roger, Alonzo methodically kills him with a shotgun; but the fabricated and collaborated story will be that Jake shot Roger after another officer was shot twice by Roger.

Despite Alonzo's statement to Jake: "Congratulations. You're gonna get a medal of valor for this," Jake refuses to claim any responsibility for Roger's death and repeatedly insists that Alonzo shot Roger. Here we have the most important struggle in the film; a rookie detective who is in serious conflict with his superior officer and the other members of the detective squad over a premeditated murder and theft of evidence. Alonzo has by now also exposed Jake to a number of his illegal activities (and those of his superiors who support and condone Alonzo's illicit activities). Jake bluntly informs Alonzo: "I did not sign up for this." Sensing the seriousness of the situation (all the detectives must have the same story when other senior detectives come to investigate this police shooting, especially if a former police officer is shot), Alonzo with a shotgun pointed at Jake suggests another lethal scenario that involves Jake being killed in the line of duty and leaving behind a wife and an infant child. Enraged by yet another threat and upset because this represents the second time that Alonzo has pointed a gun at him, Jake grabs the shotgun and threats to shoot as Alonzo looks up at the gun. Now with this reversal in roles, the confrontation has been elevated to its extreme level because now the other detectives are poised to shoot Jake despite Alonzo's passionate pleas for everyone to relax. Indeed one detective suggests that Jake is an informant working for the Feds; except for Alonzo who is a vulnerable position, all of the other detectives want to kill Jake to protect themselves and their money. The stakes are extremely high. Now comes Jake's final lesson; Alonzo informs him "that this is the nature of the business" and that he has to be willing to go all the way. More importantly, Alonzo reiterates that five decorated officers will testify that Jake shot Roger and then reminds Jake that he has been smoking PCP and drinking alcohol all day; all this will be significant because Stan Gursky leads the D.A shooting investigation team and he controls the testing of officers involved in police-related shootings. Now Jake has an epiphany, puts all the pieces together and realizes that Alonzo has been planning this scenario all day. Alonzo corrects him to say that he has actually been planning it all week, and part of the plan was to place Jake in a vulnerable position with regard to drugs and alcohol. Assuming the role of the superior officer, Alonzo tells Jake: "You give me eighteen months and I will give you a career." Amazingly, despite having a shotgun being pointing at him, Alonzo continues to talk as if he is in control of the situation; and again places Jake at an Oedipal fork in the road. He tells Jake to either go outside and clear his head (which means going along with the fabricated scenario of the shooting and taking the money) or shoot him; the clear issue here is that Alonzo is giving Jake the choices and at no point does Jake articulate or make his own choices. However, once he gives the shotgun to Alonzo, Jake does make one choice. He hits Paul (Dr. Dre), the Black detective who twice threatened to shoot him. We get the clear sense that this represents Jake's displaced rage; Alonzo is the person that Jake would really like to punch in the face, but he still believes that there is some hope for his inclusion on the team (on leaving his house, Jake compared this training day to trying out for the football team).

The deeper paradox of Jake's learning a lesson of Alonzo's type of justice is that oftentimes white drug dealers are allowed to operate because they have the resources to pay off police and other legal authorities whereas small time drug dealers such as Blue and Sandman are arrested and do significant time in prison. Roger's stash of $4 million represents an extremely long history of drug dealing. This is why Alonzo becomes annoyed when Jake jumps out of the car to help the Latina girl who is being assaulted by the two crackheads; Alonzo's focus is on the serious crimes because they represent his opportunity to receive enormous illegal monies. This recalls the Los Angeles Police Department's Rampart corruption scandal, which involved police officers stealing illegal drugs, framing gang members and committing extortion.

Back in the "office" the debriefing begins, and it is clear that Alonzo and Jake represent two totally different worldviews: Alonzo views the killing as "justifiable homicide" or "street justice," and Jake views it as "murder and armed robbery" by individuals with badges. Moreover, Jake refuses to take his share of the blood money and says: "I go back to the Valley, I'll cut parking tickets" because he views Alonzo and his team as "fucking insane." Here Alonzo makes his final offer, telling Jake that he is a leader compared to the other members of the team ("clowns") and that Jake can have his position in time. Although Alonzo with his bullying perfidy seems to be convinced that Jake will go along with the scenario, he makes another stop in the Latino section of town with the ruse of bringing some things to a family. Jake discovers that these three Latino individuals know about Roger and also know that Alonzo has killed a Russian in Las Vegas and that he has to pay the Russians $1 million if he wants to survive the night. Even worse Jake discovers that Alonzo has abandoned him, and the money that Jake refused has been given to these individuals to kill him and dispose of his body. What saves Jake from a bloody shotgun death in the bathtub is that upon searching Jake, they discover the wallet of the Latina high school girl he saved from being raped by the two crackheads. It turns out that she is the niece of one of these gangbangers, who upon releasing him tells him that "this was just business, right?"

At this point, Jake understands that his training day and quest for the American Dream (a promotion and a big house) are over and that Alonzo tried to have him killed; this realization causes Jake to provide his own training day. Ironically, it is the single incident with the Latina girl, where Jake made his own courageous choice that saves his own life whereas all of the choices that Alonzo has given him have put him in compromising, precarious, and deadly situations. Without a doubt, this has been the most traumatic episode in his training day because as he is tied up and about to be shot, he constantly screams that he has a little girl. Like Clint Eastwood in *Fist Full of Dollars,* and *The Good the Bad, and the Ugly,* Jake Hoyt returns to the "Jungle" with his 9mm Beretta, and his entrance pass is his announcement, "I am here for Alonzo." Both the Latinos and the Blacks despise Alonzo, despite the relationships they have with him; so the white boy, Jake coming to the "Jungle" to do some damage is welcomed. Damage is done in Alonzo's mistress' apartment as Alonzo and Jake exchange gunshots putting Sara and her son in danger. Surprising Alonzo and the butt-naked Sara, Jake announces: "Fuck your appointment with the Russians." Here, Alonzo still feeling the need to school the rookie, states that "It is not what you know. It's what you can prove." Jake is reminded that he has no witnesses to confirm his version of Roger's death. Instead of *High Noon* this urban battle of Black and white occurs close to midnight as Alonzo and Jake trade blows on the rooftops in the hood. Flipping the script on

Alonzo, Jake, once he has the upper hand, asks: "It's no fun when the rabbit has the gun, is it?" The racial connotations are clear: the nontraditional Black-on-top-white-on-bottom paradigm has shifted as Jake with the money and the gun stands over a bleeding Alonzo. This battle escalates in front of a crowd of Black male residents as Alonzo encourages someone to shoot Jake and become rich. Instead while reaching for a 357 magnum, Jake, in a scene that recalls the accidental mishap in *Bad Boys II*, deliberately shoots Alonzo in the buttocks and says his next shot will kill him. The symbolic act of sodomy is reinforced and reinscribed when Jake emasculates Alonzo by ripping the badge from his neck as he uses the language police use for criminals: "You want to go home or do you want to go to jail?" Once Alonzo is castrated the Black gangbangers step forward and tell Jake to bounce because they have his back. This community betrayal completely enrages Alonzo as his Machiavellian god complex is fully revealed:

> All right! I'm putting cases on all you bitches! Huh? You think you can do this shit? You think you can do this to me? You motherfuckers will be playing basketball in Pelican Bay when I get finish with you. Shoe program, nigga! Twenty-three hour lock-down! I'm the man up in this piece! Who you think you fucking with? I'm the police! I run shit here! You just live here! That's right you better walk away. I'm gonna burn this motherfucker down! King Kong ain't got shit on me!

Like Victor Frankenstein and Robert Walton the two egotistical white males with god complexes in Mary Shelley's surreal novel *Frankenstein* (1818), Alonzo Harris has deluded himself into believing that he is more than human. Alonzo's attempts to create another monster detective by changing Jake Hoyt from a rookie to a rogue have failed as Jake tells him that he has learned that he is nothing like Alonzo, that he will not commit premeditated murder and armed robbery just because he has a badge, that he will not be swayed by white superior officers and individuals in the district attorney's office who will support him if they get paid off, that he will not intimidate criminals, that he will not harass criminals and take their property and keep it for himself. Essentially, Jake realizes his fatal flaw (unbridled ambition) and that he has made some profound mistakes in judgment but declares that he will not be a criminal cop who breaks the law for personal profit or promotion in order to provide for his family. Unlike and Joe Friday and Bill Gamnon in the iconic television series about L.A. police *Dragnet*, Alonzo Harris and Jake Hoyt are always in conflict with each other and the L.A.P.D. Thus unlike Jake, Alonzo has become analogous to the gangbanger described in Sanyika Sakur's *Monster: The Autobiography of an L.A. Gang Member* (2004). Better still, Alonzo Harris can be viewed as a black version of the sadistically violent and racist Mark Furman and his anything-goes philosophy of criminal justice.

Like Clyde Barrow's bloody death in a matrix of bullets (in the classic 1967 film *Bonnie and Clyde* starring Warren Beatty and Faye Dunaway), Alonzo Harris' equally violent and bloody death at the hands of the Russian mafia announces the limits to criminal behavior within or outside the law; Alonzo's status as a detective is meaningless. In the film, Alonzo's graphically violent demise is again immediately foreshadowed by a police cruiser and an ambulance going in the opposite direction of Alonzo's now bullet-ridden and window-smashed Monte Carlo; as a phallocentric representation of his masculinity and hyper-sexuality the wrecked car represents his emasculation and castration. Harris became an outsider within a system designed to uphold certain social and ethical conduct both on duty and off duty. And it is Jake at the end of the film who tells the Three Wise Men who come looking for the money that he turned the money in to the department (in an alternative ending of the film). The final text in the film is an announcement that "An L.A police officer was killed today serving a high risk warrant near LAX. An L.A.P.D. spokesperson said Officer Harris was survived by his wife and four sons," and this provides the dramatic irony because Alonzo used similar verbiage when he talked to Jake, and Stan Gursky warned him not to get himself on the front cover of the newspaper like the other corrupt Los Angeles police officers. While the film does not provide much background on Alonzo, there is one scene that suggests how his arrogant lawlessness persona came into existence. When Jake accompanies Alonzo to Roger's house, Alonzo and Roger tap their glasses together and toast with the statement "Back to the World." This statement reinforces and reinscribes Conrad's *The Heart of Darkness* and is associated with the bloody war in Vietnam and veterans who returned home from extremely violent warfare where unexpected death and the use of drugs were extremely common. More than likely Alonzo experienced some profound trauma that had yet to be resolved. Like the brilliant foreshadowing in *A Lesson Before Dying* and *Devil in a Blue Dress,* the director places a television screen in the Quality Café: we see the woman speaking on it has the posture of a newscaster delivering the news of the day, and we recall that Alonzo's newspaper was turned to the stock market. Both the newscaster and the newspaper in the Quality Café foreshadow Alonzo's lack of moral and ethical qualities, his problems with the Russians and his subsequent brutal death. Of course the truth of Alonzo Harris' death will be concealed from the public, but those who knew him well (his mistress, his corrupt superiors, his informants, his corrupt fellow detectives) will always know the truth about his extraordinary evil ways as Jake Hoyt will have to find some new way to achieve his American Dream and find some redemption. According to a July 17, 2009, *New York Times* article,"Judge Ends Monitor of Los Angeles Police," Recent studies by the department showed that minorities were still more likely to be stopped and searched by Los Angeles police officers and that officers used force against black people and Latinos more frequently than against white people. The sweeping monitoring agreement spanned three police chiefs and three mayors. Studies conducted under the consent decree determined that the department had engaged in pattern of false arrests, unreasonable searches and use of excessive force, especially in minority communities. The court mandated more training for officers and revamped police procedures.

American Gangster (2007), directed by Ridley Scott, again features Denzel Washington playing the part of the real Frank Lucas, the king of the Harlem heroin drug trade. In this film we obtain a poignant explication of one Black man's relationship with America's legal system and the issue of redemption. Beyond being a major drug dealer, Frank Lucas was a ruthless gangster and outlaw; he lived a glamorous life, hobnobbing with famous musicians and athletes. Through his criminal connection in Asia's Golden Triangle, Lucas was notorious for using the coffins of dead GIs to smuggle heroin into the United States, and before his downfall, he played a large role in the near-death of New York City, especially Black New Yorkers. Paradoxically, Lucas, who grew up in racist and segregated North Carolina where he watched as his cousin was shot by the Klan for looking at a white girl, would eventually come to Harlem to destroy Black people by selling almost pure heroin. Unlike the Klan who brutally killed Black people by shooting, bludgeoning, and lynching them, Lucas got Black people to kill themselves as he got filthy rich, making up to a million dollars a day in the heroin trade. A fundamental method of the group of white gangsters who called themselves the Ku Klux Klan was to deny Black people any sense of economic access through relentless intimidation and murder, especially by using the sadistic sexual ritual of lynching.[1] As an American gangster, Lucas's economic subjectivity was in a similar vein; he intimidated and murdered other drug dealers, giving him the ability to kill Black people wholesale with his special brand of heroin, named "Blue Magic." Like a deadly poisonous and slimy black snake slithering through the Black community, Frank Lucas was far more pernicious than the Ku Klux Klan with their lynch-ropes, weapons, tar & feathers, gasoline, and vicious dogs.

In the historically based *American Gangster*, Frank Lucas's graphic depiction reinforces and reinscribes some fundamental aspects of America's white supremacist culture and iconography where Black people, especially Black men, are characterized as criminals. Here Frank Lucas is mentored into criminal activity by the elder Ellsworth ("Bumpy") Johnson (Clarence Williams III). Not surprisingly, Scott begins his film with a reference to the Ku Klux Klan—a bloody and beaten Latino is tied to a chair while someone pours an entire canister of gasoline on him. As Bumpy Johnson watches, Lucas lights up a long, thick cigar (a phallic symbol); we then view Lucas nonchalantly throwing a lighter on the gasoline-drenched man, who curses his tormentors before he agonizingly burns to death. The Ku Klux Klan-like overkill and heavy-handedness become sadistically apparent when Lucas whips out his revolver and fires six shots into the head of the burning Latino's head. Like the graphic lynching-burning and castration of a nameless Black man in Richard Wright's surreal poem, "Between the World and Me (1935), lynching in its many sadistic forms has been as American as white women, apple pie, baseball, and fast automobiles. Welcome to the Terrordome of American Gangsters announces this film. To juxtapose this sadistic scene, Scott depicts Johnson giving away Thanksgiving turkeys to Black people, who wildly cheer his seemingly benevolence handouts. In Bumpy Johnson's final scene in the film, his philosophy of American commercialism is evident in his mournful pronouncements to Lucas: "This is the problem, what's wrong with America. America has grown so big that you cannot find your way....Where is the pride of ownership? Where is the personal service?" Commenting on the rise on corporations and franchises like McDonalds, Johnson asks: "What right do they have in cutting out the suppliers, pushing out all of the middle men, buying direct from the manufacturer?" These pronouncements along with prejudicial remarks about the "Chinks" plant the seeds for Lucas to take over Johnson's criminal enterprise, cut out the Italians, the middlemen in the drug trade, and make a deal with the Asians to clandestinely bring 100 percent pure heroin into the country. With Johnson's death, Lucas becomes his own man and begins dealing up death and destruction to the Black community. If we extend the analogy of the Ku Klux Klan, white America has used the Ku Klux Klan and other white supremacist terrorist groups as the intermediaries in its attempt to keep Black people, especially Black men, in a perpetual state of economic disenfranchisement. What racist white America could not accomplish by legal means such as the Supreme Court's *Dred Scott* decision (1857) and the *Plessy vs. Ferguson* (1896) and other laws, extra-legal measures were used, resulting in over 5,000 Black people being lynched from the latter part of the nineteenth century to the first third of the twentieth century.

Contemptible Black and white male drug dealers are juxtaposed with contemptible male white police officers; both are characterized as predators and vultures sucking the blood of Black people. Oscar-winning Denzel Washington adroitly playing Frank Lucas becomes juxtaposed with another Oscar-winning actor Russell Crowe who plays the role of Richie Roberts, an incorruptible white police officer. At some point, Frank Lucas begins to draw the attention of Richie Roberts because, as John L. Cooper points out, the police have a broader range of responsibility:

> The police [then] cannot be impartial or chiefly concerned with criminals as we would normally want to believe. Instead they must be concerned with the social dissidents who might undercut the values and traditions that have come to represent the social center and thereby help to maintain the status quo. The police's immediate attention is drawn to nonconformity, any action or

behavior that can spite the norms of the social center. This puts every citizen [and especially Blacks] under the purview of the police, and makes us all potential suspects and possible dissidents in their eyes. There are whole categories of Americans who fall into this posture of being dissidents because they have been allocated certain statuses outside the mainstream of society in accordance with our stratification system. These people are nonconformists because society will not allow them to conform. Being recognized as social dissidents, the [racial] ethnic minorities are expected to fall sharply under police scrutiny and observation. (116–17)

However, the constant presence of Italian gangsters and corrupt white police officers provides a backdrop to the internal and external factors that lead to things falling apart. When Roberts discovers close to a million dollars in drug money and decides to turn the money in, his partner, Campizi (Kevin Corrigan) bluntly tells him that: "Cops kill cops they can't trust." In a real sense Roberts becomes a 'white nigger' when he is ostracized by other police officers who refuse to back him up when he radios for assistance. The film portrays white police officers as organized gangsters who arrest Black drug dealers, confiscate their drugs, dilute the drugs, and wholesale them back to Italian dealers, who in turn sell the drugs back to high-level Black dealers in a continuous cycle of corruption. More specific to the film, Detective Trupo and his gang of detectives go to the Police Department's property room and sign out drug evidence, dilute the drugs in their own laboratory and sell them back to Italian mobsters. Roberts' first introduction to Frank Lucas' "Blue Magic" occurs in the morgue when his partner Campizi dies from an overdose. Ironically, one of the mobsters complains to Frank Lucas about the police being unethical as he completes his drug deal with Lucas. Here is the critical point in Lucas' career: his attempt to cut out the Italians and the police as middlemen as he takes over the operation from Bumpy Johnson. By going to Vietnam and then into Cambodia, Lucas has done what no white drug dealer has ever done; he went to the directly to the source of the heroin. Lucas going into the "jungle" echoes the period of enslavement when Africans went into the interior parts of West African countries to capture slaves who would be sold to Europeans in exchange for guns and other goods. Drug use by American soldiers was widespread, and it is estimated that over one third of American troops were experimenting with opium and heroin. Back in America, even when Lucas cut the drugs with lactose, his "Blue Magic" was twice as pure as anything else on the streets of Harlem and cost half as much, an incredible value for long-term consumption. Lucas' operation in Harlem on 116th Street between Seventh and Eighth Avenues was making over a million dollars a day at its high point. In Mark Jacobson's *American Gangster and Other Tales of New York* (2007), Lucas reveals his internalized white supremacy as he explains his strategy:

We put it out there at four in the afternoon, when the cops changed shifts. That gave you a couple of hours to work, before those lazy bastards got down there. My buyers though, you could set your watch by them. Those junkies crawling out. By four o'clock we had enough niggers in the street to make a Tarzan movie. They had to reroute the bus coming down Eighth Avenue to 116th, it couldn't get through....On a usual day we'd put out maybe twenty-five thousand quarters (quarter 'spoons,' fifty dollars worth, enough to get high for the rest of the day). By nine o'clock I ain't got a fucking gram. Everything is gone. Sold...and I got myself a million dollars. (5)

Denzel Washington personifies this moment wearing a wig and sunglasses as he sits in an beat-up Chevy called "Nellybelle" to observe the block that he "owned." What the film astutely captures is the absolute control that Lucas had over his family-run business. True to his North Carolina roots, Lucas did not trust "city boys." With the brilliant Ruby Dee playing Mama, Lucas brings his mother, brothers and cousins to New York so that his brothers could play critical roles in the distribution of the heroin and collection of the monies.

In the film, Lucas becomes a better reincarnation of Bumpy Johnson; he retains the core values of his mentor—honesty, hard work, respect for family, loyalty, and respect for tradition, and never forgetting where one comes from. One poignant example of this is Lucas handing out turkeys during the week of Thanksgiving to people in Harlem, a ritual that Bumpy Johnson had established to garner community respect. What makes Lucas more sophisticated and more dangerous is his desire to be his own man, a distinction he makes clear to his brothers from North Carolina: "The man I worked for had one of the biggest companies in New York City. He didn't own his own company. White man owned it, so they owned him. Nobody owns me, though." Again the enduring echoes of Black people's enslavement by whites become evident, as Lucas has learned from his mentor that owning a company is analogous to having total freedom. Federal Judge Sterling Johnson, who served as New York's special narcotics prosecutor, aptly defined Lucas as "one of the most outrageous international dope smugglers ever...an innovative guy who broke new ground by getting his own connection outside the U. S. and then selling the stuff himself in the street...a real womb to tomb operation" (Jacobson 6). Johnson's quote resonates as Lucas stuffed heroin into the coffins of dead soldiers and produced coffins in Harlem for drug users who overdosed. Reflecting upon the death and destruction that he once reigned over, an aged Lucas recounts life on 116th Street: "You'd see a hundred junkies, lined up, sitting there sucking their own dicks....That's what you called it, sucking their own dicks...their heads on their laps, down in the crotch, like they was dead. People saw that, everyone knew that shit was good" (8). The utter contempt that Lucas had for drug users becomes juxtaposed with the pride in his deadly product.

In the film *American Gangster* and the chronicle of the real Lucas' life in Jacobson's book *American Gangster,* the conflicts and perils of a Black man operating outside the law foreshadow the thematic issues characterized in the four novels discussed in this book, especially with regard to intraracial and interracial conflicts. In one of the film's most violent scenes Frank Lucas has a deadly encounter with the six-foot-five, 270-pound Tango over control over a part of a Harlem's street. Using the rationale that Tango had messed up $5,000 that Lucas gave him, Lucas has an opportunity to establish himself and send fear throughout the community. In the film and Lucas' statement, Tango is killed at four o'clock in the afternoon during the summer of 1965. Proud of his bravado, Lucas using hyperbole to characterize Tango states: "Right there...the boy didn't have no head in the back. The whole shit blowed out....That was my real initiation fee into taking over completely down here. Because I killed the baddest motherfucker. Not just in Harlem, but in the world" (10). His reasoning was clear: "When you're in the kind of work I was in, you've got to be for real. When you say something, you've got to make sure people listen. You got to show what exactly you're willing to do to get what you want" (9). With this philosophy and the action to back it up, Lucas became the richest and most sophisticated Black drug dealer in American history. However, the "Blue Magic" that was twice as powerful and cost half as much as other offerings began to garner the attention of detectives in special units and the attention of white mobsters. Detectives like Trupo of the Special Investigation Unit represented the corrupt police officers and Roberts represented the honest police officers; both began to focus on Lucas for different reason, Trupo because Lucas represented a cash cow and Roberts because criminals needed to be stopped. A brazen Detective Trupo stops Lucas' Rolls-Royce after his wedding to introduce himself and to inform Lucas that a $10,000 payment is due on the first of the month. Lucas's violent response to this insult was to place a caged turkey on Trupo's front steps and to blow up his favorite sports car. On the other hand, Detective Roberts' focus on Lucas begins after seeing Lucas wearing a matching chinchilla coat and hat while sitting in the first row at the Madison Square Garden spectacular boxing match of Joe Frazier and Muhammad Ali. As a gift from Lucas' Puerto Rican beauty-queen wife, Eva (Lymari Nadal), the coat and hat are antithetical to Lucas' manner of always being discreet, something he learned from Bumpy Johnson. In a dramatic scene in the film, Lucas throws the chinchilla hat and coat into the fireplace because he has been marked by both sides of law enforcement for this ostentatious display of wealth. Yet, as Jacobson's book relates, Lucas was one of the richest drug dealers and according to his own records had "at least fifty-six million dollars." Lucas' immense real estate holdings included two twenty-plus-story buildings in Detroit, garden apartments in Los Angeles and Miami, another apartment house in Chicago, and property in Puerto Rico. In Lucas's New Jersey home, the film highlights the perverse nature of Lucas' drug empire when he shows his soon-to- be-wife, Eva, a picture of Bumpy Johnson (for whom he worked as chauffeur and collector for over fifteen years) and states that he was Martin Luther King Jr. and finally straightforwardly states that Johnson was just as important to him as the courageous and self-sacrificing civil rights leader. Roberts' relentless focus discovers to his amazement the depth and diversification of Lucas' drug empire—a dry cleaners, a hardware store, a tire shop, a, auto body shop, and a custom furniture store were all used in Lucas' drug operation. Roberts and his Special Narcotics Unit had been looking for the person who was bringing the heroin into the country, never initially suspecting that it was Lucas. Race and the drug business become even more specific when Roberts informs the head of the DEA that Lucas is "above the Mafia, buys direct and uses military planes to smuggle in the heroin." With an incredulous tone, the head of the DEA responds that "No nigger has accomplished what the American mafia has accomplished in a hundred years." Simply put, Frank Lucas did accomplish this feat. Roberts also makes the profound and damning statement that certain people do not want the drugs to stop coming into the country because police officers, lawyers, judges, prosecutors, politicians, probation officers, and prison guards would be unemployed if the drugs stopped. He concludes that 100,000 people would be out of work if the drug flow came to an end. Criminal police officers and the honest police officers simultaneously take down Lucas; Detective Trupo and his gang invade Lucas' home in New Jersey while Roberts and his unit break into Lucas' drug laboratory. Trupo steals Lucas' hidden money after shooting his dog, and after a bloody shoot-out, Roberts and his unit confiscate the drugs, money, and weapons at Lucas' lab.

Conflict with other drug dealers such as Leroy ("Nicky") Barnes was also a consistent issue. When Lucas becomes aware that Nicky is selling diluted packages of "Blue Magic," he confronts him in his own club. Like a CEO with a serious case of product infringement on his hands, Lucas tells Nicky that his product is analogous to the brand names of Pepsi and Coca-Cola and that any tampering with it is a commercial violation. Despite this not so bizarre analogy, here we have a portrait of the Black man as an outsider who believes that he has the same rights and privileges as a legitimate businessman and an illegal product masquerading as a legal commercial product. Before leaving Nicky's cub Lucas adamantly tells him to change the name of the drug he sells so that "Blue Magic" remains true to the Lucas copyright. In discussing Nicky Barnes, Lucas marks himself in the mode of the reserved Bumpy Johnson as a more conservative drug dealer. In the film Lucas tells his brother that "the loudest person in the room is always the weakest person in the room." Moreover, Jacobson states that Lucas "never liked the grandstanding (Nicky) Barnes, who Lucas thought brought unneeded heat by doing things like appearing on the cover of the *New York Times Magazine* wearing his trademark goggle-like Gucci glasses bragging that he was 'Mr. Untouchable'" (23). This utter contempt is again shown in the film when Lucas and Eva pass by their club and see the gaudy Nicky go in with his entourage; minutes later Lucas is shot and wounded during a drive-by shooting as they stop to get some Chinese food. Here Lucas understands the malicious nature of his business where other drug dealers are willing to kill him and his wife because he has profoundly disrupted the natural order of things, where there was not a huge disparity in the price and quality of the drugs. This incident does not, however, diminish Lucas' patriotism or his desire for the American Dream: "This is my home. My country. Frank Lucas don't run from nobody. This is America....This is where my business is, my wife, my mother, my family. This is my country. I ain't goin nowhere." Like the thousands of Black men who fought and died in America's many wars overseas (especially the then-current conflict in Vietnam), Lucas has a similar philosophy despite his criminal enterprise.

In the film, the paradoxes are profound and conclude with Frank Lucas being arrested by Richie Roberts while coming out of Sunday church services, a weekly ritual at which he accompanied his wife and mother. This scene reinforces the contradiction of Frank Lucas having dinner with his family while drug users are dying from "Blue Magic." The fall of Saigon in Vietnam also prefigures the fall of Lucas and the corrupt police officers. Based on Lucas' statements, more than half of the police involved in drug investigation were arrested; three quarters of the New York City's Drug Enforcement Agency were convicted, and Detective Trupo committed suicide. Thirty members of the Lucas family were convicted of drug trafficking and sent to prison; his wife returned to Puerto Rico, and Frank's mother went back to North Carolina. Federal authorities confiscated over $200 million and assets in U.S. and foreign banks. Lucas was initially sentenced to 70 years in prison, but amazingly was released after serving only 15, and Roberts became a defense attorney with Lucas as his first client. The bond between the drug dealer and the police officer became established when Lucas began to reveal evidence against other drug dealers and corrupt police officers. Beyond this Lucas reveals the trauma that he experienced as a child that led to his hatred of the police and his long life of criminal activity. When he was six years old, he witnessed the brutal killing of his cousin by five white males; the allegation was looking at a white girl walking down the street. Recalling the 1936 incident in La Grange, North Carolina, as if it was yesterday, Lucas states:

> Obedai was like twelve or thirteen, and he come out the door, all sleepy and stuff. 'You been looking at somebody's daughter. We're going to fix you,' they said.

They took two ropes, a rope in each hand, they tied him down on the ground, facedown on the porch, and two guys took the rope and...pulled it tight in opposite directions. The other guy shoved a shotgun in Obedai's mouth and pulled the trigger simultaneously. (12)

One immediately thinks of the sadistic killing of Emmett Till some 19 years later; however, unlike many Black people subjected to trauma, Lucas turned his rage into a criminal activity that would do much more damage than this one incident. What is significant about the Klan killing of young Black males for supposedly looking at white girls is the larger context of the Jim Crow culture eradicating all avenues for socioeconomic advancement. Blacks seeking to advance themselves through education were met with the same violence and hostility as any appearance of miscegenation between Black males and white females. At no point in the film do we get any sense of Lucas' formal education; subsequently, there exists a direct social correlation between a lack of an education, miseducation and the propensity for involvement in criminal activities. Paradoxically, when Roberts and Lucas are sitting across the table, we understand how similar they are because they are both disciplined, hard working, committed to their dreams, and honest. Both men are trying to better themselves; Roberts is studying for a law degree, and Lucas wants to help himself and his family. Frank and Richie are both outsiders playing by rules and regulations everyone else ignores. But it is Frank Lucas who resembles F. Scott Fitzgerald's Jay Gatsby, who attempts to transform the past by engaging in criminal activities that lead to his tragic downfall.

Thus, we understand why the film is entitled *American Gangster* because too often white America represents a gangster culture, a thug culture that has produced Bumpy Johnson, Frank Lucas, Nicky Barnes, and other Black gangsters. There is no other modern-day country in the world that has a culture with such a long history of national and international criminality. The Ku Klux Klan, the bombing of the church in Birmingham, Alabama, where four Black girls were killed, the bombing of Wallstreet in Tulsa, Oklahoma, the Co Intel Program, the massacre in Rosewood, Florida, the Red Summer of 1919, the beating and killing of civil rights activists, the killing of James Byrd in Jasper, Texas, the beating and sodomy of Abner Louima in New York City by Justin Volpe, a white police officer, the February 4, 1999, murder of Amadou Diallo in New York City by a gang of four white police officers, the Jim Crow laws, the castration and killing of Emmett Louis Till in Money, Mississippi,[2] white America's genocide against the Black Panthers, the ongoing genocide of Native Americans, the killing of Patrick Dorsmond by white New York City police officers, the tragic and senseless killing of Sean Bell in Queens, New York by another gang of New York City police officers, the bombing of Black churches, the murder of Fred Hampton in Chicago, Illinois by the police, the over 3,500 Black people lynched and some lynched and burned to death, the abandonment of Black people and the poor during Katrina, the lynching of Black soldiers who returned from World War I, the shooting of Eleanor Bumpers by white New York City police officers, the Black Codes, the internment of Asians during World War II, America's foreign policy in the Middle East, Latin America, Central America, Africa, and Asia—represent just a few examples of the systematic gangster-like behavior of a too often racist country that has shown little respect for the lives of its citizens of color or for the non-white citizens of other countries. In terms of American culture and representations of Black males it is interesting to note that Denzel Washington received an Academy Award for Best Actor for *Training Day,* and a few years later the film *Hustle and Flow* (2005) received an Academy Award for the song "It's Hard out Here for a Pimp."

It would not be a literary stretch to think of Alonzo Harris and Fred Lucas as more modern-day versions of Jay Gatsby. Gatsby, the protagonist in Fitzgerald's novel, was a bootlegger; Harris was a corrupt police officer confiscating drugs for his own personal profit, and Lucas was a heroin dealer: all of these men worked outside the law to amass tremendous wealth and power. In my first book *The Tragic Black Buck: Racial Masquerading in the American Literary Imagination,* I argue that Fitzgerald characterizes Jay Gatsby as a light-skinned Black man passing for white. Regardless of the racial aspects, both the fictional Gatsby and the non-fictional Lucas as well as Harris represent cunning and corrupt individuals seeking the American Dream.

With these films in mind, this project *Black Outlaws: Race, Law, and Male Subjectivity in African American Literature* examines Black male characters as outside the law of America's white supremacist culture. The films have a much greater significance because of their worldwide distribution; the images associated with these two characters played by Denzel Washington will have a lasting impact and tend to reinforce and reinscribe problematic notions of Black male subjectivity often presented in novels by great writers. The African American literary texts examined here are Richard Wright's *The Outsider* (1953), Chester Himes' *The Third Generation* (1954), Walter Mosley's *Devil in a Blue Dress* (1990), and Ernest J. Gaines' *A Lesson Before Dying* (1993). As Margaret Walker states so emphatically: "I believe that every issue in the country now boils down to race. Whether it's education, unemployment and labor, health, politics, religion, or the family—all the social institutions are now affected toward race" (Maryemma Graham 281). Considering African American literature, Michele Wallace makes an astute point:

> In most influential twentieth-century Afro-American literature, portrayals of black community are deeply ambivalent. On the one hand, the community may offer certain protections and compensations. On the other, the community is a result

of segregation and poverty, not fraternal feelings or collective purpose. And so the protagonist, usually radically individualistic, either endures some degree of spiritual alienation from the community as the price of creative identity or is destroyed/consumed. Even when deliverance comes, it is apt to be in the form of exile, hibernation, catastrophe, madness, or death. (69)

While Wallace's analysis holds true especially for Richard Wright's *The Outsider* and Ernest J. Gaines *A Lesson Before Dying,* Chester Himes' *The Third Generation* and Walter Mosley's *Devil in a Blue Dress* are much too complex for this formation. Jim Crow segregation plays a significant role in the spiritual/psychological alienation and subsequent destruction/consumption of these Black male characters. Like a persistent and soul-crushing force, Jim Crow segregation has kept many Black men in a perpetual state of apprehension and anxiety, leaving them to make difficult and precarious choices in order to survive. Perhaps there is not better articulation of the soul-crushing effect of Jim Crow segregation than Martin Luther King Jr.'s "Letter from a Birmingham Jail" in which he describes the insidious and immoral nature of white supremacy and its psychological impact:

> When you have seen vicious mobs lynch your mothers and fathers at will and drown your sisters and brothers at whim, when you have seen hate-filled policemen curse, kick, brutalize and even kill your black brothers and sisters with impunity..... when you are humiliated day in and day out by nagging signs reading 'white' and 'colored'; when your first name becomes 'nigger' and your middle name becomes 'boy' (however old you are) and your last name become 'John,' and when your wife and mother are never given the respected title 'Mrs.'; when you are harried by day and haunted by night by the fact that you are a Negro, living constantly at tip-toe stance never quite knowing what to expect next, and plagued with inner fear and outer resentment; when you are forever fighting a degenerating sense of 'nobodiness'—then you will understand why we find it difficult to wait.[3]

Again and again we understand the plethora of indignities and assaults that are a part of Black people's daily existence; violence and the apprehension of violence shaped Black lives and psyches. In America's patriarchal society a man's ability to provide and protect himself and his family are fundamental to any definition of manhood; however, as Martin Luther King Jr. makes clear, America's racist culture of violence and disrespect makes Black people's existence a day-to-day battle, leaving them in a constant state of anguish and anxiety. Moreover, there is a transgenerational trauma in which the psychological impact is passed on to succeeding generations. Within a legal context, Black people's fundamental disenfranchisement can be traced back to the United States Supreme Court's 1857 *Dred Scott* decision, where Justice Taney and the Court forcefully ruled that "a black man had no rights which a white man is bound to respect," and this remained a defining principle of race in America a century after the ruling. Indeed, the relationship between Blacks and racist whites can be truly characterized as warfare, with Black people sustaining the heaviest physical, psychological, and economic casualties.

In the second chapter, "Cross Damon Dangerously, Freedom and Black Male Subjective: The Ultimate Urban Outlaw in Richard Wright's *The Outsider,*" I examine the heavily pressured life of Cross Damon as he transforms himself to escape a reality too difficult to face. Violence becomes fundamental to Cross' negotiation with his new identity until he reaches a point of no return, and it is only when he is confronted with another outsider that he comes to terms with his tragic life.

"A Black Man's 'Veil of Horror': Oedipal Trauma and Psychic Redemption in Chester Himes' *The Third Generation,*" the third chapter, represents Himes' *Bildungsroman* as Charles Taylor fights his way of a psychological family drama where the mother, Lillian Taylor, becomes fixated on her youngest son, Charles. This fixation causes enduring psychological trauma and violence for Charles as he moves into manhood. With psychological depth and a clear sense of the historical period, Himes portrays the transgenerational trauma.

The fourth chapter, "Black Male Subjectivity and the American Dream: Working Outside the Law in Walter Mosley's *Devil in a Blue Dress,*" combines the detective novel with the racial passing narrative to explore how a Black man can survive and thrive despite America's racism after World War II in California in the 1940s. Easy Rawlins, a war veteran attempting to hold onto his part of the American Dream, places himself in a precarious situation outside the law as he endeavors to locate Daphne Monet, a blonde beauty with a secret past. With his alter ego, Mouse, Easy Rawlins undergoes a permanent transformation from a factory worker to a private investigator.

Lastly, the fifth chapter, "From a Hog to a Black Man: Black Male Subjectivity and Ritualistic Lynching in Ernest J. Gaines' *A Lesson Before Dying,*" examines the transformation of two Back men within the context of a legal lynching. Jefferson, who is labeled a "hog" by his white defense attorney, must learn how to die like a man, and Grant Wiggins, his teacher, must learn how to live despite the crushing aspects of Jim Crow segregation. Here three Black women—Tante Lou, Emma Glenn, and Vivian Baptiste—play critical roles in the transformation of these two Black men, who discover they need each other in order to be the men they need to be.

These four prolific Black novelists—Richard Wright, Chester Himes, Walter Mosley, and Ernest J. Gaines—represent the most captivating and creative writers documenting the psychological and socioeconomic realities of Black life in America, especially those facing Black men. The two older naturalistic novels and the two more postmodern novels illustrate the ongoing continuum that many Black men face in America's materialistic white supremacist and racist culture in which Black males are the primary targets for eradication beginning in the educational system and ending in long years of incarceration. America's legal system becomes fundamental to any examination of the political, social, and economic realities facing Black male inside and outside the law. Too often Black men, whether by their own actions or by societal forces beyond their control, become outsiders.

Notes

1   V. P. Franklin's *Black Self-Determination: A Cultural History of African-American Resistance* (New York: Lawrence Hill, 1992), the author provides an overall assessment of white supremacist groups: "Through violence, brutality, and terrorism, the Night Riders had seared into the consciousness of thousands of southern blacks the true meaning of 'white supremacy.' The Klan had violently opposed the continuation of basic civil rights for Afro-Americans. (The Klan's spreading their hatred to include southern European immigrants, Catholics, Asians, and Jews did not diminish the black community's feelings and sentiments about their self-professed enemy)....But to Afro-Americans in the United States the Klan represented much more historically, economically, socially, and culturally than white racial purity" (200–201).

2   Ironically, in June 2005, fifty years after Emmett Louis Till's swollen, tortured, and mutilated body was retrieved from the muck and mire of the Tallahatchie River in Mississippi, it was exhumed for an autopsy. According to Monica Davey and Gretchen Ruethling in their *New York Times* article, "Federal authorities ordered the exhumation as part of their new investigation into Emmett's kidnapping and death, one of more than 20 cases of killings in the Jim Crow South that have been reopened in recent years. The new inquiries have been prompted by a new generation of prosecutors and investigators, by the work of historians and filmmakers, by witnesses who have unexpectedly come forward and, simply, by the interest that has grown with each new investigation."

3   Martin Luther King Jr. "Letter from Birmingham Jail," in *A Testament of Hope: The Essential Writings and Speeches of Martin Luther King Jr.,* ed. James M. Washington (New York: Harper Collins, 1986) 292–93. Also see James Baldwin, "In Search of a Majority," in *Nobody Knows My Name* (New York: Vintage, 1960) 127–37.

2. Cross Damon—Dangerous Freedom and Black Male Subjectivity: The Ultimate Urban Outlaw in Richard Wright's The Outsider

> So, in leaving, I was taking a part of the South to transplant in alien soil, to see if it could grow differently, if it could drink of new and cool rains, bend in strange winds, respond to the warmth of other suns, and perhaps to bloom....And if that miracle ever happened, then I would know that there was yet hope in that southern swamp of despair and violence, that light could emerge even out of the blackness of the southern night.

> —*Richard Wright, Black Boy: A Record of Childhood and Youth*

If there is one aspect that absolutely defines much of Richard Wright's literary work it is his documentation and characterizations of the nefarious system of Jim Crow segregation and its enduring and tragic impact on Black people, especially Black men. For Black people who recently liberated themselves from the demonic and iron-spiked shackles of enslavement, the institutionalized system of Jim Crow segregation brought a pernicious plague of despair and violence that cast its dark shadow on every aspect of Black life in America, especially in term of economics.[1] For many Black people, slavery represents and speaks to the transgenerational transgression of trauma, and for many whites it represents the transgenerational transgression of tremendous wealth and leisure. The "particular institution" and its legacy of segregation and de jure segregation created tremendous wealth and leisure for many moneyed and propertied whites, and these institutions were fundamentally about the socioeconomic disenfranchisement of Black people. Within the context of the period of Black people's enslavement by whites and ongoing de facto segregation, for better or for worse much of Black people's identity has been formulated. Indeed the "American Dilemma" of white supremacy has had a profound impact on Black writers and the works that they have produced. In many ways, Wright stands alone in the sagacious manner and complex depth of his depiction of the harsh realities of Black people's existence under de jure segregation. Looking at Black people's proud history before the Romans, the heinous "Middle Passage," and beyond, Wright articulates the painful paradox of our condition: "We black men and women in America today, as we look back upon scenes of rapine, sacrifice, and death, seem to be children of a devilish aberration of an interval of nightmare in history, fledglings of a period of amnesia on the part of men who once dreamed a great dream and forgot" ("Our Strange Birth," 13). This American Dream with its entire "fresh green breast" of promise was significantly constructed on the bloody backs and raped bodies of Black men, women and children. Wright is clearly distinguished from many Black writers by not only living under Jim Crow but by his candid autobiographical documentation. In the section "The Ethics of Living Jim Crow: An Autobiographical Sketch," Wright with bitter indignation describes the brutally violence of this system—from fights with white boys to random acts of violence. Wright recounts numerous incidents where he and other Black people were constantly terrorized. A consistent theme of this enduring racial bigotry was keeping Black people "in their place" by legal and extra-legal measures. In one fight with white boys, Wright sustains a deep gash requiring three stitches, but it is his mother's response to his fighting white boys that teaches him a significant and brutal lesson about Jim Crow segregation:

> She grabbed a barrel stave, dragged me home, stripped me naked, and beat me till I had a fever of one hundred and two. She would smack my rump with the stave, and, while the skin was still smarting impart to me gems of Jim Crow wisdom. I was never to throw cinders any more. I was never to fight any more wars. I was never, under any conditions, to fight *white* folks again. And they were absolutely right in clouting me with the broken milk bottle . . . She finished by telling me that I ought to be thankful to god as long as I lived they didn't kill me. (248)

Traumatized by his mother's violent reaction and alliance with whites, Wright recounts: "All that night I was delirious and could not sleep. Each time I closed my eyes I saw monstrous white faces suspended from the ceiling, leering at me" (248). Wright's nightmare reflects the dual trauma of being physically hit by the bottle and the physical and psychological trauma that his mother dispenses in support of a Jim Crow system designed to disenfranchise all Black people. Black parents played a critical role in socializing their children to either kowtow or challenge white supremacy; in this incident, it is clear that Wright's mother has been psychologically beaten down and attempts to instill in her son a perspective of total submission and abject obedience to whites. This sense of total submission is evident in the area of housing. Describing the psychological and the physical geographic aspects of white supremacy, Wright states:

> Negroes who have lived South know the dread of being caught alone upon the streets in white neighborhoods after the sun has set. In such a simple situation as this the plight of the Negro in America is graphically symbolized. While white strangers may be in these neighborhoods trying to get home, they can pass unmolested. But the color of a Negro's skin makes him easily recognizable, makes him suspect, converts him into a defenseless target. (*Black Writers of America* 546)

When we consider the concept of "whiteness as property" as articulated by Cheryl Harris, a Black individual in a white neighborhood after dark becomes a dangerous threat. White privilege is a sociological term for the advantages purportedly enjoyed by most white persons beyond what are commonly possessed by Black people in the same social, political, and economic spaces (nation, community, workplace, income, etc.). It differs from racism or prejudice in that persons benefiting from white privilege do not necessarily hold racist beliefs or prejudices themselves. Often, the person benefiting is unaware of his or her supposed privilege. Indeed most white people never think about having any privileges and just accept the benefits of whiteness and pass on the spoils to succeeding generations. As Tim Wise elegantly explicates in *White Like Me* (2008): white privilege allows the majority of white people to live in a state of denial in the face of a looming danger:

> The ability of whites to deny nonwhite reality, and indeed to not even comprehend that there is a nonwhite reality (or several different ones), is as strong as any other evidence of just how pervasive white privilege is in this society. It determines the frame, the lens, through which the nation will come to view itself and the events that take place within it. It allows the dominant perspective to become perspectivism, by which I mean the elevation of the majority viewpoint to the status of unquestioned and unquestionable truth.... By allowing white America to remain in this bubble of unreality, white privilege ultimately distorts our vision, and makes it difficult for us to function as fully rational beings. It protects us from some of life's cruelties, and allows us to wander around, oblivious to the fires, that for others burn all around them. In the end...this bubble of unreality can be dangerous place to reside. (60)

However, despite this ever-present danger most white people are committed to and expect their "whiteness as property" to bring them privileges in employment, education, and housing; indeed, this privilege extends into every aspect of human life and this privilege begets power. Segregation in housing helps keep white people in the voluminous bubble of racial denial, and it makes them willing to engage in violence to protect their racial space. Thus, Wright's discussion reinforces the fact that the only reason a Black individual would be in a white neighborhood during the daytime would be to work as a maid, gardener, cook, or housekeeper; under Jim Crow there would be no legitimate reason why a Black person should be in a white neighborhood after dark (without written permission) because living here or visiting a white person was absolutely impossible for Blacks. Economically, white people had the very best schools, the most lucrative employment, the greatest health care, and the finest housing. Legal statutes strictly enforced by the white police and cultural practices violently enforced by white supremacist organizations such as the Ku Klux Klan maintained white people's privilege and Black people's marginality.

Beyond the economic and legal aspects, the prevailing intent of America's white supremacist culture was to restrict miscegenation, especially between Black males and white females. For example, segregation in the sphere of public transportation was, as one white judge argued, to prevent "contacts and collision" from "a promiscuous sitting." The paradox of miscegenation represents a long and bloody history in which Black females were raped by white males, and any real or rumored miscegenation between Black males and white females would result in the Blacks being brutally lynched, castrated, or imprisoned. As we know this, situation began in the period of enslavement when the legal status of the child was determined by the legal status of the mother. With Black females being raped by their white masters and overseers or being forced to have sexual relations with male slaves, it is obvious that the institution of slavery was based on the reproduction and consumption of Black bodies. Wright has captured this sadistic sexual paradox in *Uncle Tom's Children* (1938), *The Long Dream* (1957), and most prolifically in *Native Son* (1940), in which Bigger Thomas, a twenty-year-old Black male from Chicago's South Side becomes involved in a tragedy. As his name suggests, he represents the stereotypical "bad nigger," who in the minds of many racist whites is inherently criminal and will eventually commit some heinous crime and be sent to jail or worse. A panic-stricken Bigger Thomas accidentally kills, Mary Dalton, a liberal white who wants to become friends with Bigger. In Bigger's mind, a young Black man in a white female's bedroom would always be seen as a violent and deranged rapist despite the innocence of the situation. This engrained apprehension causes Bigger to accidentally suffocate Mary when her blind mother comes into her bedroom after Bigger placed the drunken woman in her bed. As the jury eventually decided, Bigger suffocated and strangled Mary while raping her. On the other hand, his grotesque murder of his girlfriend, Bessie Mears, is deliberate and totally brutal as he bashes her in the head with a brick and dumps her body down a shaft. Bigger's only regret is that the money she brought him was still in her pocket. Bigger's response to all whites is trepidation, hatred, rage, and humiliation, and these emotions culminate in increasing violence; Mary's suffocation leads to her decapitation and her body being consumed in a furnace. Like his friends Gus, G. H., and Jack, Bigger is a victim of white oppression. While waiting for his execution, Bigger Thomas comes to terms with his tragic fate, and this coincides with his early speculation that he would either kill himself or kill someone else. Bigger Thomas' subjectivity is achieved through murder. *Native Son* can be ultimately characterized as naturalistic and existential, not because Wright is intent on holding fast to certain philosophical structures, but because he found Black life in America both naturalistic and existential. The wooden cross that Reverend Hammond gives Bigger in prison is discarded when he sees the burning cross of the Ku Klux Klan. As he does in his lynching poem "Between the World and Me," in which a battered Black man is "baptized with kerosene," Wright makes the point here that Christianity and racial oppression go hand in hand. At the end of the novel, we understand why Bigger has killed twice and that he begins to feel only after he has murdered, and this is worthy of our understanding and compassion. America's enduring corrupt system of racism is under attack here,

> but [until Wright] no one had linked this corruption so pervasively to racism. Wright also explored some terrifying ideas. *Native Son* suggested the inevitability of black hatred of whites; the desire for violent revenge; and, most appalling, the idea that violent revenge might be essential therapy for the black mind. (Rampersad, 119)

Wright uses this terrifying aspect with incredible power in the character of Cross Damon, the most intellectual and literate of all of Wright's heros and the most violent. Like the peripatetic Ex-Colored man who travels throughout America, Cross Damon is characterized by constant movement in his attempts to maintain his masquerade.

Murder in its metaphoric and literal sense propels *The Outsider* (1953) forward. As he has done in all of his previous work, Richard Wright illustrates the violent and repulsive nature of white supremacy and the too-often horrifying and paralyzing effect it has on Black men. Here we encounter Cross Damon, a Black man caught in the midst of suffocating personal and societal pressures. With a demanding wife, an oppressively religious mother, a pregnant girlfriend, and a racist supervisor at the Post Office, a beleaguered Cross Damon is at odds with himself and looking to escape his bleak reality. Cross Damon begins and ends his epic journey with death and murder. Similar to Fyodor Dostoevsky's *Crime and Punishment* (1866), Franz Kafka's *The Metamorphosis* (1915), and Albert Camus's *The Stranger* (1942), other novels that address alienation, social responsibility, authoritarian structures, and existentialism, Wright's novel examines life in the light of modern philosophies. The protagonist of *The Outsider*, Cross Damon (a name heavy with symbolism) represents the modern man in frenzied pursuit of freedom from all systems and institutions of oppression. Cross is an

intellectual, the product of a culture which rejects him. He is further alienated by his "habit of incessant reflection" and his thoughts that the
experiences and actions of his life have so far taken place without his free
assent, and a profound conviction that there must be more to life, some
meaning and justification which have so far eluded him. Caught up in a
psychological battle with himself and relentless oppressive forces, the psychologically burdened Cross, true to his demonically religious name, commits four murders before he is violently killed by members of the Communist
Party.[2] Representing the white legal establishment, the physically
handicapped white district attorney, Ely Houston, becomes Cross's
consciousness and pursuer. Thus this epic novel represents Wright's master
narrative on crime and justice within the context of America's white supremacist culture, and as we will see here and in the three other novels considered in this book, more often than not for Black men the white establishment
is an element in one's elevation or demise. Structurally, we recall "Fear,"
"Flight," and "Fate" were the character-defining sections for *Native Son*, and
Wright provides "Dread," "Dream," "Descent," "Despair," and "Decision" as
the progressive segments of this epic narrative. This structure reflects the
trajectory of Black fears and desires associated with their unwavering quest
for the respect and material wealth of the American Dream.

For Cross Damon a critical aspect of the American Dream will come to
symbolize his enduring desire for freedom and peace of mind because as
this novel opens, Cross has neither freedom nor peace of mind. While
Damon has been characterized as the ultimate Black male outsider in
African American fiction, he provides us with a deeply personal perspective
of the working class and Black people's existence. Indeed, by his extremely
violent actions (external manifestations of intense internal turmoil), Cross
places himself outside the normal psychological realm of most Black men
during this period, but his behavior reflects the larger discontent felt by all
of them due to societal limitations. As in *Native Son* Wright makes the point
in *The Outsider* to a lesser extent that the fate of Black men is determined by
a hostile environment and a deep sense of alienation. Wright emphasizes
the hatred, apprehension, rage, and vindictiveness in America's racial bat-
tleground. Accordingly, his books are bullets fired as warning shots of an
impending doom if apartheid in America continues to create havoc and
death in the Black community. Ralph Ellison in *Shadow and Act* makes a
point about Wright and himself that conveys their individual yet joint mis-
sions as writers. Ellison writes:

> Wright believed in the much abused idea that novels are "weapons"—the
> counterpart of the dreary notion, common among most minority groups, that
> novels are instruments of good public relations. But I believe that true novels,
> even when most pessimistic and bitter, arise out of an impulse to celebrate human

life and therefore are ritualistic and ceremonial at their core. Thus they would preserve as they destroy, affirm as they reject. (114)

Despite narrative flaws such as some prolonged didactic moments in *The Outsider,* I would argue that this statement by Ellison (whose *Invisible Man* certainly represents a post-modernist weapon) describes Wright's ultimate goal in this somewhat bitter and pessimistic novel. Wright's characterization of Cross Damon, like those in *Invisible Man,* ultimately reflects a desperate desire for a meaningful existence without individual or collective oppression. Here Wright is much more straightforward and honest than Ellison in his depiction of an ultimate "impulse to celebrate human life." Wright and Ellison had an intimate friendship with Wright serving as a mentor for the young Ellison. In *Ralph Ellison: A Biography,* Arnold Rampersad reveals:

> The two men, nevertheless, already shared certain binding attitudes and beliefs. Both had grown up essentially fatherless boys nurtured by poor, suffering mothers whom they both loved and resented. Hating racism, both men were also haunted by what would soon be called a sense of existential chaos in life. Both were hungry for fame, in love with art and ideas, and adoring of Western learned culture. Both Wright and Ellison admired and yet had grown more and more critical of black culture. They had become especially disdainful of its political and religious leaders....Ralph's most ambitious pieces of fiction emerged directly from Wright's commanding effect on him at this time. (97, 106)

The themes of fatherlessness and natal alienation represent an enduring issue for both authors. While we may immediately think of making a comparison between Bigger Thomas and Cross Damon, there is little doubt that Cross represents a more sophisticated and without question a more deadly version of a Black individual at odds with himself and society, a Black man willing to kill for the philosophies and ideas that he views as fundamental to his existence.

Like his psychological counterpart, Bigger Thomas, Cross Damon at the start of the novel is a rat in a dirty corner, physically and psychologically trapped by his environment, and he acknowledges his need for support from his fellow Black postal workers. Self-medicating with alcohol does nothing to relieve his deep-seated emotional frustrations. One fellow worker provides an example of one of Cross's gags: he would buy a batch of magazines—*Harper's, Atlantic Monthly, Collier's, Ladies Home Journal*—and send them as Christmas gifts to his friends, but he would not sign his name, instead he signed the names of friends of people he was sending the subscriptions to. The novel's description of Damon's psyche relates: 'Any man who can do things like this is a man standing *outside* of the world. Like somebody outside of your window was looking into your house and poking out his tongue at you.' "[3] Cross is not just literally outside of society; a deep internal factor places him outside of conventional human interaction. My analysis of Cross Damon as the ultimate outsider will be done in the context of a Black male with a Du Boisian double consciousness similar to that of those light-skinned Black individuals seeking to escape their blackness by passing for white. The most appropriate literary analogy would be the nameless protagonist in James Weldon Johnson's *The Autobiography of an Ex-Coloured Man* (1912). Socialized to pass for white, the Ex-Coloured Man uses his musical ability to abandon his blackness and permanently pass as a white man. On his journey to whiteness the light-skinned protagonist experiences the death of his mother, abandonment by his white father, the theft of his money to go a Black college, and finally the sight of a Black man being lynched and burned causes him to abandon his blackness. In the first paragraph of Johnson's novel the critical aspects of racial passing are announced with the protagonist summing up his experiences:

> I know that in writing the following pages I am divulging the great secret of my life, the secret which for some years I have guarded far more carefully than any of my earthly possessions, and it is a curious study to me to analyze the motives which prompt me to do it. I feel that I am led by the same impulse which forces the unfound-out criminal to take somebody into his confidence, although he knows that the act is liable, even almost certain, to lead to his undoing. I know that I am playing with fire, and I feel the thrill which accompanies that most fascinating pastime, and back of it all, I think I find a sort of savage and diabolic desire to gather up all the little tragedies of my life, and turn them into a practical joke on society.[4]

These aspects of racial passing speak directly to Cross Damon's behavior, especially the clandestine and criminal aspects. The critical difference between the Ex-Colored Man and Cross is the psychological component. While the Ex-Colored Man is passive and extremely non-confrontational as he moves away from his Black identity, Cross is aggressive and extremely violent as he, too, moves away from his Black identity. Both narratives end tragically with the Ex-Colored Man lamenting his decision to abandon his philosophy of racial uplift and Cross, sensing the errors of his ways, attempting to return to blackness but never having the opportunity.

I want to emphasize the deep psychological alienation and the extreme acts of violence that Cross engages in to either maintain his freedom or to further escape from blackness. For Cross his blackness becomes defined by a deep sense of nihilism brought on by his divorce from Gladys and subsequent alienation from his sons, his oppressive and frustrated mother, his deadening job at the Post Office, his chronic alcoholism, and by the fact that his ex-girlfriend, Dot, out of her own loneliness and desperation, tricked him and wanted to take him to court for statutory rape. After escaping from Chicago, Damon rents a room, and the jazz records that the young Black widow plays become a metaphor for his divided subjectivity:

> He realized that this blue-jazz was a rebel art blooming seditiously under the condemnation of a Protestant ethic just as his own consciousness had sprung conditioned to defiance from his relationship to his mother, who had shrilly evoked in him exactly what she had so desperately tried to smother. Blue jazz was the scornful gesture of men turned ecstatic in their state of rejection, it was the musical language of the satisfiedly amoral, the boasting of the contentedly lawless, the recreations of the innocently criminal. (178)

This passage is emblematic of Damon's lawless behavior and nihilism all designed to further his escapism from his Black family and his culture, ultimately seeking an confrontational yet oppressive interracial world represented by the Communist Party. Like light-skinned Blacks seeking to escape blackness by passing for white, Damon passes while maintaining his tormented Black identity. Wright's characterization of Damon is that of a man seething with anxiety: "He twisted on his crumpled bed...trying to purge his mind of anxiety, beseeching sleep....Then convulsively, his entire body jerked rigidly to stem a fearful feeling of falling through space. His rebellious nerves twanged with a terror that his mind sought desperately to deny. He shook his head, his body seething with hate against himself and the world (15). Cross' antipathy and self-hatred are analogous to the unspoken frustrations of his nameless father who met his death after a drunken brawl.

Like many "passing" narratives in which Blacks assume a white identity, a death must occur for a new identity to be born. For the characters who pass, the realization of desire comes in a sinister form, destruction of the self. Death and desire become intertwined and interconnected because passing involves a death-within-life in order to preserve life-within-in-death. Beset by an estranged wife, Gladys, and two sons, a pregnant underage girlfriend, Dot, a religious suffocating mother, and problems at work, Damon is in a desperate state. A violent subway crash in Chicago occurs in a critical point in beleaguered Damon's life: He is ready to do something desperate because, despite her having misrepresented her age to him, Dot is considering getting a lawyer, accusing Damon of rape, and confronting Damon's overbearing wife, who will, in turn, confront his zealous Christian mother. Damon, contemplating how Dot "tricked him" and the dire consequences of her legal actions, considers that, "He ought to buy a railroad ticket for as long a journey as the money would cover and vanish. There was no doubt now but that Dot had made up her mind, and from now on he had to regard her as his enemy" (51). In African American literary discourse from the slave narratives to the present, the train has always represented escape and freedom from oppressive conditions. Here the conditions are more psychological, especially Damon's shame as it relates to his mother's probable reaction. This conflict highlights the larger issue of Damon's problems with all Black women, who are characterized as oppressive, manipulative, vindictive, and deceptive. Wright's simultaneous characterization of Damon's "deepening mood of desire for the desirable" for females, of "woman as body of woman," is purely sexual, but it has an objectifying context involving Black and white women. Indeed it is the objectified "woman as body of woman" that gives Damon his freedom. After the train crashes, a dazed and bewildered Damon struggles to liberate himself from the wreckage, and it is a woman's body that provides the foundation for his freedom, especially from his mother, Gladys, and Dot:

> He crept forward over the ceiling of the overturned coach, past twisted and bloody forms, crunching shattered electric bulbs under his feet, feeling his shoes slopping through sticky liquid. He moved on tiptoe, as though afraid of waking the sleeping dead. He reached the window and saw that a young woman's body had been crushed almost flat just beneath it. The girl was dead, but if he was to get through that window, he had either the choice of standing upon her crushed body or remaining where he was. He stepped upon the body, feeling his shoes sinking into the lifeless flesh and seeing blood bubbling from the woman's mouth as his weight bore down on her bosom.... He crawled through and lowered his feet to the ground. (97)

Like a slave on a transport ship during the Middle Passage, Damon searches for a way to survive, and his very survival becomes dependent on using this woman's dead and deformed body as a stepladder. Simply put, death provides a false freedom. As Frank McMahon states: "In this scene the natural process of birth is evoked only to be abused: the head battered to pulp, the woman's body trampled on. This anti-birth promises, falsely, to free the intellectual Cross from the constraints associated with the body" (299). Beyond McMahon's astute analysis we also recall how Bigger battered Bessie Mears's head and throws her body down a shaft. Throughout the novel "woman as woman body" becomes to resonate a constant objectification of the female body. Also, Wright reverses and reinscribes the traditional motif of the train movement from slavery to freedom. Although the subway train "streaking through the underground" crashes, it becomes Damon's literal and metaphoric vehicle for physical and psychological liberation with economic implications. This scene becomes Wright's literary tool for Damon's identity reformation and reconstitution as he assumes the identity of a dead Black man, who Damon notices has the same "color and build" sitting across the aisle from him. In a surreal moment, Damon eats at a restaurant and hears a radio newscast that relates:

Ladies and gentlemen, the police have just informed me of the identity of the last victim taken from the subway crash at Roosevelt Road. His name is Cross Damon, a 26-year-old postal clerk who lived at 244 East 57th Street on the South Side. Mr. Damon's body was crushed and mangled beyond recognition or hope of direct identification. His identity has been established, however, by his overcoat, private papers, and his post office badge... His body is being taken directly to the Cook County Morgue. Relatives must address all inquiries there. (103–04; author's emphasis)

Damon's first thought is to share the bizarre joke with his friends, but after some reflections about the consequences of his death would affect the three women in his life, "a keen sensation of vitality invaded every cell of his body and a slow strange smile stole across his lips" (106). With $800 in his shirt pocket from a Post Office loan and the work day off, Damon realizes that his announced death will provide him total freedom from all of his family responsibilities. "He would be a damn fool if he did not try it. All of his life he had been hankering about personal freedom and now freedom was knocking on the door, begging him to come out" (107). The subway death scene and the assumption of the identity of Lionel Lane, a name he finds by searching through a snowbound cemetery in New York provide for the death and birth of a new Cross Damon, who, as he states, has become a criminal: "In a way, he was a criminal, not because of what he was feeling. It was for much more than merely criminal reasons that he was fleeing to escape his identity, his old hateful consciousness" (109). Like the Ex-Coloured Man in Johnson's novel, Damon develops a deep ambivalence as a Black man in the context of all the socioeconomic and psychological restrictions in a society deeply segregated by racism. Like black bugs trapped in a ventilated jar, both Black men are trapped by their circumstances. Johnson's character frees himself using his musical ability and his light-skinned phenotype, and Damon uses the dead bodies of other Black males, the nameless man killed on the train and Joe Thomas, a fellow Post Office worker.

While the death of the Ex-Colored Man's Black mother, the symbolic death of his white father, and the bloody death of the white widow in the club all have a traumatic effect on him, Damon creates his own trauma by his enduring deception and murderous acts. After becoming "Charles Webb from Memphis, Damon commits his first murder at a hotel after seeing "big, fat, black Joe Thomas," a Black man who served as a pallbearer at his funeral. Realizing that Joe is going to "smash all he had so laboriously built up" (135), Damon picks up a bottle, smashes Joe in the head, and throws his body out the window unto a snow-covered roof. Killing Joe in order to keep alive his new identity and freedom represents a more direct destruction of Damon's troubled past because he had known Joe for over six years, an individual who symbolized the restricted Black life he is rejecting,.

Similar to Johnson's train scenes in *The Autobiography of an Ex-Coloured Man,* Wright's second train scene in *The Outsider* serves a dual purpose in reinforcing Damon's freedom journey away from blackness and a transition to a more intellectual intraracial society. Damon's connection to and distance from the Black world are established in his relationship with Bob Hunter, a short Black waiter on the train, who announces to Damon that he has his "hand full of white shit" because his partner got sick and got off in Cleveland. Like the unexpected meeting and then deliberate murder of Joe Thomas at the hotel, Cross Damon's desire for freedom comes is conflicted when a white woman passenger screams at Bob: "Nigger, you're burning me'" Considering America's long history of extra-legal lynching of thousands of Black males for having real or imagined contact with white females, this white woman's exclamation represents generations of racist white males burning "niggers" for bothering white females. Full of his sense of newfound freedom, Damon jumps up to confront the white woman who is about to assault Bob. Damon defiantly responds with "You're not hitting anyone either" when the woman tells him "You're not hitting me, nigger" (158). The dynamics of race are made clear here when Damon jumps up to stop the woman from hitting Bob and the white priest who Damon was talking to jumps up to defend the white woman. "Both of them had acted before they had been fully conscious of what they had wanted to do" (159). Bob requests that Damon serve as a witness because the white woman is threatening to sue the company. Keeping true to the masquerade, Cross Damon or at this point Lionel Lane gives his name as Addison Jordan with a false address in Harlem. Unknown to Bob, Cross's deception is a source of anguish to him:

> Hunter was believing that he had his help, that he would be a friend. He had made Hunter a promise that he could not keep, just as he had made his mother, his sons, Dot, Gladys, and Jenny (a white prostitute at the hotel where he killed Joe) promises that he could not keep.... His nonidentity was making Hunter believe in the unreal.... He had to break out of this dream, or he would surely go mad. He had to be born again, come anew into the world. To live amidst others without an identity was intolerable. (167)

Damon articulates the fundamental aspects of a Black man who is an outsider; in every aspect of his life he must be disingenuous if he is to survive and maintain his freedom from his past. In Johnson's novel the train scene is reversed: the Black porter befriends the Ex-Coloured Man, then steals his money for college from his trunk, only to later loan him $15, presumably part of his own money. Upon meeting the porter again much later, the Ex-Colored Man returns the loan and notices that the porter has on his lamented black and gray tie that had also taken from the trunk. Unwilling to take any action on this theft that had drastically changed his life, he states:

"My astonishment and the ironical humor of the situation drove everything else out of my mind" (52). On the other hand, Cross is fundamentally deceptive as evidenced in his beating his wife and feigning amnesia all in order to end the relationship. Cross plans his attack: "He was far from planning anything criminal; it was a complicated psychological attack whose consequences would clarify Gladys' feelings about him.... His self-hatred, his aversion for Gladys, his perpetual toying with his own feelings had resulted in there flashing into his mind a confoundingly luminous image" (72). Without saying a word, Cross repeatedly slaps Gladys, returns to the bar, and then comes home acting as if nothing has happened. After the second attack, Cross achieves his objective when Gladys says: "I can't bear with you another minute. Pack your things and get out *now*! You're crazy, a danger to yourself and others" (82)! These incidents foreshadow the cool and cunning behavior that Cross displays in his interactions with the Communists. Beyond abandoning his mother, Gladys, and his pregnant girlfriend Dot, Damon has abandoned his sons. Damon's guilt and shame (and guilt in regard to Bob Hunter) are magnified ten-fold when he thinks about his family, especially his small sons—Cross Junior, Peter, and Robert—not just abandoned but deliberately made to believe that he is dead.

Damon's dread and deference are evident when he meets another outsider on the train, District Attorney Ely Houston of New York City. Houston represents a physical and psychological paradox in that he is a hunchback but possesses an acute mental awareness. Wright's description of Houston captures the paradox along with the dread that Damon has for this white man who represents a high level of law enforcement:

> The hump on his back was prominent but not in any way as noticeable as Cross would have thought it would be, so naturally did it blend in with the man's general build. Cross had not particularly noticed this deformity when Houston had first sat down, but now he remembered that Houston had moved forward to the table with a motion that slightly resembled that of a creeping animal, holding his body still as he walked. He reminded Cross of a giant, patiently waiting white spider whose temper was never ruffled but whose mental processes ground fast and exceedingly fine. He had the impression of a man possessing stealthy reserves of physical and emotional strength, and he felt intuitively that this was exactly the kind of man whom he had to fear not only because he was a defender of the law, but because Houston had an ability to delve into life. He was afraid of this man and yet his fear made him want to know him. (161–62)

Damon's immediate reaction to Houston is to consider that the Chicago police had wired the train and sent the district attorney to apprehend him. Beyond his apprehension, Damon is attracted to Houston's ability to delve deeply into human psychology. Although white male privilege is obviously an element in the relationship between Damon and Houston, Damon understands that Houston views himself as an outsider who has the ability to comprehend that Black people are perpetual outsiders. Houston states:

> Negroes, as they enter our culture, are going to inherit the problems we have, but with a difference. They are outsiders and they are going to know that they have these problems. They are going to be self-conscious; they are going to be gifted with a double vision, for being Negroes, they are going to be both inside and outside of our culture at the same time. Every emotional and cultural convulsion that ever shook the heart and soul of Western man will shake them. Negroes will develop unique and specially defined psychological types. (163)

Damon reflects the complexity of internal and external forces. In abandoning his sons, Damon follows the pattern of his father, who after returning from France during World War I, re-joined the army as a regular soldier. He used alcohol to relieve the trauma of battle and the trauma of racism at home. Finally Damon's mother learns that "somewhere in the reaches of Harlem, in a dirty, vacant lot at midnight, the police had found him lying wounded. He had been in a drunken street brawl, had lain unconscious in subzero weather and had died a day later in an army hospital" (28). Like many traumatized Black soldiers returning from war, Damon's father confronted America's ongoing racism and segregation's dire socioeconomic effects. Damon never knew his father and never had the influence, protection, and guidance that a healthy father and son relationship would provide. Providing for a family represents a critical concern for many Black men in a country defined by white patriarchy; and beyond the disruption caused by Dot being pregnant, Damon would have soon been burdened by yet another child to support. Damon's mother provides the reader a sense of the weight that he carries: "To think I named you Cross after the Cross of Jesus" (29) she tells her son. Wright's choice of a name suggests a plethora of possibilities as it relates to Black male subjectivity and legal matters. Under America's white supremacist patriarchal culture, Black males represent a critical threat as reflected by the fact that thousands of Black men have been lynched or otherwise killed. Wright's surreal poem about lynching "Between the World and Me" (1935) immediately comes to mind as Wright's religious symbolism makes an analogy between the crucifixion of Christ and the extra-legal lynching of a nameless Black man. A relevant line is "There was a charred stump of a sapling pointing a blunt finger accusingly at the sky." An analysis of this section of the poem reveals:

> Ironically, only through the ritualistic act of lynching do the fragments of the black body find some element of peace. But the "charred stump of a sapling pointing a blunt finger accusingly at the sky" personifies and provides a synthesis between the lynching and the crucifixion of Jesus Christ. While on the cross, Jesus asks God the father why He has forsaken him. With adept personifying signification,

Wright has the sapling asking God why has this African American man has been tortured and killed; also, the sapling asks why has it been tortured and killed by mankind. Both the African American man and the sapling that the man has been bound to have become sacrificial victims of white people's malfeasance manifested in ritual violence; the sapling voices a double articulation: the lost of human life and the desecration of nature. The fingers of the man become metastasized into the accusing gesture of the sapling; yet there resides some tension here. Whereas Jesus Christ has sacrificed himself for all of mankind, the African American male body becomes an ensanguined sacrifice for the furtherance of the socioeconomic subjectivity of white male supremacy. (*Eating the Black Body* 30)

Thus the name "Cross" represents the sacrifice and struggles that many Black men have made during enslavement, Reconstruction, Jim Crow segregation, and in America's foreign wars through the Civil Rights era fighting for socioeconomic justice and freedom, as Damon's father did. The name also represents the racial boundary that Damon will cross to achieve his psychological freedom. With regard to conflict between a Black mother and son a section of Langston Hughes's poem "Cross" reads: "If ever I cursed my black old mother/And wished she were in hell,/I'm sorry for that evil wish/And now I wish her well." Perhaps more than any other woman in the novel, Damon's relationship with his mother causes him the most psychological anguish, an anguish so profound that abandonment is his only recourse. In his mind, Damon's mother projects her failed relationship with his father on to him, causing him to experience a violent rage:

She had done it; she had evoked in him that shameful mood of guilt born of desire and fear of desire. He knew that she was not lamenting for him alone, but for her own betrayed maidenhood, for how she had once been so treacherously beguiled into trusting surrender; she was blaming him somehow for its having gone wrong, confusedly seeking his masculine sympathy for her sexually blighted life! Goddamn her! Hadn't she no sense of shame? He imagined himself rising and with a single sweep of his palm slapping her to the floor. And in the same instant a poignant pity for her seized him. Poor, lost, lonely woman clinging for salvation to a son who she knew was as lost as she was. He was too close to her and too far from her; much too warm toward her and much too cold.... And this image of his mother's incestuously-tinged longings would linger with him for days and he could curse her for it, and finally he would curse himself for living in a crazy world that he could not set right. (26)

Here we have another disturbing element of Damon's psyche of wanting to abandon his blackness, his mother's incestuous desire born of her own failed relationship with his father. As Damon's father is dead, she projects her shame and guilt along with the sublimation of her sexual self to her son.

Damon's own guilt and shame lead him to Bob Hunter's apartment and into a world of intense intraracial conflict and intense violent interracial conflict represented by the Communist Party. Here Bob informs Damon that he lost his job with the railroad because he was counting on Damon to be a witness in the lawsuit brought by the white woman whose arm was accidentally burned. Paradoxically, in line with death and rebirth, Bob informs Damon that he went to the address that Cross had given him, and it turned out to be funeral parlor and nobody knew him there. Damon's deception with Bob pales when compared to the arson and forgery he committed in order to obtain the identity of the dead Lionel Lane; each step to conceal his real identity solidifies his status as an outsider. Understanding the nature of white supremacy, Damon feigns the role of the slow and intellectually challenged Black man in order to obtain a duplicate birth certificate:

> Cross knew exactly what kind of man he would pretend to be in order to ally suspicions if he ever got into trouble. In his role of an ignorant, frightened Negro, each white man—except those few who were free from the race bias of their group—he would encounter would leap to supply him with a background and an identity; each white man would project out upon him his own conception of the Negro and he could safely hide behind it. (217)

Like many Black male characters in passing narratives, fair-skinned protagonists become chameleons to assume and maintain their white identities; Cross' masquerade as the stereotypical feeble-minded Black feeds into all the theories of Black inferiority allowing him to pass as Lionel Lane. With Bob, Damon realizes the full extent of his false identity: "His life had become a vast system of pretense; one act of bad faith necessitated another, and in order to prove the sincerity of a new lie he had to fall back upon lying still further" (222). Although Cross cannot physically pass for white, his quest for socioeconomic subjectivity in the white world reveals that crossing geographic boundaries, forsaking family, changing one's name, prevaricating and performing are too often critical for many black people's success in the white world. However, Bob's wife, Sarah's initial reaction to Cross and his undeclared desire to join the Communist party "to find some disguise for his outlaw existence" (224) causes uncontrollable laughter; the idea of Cross as an intellectual is hard for her to believe. Deeply offended but able to keep up the masquerade of blackness, Cross conceals his seething rage with laughter.

In the section describing Cross' relationship with the Communist Party, Wright solidifies his characterizations of his status as an outsider as the excitement and thrill of masquerade becomes intertwined with violence. Cross's relationship with the Communist Party turns violent when Bob Hunter is driven out of the Party and when Damon discovers how Eva, a twenty-four-year-old white woman married to Gil Blount, a Party leader, has been manipulated. Here unlike the Ex-Colored Man, Cross's delusions of embracing whiteness are totally eviscerated his violent behavior envelops everyone. For the Ex-Colored Man the scene that seals his fate in whiteness occurs when he witnesses a nameless Black man being lynched and burned alive. Like the light-skinned Walter White who passed for white when he investigated lynchings while working for the NAACP, the Ex-Colored Man understands that he could easily be lynched for passing as a white man. Articulating his rationale for permanently passing as a white man, the Ex-Colored Man discusses his deep sense of humiliation and shame in being Black:

> A great wave of humiliation and shame swept over me. *Shame that I belonged to a "race" that could be so dealt with; and shame for my country, that it, the great example of democracy to the world, should be the only civilized, if not the only state on earth, where a human being would be burned alive.* My heart turned bitter within me. I could understand why Negroes are led to sympathize with even their worst criminals and to protect them whenever possible. By all the impulses of normal human nature they can and should do nothing less. (137; emphasis added)

For Cross the emasculation and symbolic castration of Bob Hunter in front of him and Bob's wife by Jack Hilton, a leader of the Communist Party illustrates a similar Lacanian scene for Cross Damon with a similar feeling of humiliation and shame. Deciding that Bob will no longer organize the Dining Car Waiters' Union, Jack Hilton's tone is beyond arrogance as he tells Bob that he must stop his activities and that he would be disciplined, expelled from the Party or even killed if he refuses. Without flinching, Jack tells Bob:

> You are an instrument of the Party. You exist to execute the Party's will. That's all there is to it.... And being a Communist is not easy. It means negating yourself, blotting out your personal life and listening only to the voice of the Party.... The Party hopes that you can understand *why* you must obey; but even if you don't understand you *must* obey. If you don't, then the Party will toss you aside, like a broken hammer, and seek another instrument that will obey. Don't think that you are indispensable because you're black and the Party needs you. The Party is conducting this fight on your behalf and you must fit into it. (248)

Jack's strategic discourse places the demeaned Bob in his place and shows Cross what he is in for if he desires to become a member of the Communist Party. Indeed the point is clear: "Cross felt that a better demonstration of what he was in for could not have happened even if it had been arranged" (249). For Damon this hegemonic and arrogant discourse is analogous to that of his white supervisor at the Post Office and the white workers at the office where he got his false birth certificate. Moreover, Bob's shame and humiliation also affect Damon because of the racial and emotional bond they have; Damon's equivocation caused Bob to lose his job in the very place that he is now organizing. However, Damon's unqualified contempt for the Communist Party has been established long before this incident. When Bob suggests that Damon meets his Communist friends, Damon considers that the Party would be the perfect place for him:

> Did not the Communists, like he, have a secret to hide. And what was the Communist secret? Cross felt that at the heart of a political movements the concept of the basic inequality of man was enthroned and practiced, and the skill of politicians consisted in how cleverly they hid the elementary truth and gained votes by pretending the contrary.... If, by pretending, he could find a hiding place, why, he would pretend that he believed in the Communist pretensions. (224)

Like the Ex-Colored Man's embrace of whiteness, for Damon the Communist Party represents a similar place of privilege and protection along with the illusion of inclusion. In Johnson's novel the protagonist's white wealthy benefactor tells him that aside from his pigmentation he is a white man, and his questioning makes the racial differences clear: "My boy, by blood, by appearances, by education, and by tastes, a white man. Now why do you want to throw your life away amidst poverty and ignorance, in the hopeless struggle of the black people of the United States?" (86). Although the Ex-Colored Man has some specific desires with regard to music and making an impact on Black culture, Damon, who cannot pass for white, does want to escape the poverty and ignorance associated with Black people who live under the thumb of white supremacy. Indeed the white millionaire makes an astute analysis of the racial situation in America:

> We hit slavery through a great civil war. Did we destroy it? No, we changed it into hatred between sections of the country in the South, into political corruption and chicanery, the degradation of blacks through peonage, unjust laws and cruel treatment; and the degradation of the whites by their resorting to these practices, the paralyzation of the public conscience, and the ever overhanging dread of what the future may bring.' (87)

Perhaps this reinforces and reinscribes Damon's view of the Communist Party when he views Bob's humiliation in front of his wife and later understands the degradation that Gil's wife, Eva, experiences under the Party's leadership. Eva's diary reveals her lifeless marriage based on deception and betrayal in that Gil was ordered by the Party to marry her for "prestige purposes" because she had "a stunningly successful exhibit in New York." More shocking than this, Eva's diary reveals that "Gil's secretary, Rose Lampkin [who accompanied them to Paris on their honeymoon], was his mistress and had been for years, and that at the same time she was spying on Gil" (279). Like Cross's father died, who died when Cross was an infant, Eva's father died when she was six and she became an orphan. Gil drowns his feelings in alcohol because he is ashamed to face Eva sober; as a result, Eva resolves that "Gil will *never* touch me drunk or sober" (282). While Cross's instincts about the Communist Party were accurate, he had no idea about the personal levels of deception that Party members are involved in. The last diary entry that Cross reads concerns himself—speculations on his past and a warning:

> He is a young Negro, living under an assumed name, a fugitive from southern racist. He is, according to Bob, who swore me to secrecy, a bright young Negro intellectual who had some dire trouble with whites and committed some crime and is in hiding to save his life. Bob met the young man on the train and is certain that he has killed a white man, and that there is a price on his head.... It sounds so exciting, terrible, pitiful.... And they're bringing him into the Party! Another victim? I wish I could talk to him and tell him something... Colored people are so trusting and naïve... He's going to be misled by Gil just as I have been. (285)

Eva's entry serves two narrative functions. First, it essentializes Black male subjectivity with regard to Black status in America's white supremacist society. There is the idea that Black men are in a constant violent battle with racist white men. Second, this diary entry foreshadows the killing of three white men, one a rabid white supremacist and the two others more benign white supremacists—all three have a god complex and all three have ideologies of supremacy. Cross's reading of Eva's diary is significant in terms of traumatic countertransference or vicarious traumatization, a process whereby one person's traumatic experience can revive another person's traumatic experience. Framing her analysis in terms of a patient and therapist encounter, Judith Herman's analysis can extend to Eva and Cross. Herman states:

> Traumatic countertransference includes the entire range of the therapist's emotional reactions to the survivor and to the traumatic event itself.... In addition to suffering vicarious symptoms of post-traumatic stress disorder, the therapist has to struggle with the same disruptions in relationship as the patient. Repeated exposure to stories [diaries] of human rapacity and cruelty challenges the therapist's basic faith. It also heightens her [or his] sense of personal vulnerability. She [or he] may become more fearful of other people in general and more distrustful even in close relationships. She [or he] may herself [or himself] becoming increasingly cynical about the motives of others and pessimistic about the human condition. (141)

Cross internalizes Eva's trauma because it represents his own traumas with his mother, Gladys, and Dot; he believes that they all betrayed him. Wright's narrative structure suggests a direct correlation between Cross reading the diary and the ensuing murders of Herndon and Blount.

Despite the extreme risks involved in undermining his clandestine status as an outsider, the double degradation of Bob Hunter and Eva Blount makes it much easier for Cross Damon / Lionel Lane to viciously slaughter Gil Blount and his white fascist landlord, Langley Herndon, "a dyed-in-the-wool Negro hater" (263) and later shoot and murder Jack Hilton—all whites with god complexes. Bob not only loses his role as a union organizer for railroad workers, but because of the Party's actions, he faces deportation. Sarah views her husband's degradation as worse than an extra-legal lynching: "Even in the South when the white folks lynched you, they told you why! You didn't agree with 'em, but, by God, they told you why!" And then Sarah compares the Communist Party to Jim Crow: "All my life I've seen niggers knuckling down to white people. I saw my mama knuckling down when I was a child in the South. And nothing hurt me so much as when I saw a white man kick her one day'" (257). Unknown to Sarah, Bob experiences a more metaphorical kicking when he comes to Gil and Eva's apartment after the Party expels him and Immigration officers come to his apartment. Cross watches Bob sobbing and pleading with Gil, who shows absolutely no compassion for Bob's fear of doing ten years in "jail in the tropics" for former Party activity. Cross again registers the shame and rage of seeing another Black man kowtowing to power: "Cross was stunned. He wanted to rise and place his foot on Bob's neck and cut off the flow of whining words. Gil watched Bob with calm placid eyes and Cross wondered how many men and women Gil had seen in such prostrate positions of penitent surrender to enable him to stare at Bob with so aloof and yet engrossed a passion" (296). Gil true to his god-like posture, informs the men from Immigration and Bob is arrested and will most likely die in a prison in Trinidad. Like a tool no longer able to serve its purpose, Bob is discarded. The Party has no regard for him or his wife; even more malevolent is the clandestine role that the Party has had in his arrest and deportation.

With little regard for Bob's life, Cross represents another tool to be used by Gil, Jack, and the Communist Party, but Cross's masquerading posture results in two separate yet deliberate deadly encounters. First, knowing the racist and fascist perspectives of his landlord, Langley Herndon, Gil Blount informs Cross that he will be a pawn of the Party against race based housing segregation in their apartment building, and this leads to a confrontation between Langley and Cross. Here Wright establishes Langley's self-righteous and god-like persona as he informs Cross about his building's policy: "You're black and you don't belong there and you goddamn well know it" (287). Cross informs Herndon that he is not a Communist and warns him that he has a gun and is willing to use it if Herndon pulls a gun; later Cross tells Eva that "I like his kind" (289). The obvious paradox here is that Wright makes a distinction between those whites like Herndon who are open white supremacists and those whites like Gil and Jack who are the more benign white supremacists; perhaps it is easier to deal with the former because they are more honest in their contempt for Blacks, whom they perceive as innately inferior.

When Cross kills both Herndon and Gil after they were fighting each other, the novel provides us with a racial synthesis. Wright suggests that any individual can become an outsider within his or her particular racial or ideological perspective, especially if that person believes himself superior in some manner. As Herndon and Gil are exchanging blows in Herndon's apartment, Cross contemplates: "Which man he hated more? Many times during the past twenty-four hours he had wished both of them dead and now he was looking at them batter each other's brains out.... Let 'em fight it out, he said to himself" (300). Instead of leaving them alone Cross plays god and bludgeons them both to death with a "heavy oaken leg of the table" (303). Like Shakespeare's famous line about little boys and wanton flies, Cross, assuming a god-like persona, concludes that after bludgeoning Herndon so hard that his muscles ached and seeing a bloody Gil struggling to his feet: "Yes, this insect had to be crushed blotted out of existence" (303). With both white men dead ("bloody forms stretched grotesquely on the smeared rug") (303), Cross understands how these white men have transformed him into the very individual that he despises. In the conclusion of the book "Descent," Wright characterizes Cross as a man infected by the same disease he sought to destroy:

> Like Hilton and Gil had acted toward Bob, so had he acted toward Gil and Herndon; he had assumed the role of policeman, judge, supreme court, and executioner—all in one swift and terrible moment. But, if he resented their being little gods, how could he do the same? His self assurance ebbed, his pride waned under the impact of his own reflections. Oh, Christ, their disease had reached out and claimed him too. He had been subverted by the contagion of the lawless; he had been defeated by that which he sought to destroy.... He had become what he has tried to destroy, had taken on the guise of the monster he had slain. (309)

Cross's killing of Jack Hilton represents a continued descent into lawlessness and the death of his dream of a life as an outsider in the Communist Party. Once Cross realizes that Jack suspects him and discovers evidence of his crime (a bloody handkerchief which he thought he had burned by dropping it in the incinerator) in Jack's hotel room, Cross realizes that he must kill again, but his reasoning is more complex here because he understands that Jack would use the bloody evidence to make Cross his slave. Even in the Communist Party there is the need for the proverbial "hewers of wood and drawers of water." Like Johnson's Ex-Colored Man who after deep consternation terminates his relationship with the wealthy white millionaire because he also realized his role in the Hegelian master and slave dialectic (the Man played the piano for his master who later provided travel, clothes, and lodging on their overseas trip), Cross is willing to kill to be maintain his freedom as an outsider. While Gil Blount's attempts to manipulate Cross are arrogantly straightforward in terms of the ideology and philosophy of the Communist Party, Cross realizes that Jack Hilton, a much more sinister individual, would be more ruthless and demanding in making him his personal slave. Wright's description of Jack Hilton makes clear his enduring threat to Cross Damon's freedom:

A disciplined man, cold precise, farseeing ruthless; Hilton was free of such infantile stupidities as racial hatred; he was no frightened, white American dope worried about a white girl who slept with a colored boy.... Hilton was after power and his keeping his mouth shut about Cross' guilt was but one more step along the road to getting hold of a young bright man whose life he would own and whose talents would serve him in his struggle for power. (395)

With the confidence and candor of an experienced assassin, Cross explains to the power-driven Jack (a name that recalls the manipulative and highly deceptive white male communist with a glass eye in Ralph Ellison's *Invisible Man*) that he was responsible for Bob Hunter being sent back to Trinidad and a sure death sentence. Jack's sincere yet arrogant response seals his fate when in responding to Cross' concern about Bob's fate, he says "So what there are a million Bob Hunters. What do you mean? They don't count." (399) Cross understands that he and other Black men only count in terms of their utility to white males in the Communist Party and that their struggles against America's white supremacy and too often violent racism will only be used to advance another form of white male supremacy. Not surprisingly, Jack reveals that he is pleased that Gil is dead because he stood between him and "one of the most important assignments on the Central Committee" and that he always wanted Eva. For Jack, "Gil's death was like a gift dropped from the sky" (397). Equally important, Jack reveals that he was able to see beyond Cross's masquerade for the white police officers. Jack tells Cross: "I'm not so stupid a white man that I cannot tell the difference between fear and self-possession in a Negro. You were self possessed. The cops thought you were just another scared darky" (397). However, Jack is completely wrong when he believes that the violent murders of Gil and Herndon were all about Cross killing to have Eva; the possibility that Cross or any Black man would resent and be willing to kill god-like white male individuals like Gil and Herndon purely on the basis of ideology is unfathomable. Jack's perception that Cross is strictly motivated by physical desires misses the point. Cross's motivations are foremost his psychological and physical freedom—characterized as an escape from blackness. Jack is clueless about the fact that many Black individuals would view Gil and Herndon as two different versions of white male supremacy. Like an ex-slave on the run and echoing back to the days of the Middle Passage, Cross articulates his desire for freedom in a collective sense when he states: "I won't ever feel free as long as you exist, even if you are not hunting me down. You and men like you are my enemies. Bob Hunters will go on being shipped to their deaths as long as you live.... And don't give me that goddamn argument about helping me. You help others when it suits you, and when it doesn't, you don't" (400)! Wright's point in the ongoing and prolonged discourse between Cross and Jack underscores that psychological trauma has a more devastating effect than physical violence. In explaining to Jack his rationale for killing him, Cross says:

> I might forgive you if you had been going to kill me. But, you were going to make me a slave. I would never have been able to draw a free breath as long as I lived if you had had your way. I'd have suffered, night and day. You would have dominated my consciousness.... If you had killed me, that would have been a simple act. Killing Bob might have been in a way merciful. He wasn't happy. But to make him suffer ten long years! (402–3)

In the killing of Jack, Wright provides a synthesis in Cross's attempts to embrace whiteness as symbolized by Eva and the escape from blackness symbolized by the loud radio's "dancing waves of jazz music that swirled around the room" (405) before he shoots Jack in the temple, leaving another bloody body to symbolize Cross's intense desire to be his own man. As with the killing of Gil and Herndon, Wright presents the larger ideological conflict with all hegemonic dictates, especially those discourses that appear to have a liberatory epistemology. Even in sensing his own doom, Cross understands the many reasons for this final killing: "He killed Jack Hilton for many reasons: to redeem Bob's betrayal, for the sake of Sarah's indignation, for Eva's deceived heart; but mainly it had been to rid himself of the sense of outrage that Hilton's attitude had evoked in him, Hilton's assumption that he could have made a slave of him" (409). Thus in Cross's mind, Jack represents the last barrier to his overall embrace of whiteness and freedom from his Black past, but "each step he took carried him deeper into a morass of lies and deceit" (461).

Wright synthesizes the theme of the Black man as the ultimate outsider when he brings Cross Damon and the white outsider District Attorney Ely Houston ("the old outsider who trapped himself with the law") together in the fifth and last section of the novel. This relationship between two outsiders illustrates how Cross's extreme circumstances of murder and deception place him inside and outside of the legal process. Laying out the foundation for this encounter, Wright raises critical questions about legal jurisprudence—most noticeably that Cross's psychological motivations are atypical, so abnormal that anyone would have a problem suspecting him, much less pronouncing any judgment:

> Who could possibly suspect him of being guilty on the basis of his real motives unless he himself had wrestled fatally with the same serpentine motives in his own heart? And if one had so wrestled, might he not, on finding Cross guilty, feel inclined to cross the line of the law and arraign himself on Cross' side....His crimes constituted so decisive a divergence from the plane of ordinary moral consideration, stemmed from so weird an angle of perspective that he who would find him guilty must needs go so far as to place himself as the same point of vision that he had had

while committing his crimes, and that person, his accuser, would automatically and of necessity have to become entangled in the very guilt he would denounce! He who would judge him would have to be as much outside of the canon of normal living as he before his guilt would become evident to that judge! (410–11)

Cross's rationale centers on the fundamental desire to achieve freedom, a desire that speaks to the essence of being an American and the most difficult existence for a Black man to achieve within a white male-dominated society. The metaphorical killing of the old Cross Damon along with the murders of Joe Thomas, Gil Blount, Langley Herndon, and Jack Hilton—all were designed to keep him free from his Black past and to ensure a new-found freedom in whiteness characterized as a violent and chaotic movement from segregation to integration. However, at the center of this white world, Cross is constantly confronted with ruthless ideological power inside and outside of the Communist Party and those white males who insist that he submit to their dictates. In a very real sense, Ely Houston places Cross Damon on trial and serves as the judge and executioner. With the three brutal murders of Blount, Herndon, and Hilton all being connected to Cross, Houston discovers the real identity of the Black man he knows as Lionel Lane—Cross Damon, a Black man presumed to have been killed in a subway crash. Cross Damon's planned dinner with Ely Houston to discuss philosophy, ideology, and the inner workings of the mind turns out to be an extraordinary inquest, at which all of Cross' secrets and "monstrous deeds" are revealed. On his way to Houston's office, Damon "wondered how much of his path of blood and deception had they uncovered; but his wonderment was devoid of any desire to erect a strategy of legal defense for himself" (501). At this point, Cross realizes that there is no defense or acceptable rationale for his crimes; he silently accepts his status as a Black man living outside of civilized society but lacks the ability to acknowledge his tormented status. Like Shadrack, the Black outsider and psychologically tormented veteran in Toni Morrison's novel *Sula* (1973),[5] Cross Damon "had no party, no myths, no tradition, no race, no soil, no culture, and no ideas—except perhaps the idea that ideas in themselves were at best, dubious" (504–5)! The elaborate cat and mouse session between Houston and Cross begins with Houston asking a series of questions that leads to Cross' repeated statement that he would neither deny nor acknowledge anything. A stoic demeanor remains Cross' psychological posture even when Houston informs him that his mother has died of shock when she learned that he is still alive. This news has no effect on Cross; in fact: "not a facial muscle moved as he gazed into the eyes of Houston" (511). Cross thinks "his mother had been dead for him for years, and that was why he had been able to reflect upon her so coldly and analytically while she had still been living" (512). Without doubt the most psychologically disturbing moment in the novel occurs when an enraged Houston shouts: "Godammit,

I'll break your spirit yet!" He brings forth Cross's wife and his sons—all of whom believed that he was dead and had attended his tragic funeral. While his mixed feelings of antipathy and concern for his mother cause no physical reaction, the sight of his wife and sons produces intense internal anguish and intense anger at Houston for subjecting him to this trauma. For Cross, Houston's behavior is analogous to that of Gil, Langley, and Jack as he vows to be unbroken:

> Yes; Houston, too liked to play at being a little god, liked to ravage the souls of others. That was why he was District Attorney.... And Cross vowed that Houston would never see him humbled, unnerved, or weeping. Houston had thought that the sight of Gladys would make him break down and talk. Well he would not react. He would show Houston that he had miscalculated. Then Cross sucked in his breath sharply; from the open door behind Gladys, being led by Neil, came his three sons, Cross Jr., Robert, and Peter. He whirled to Houston and saw an expression of sensual excitement upon the hunchback's lean face. (519)

Here again Wright emphasizes the theme of natal alienation as Cross comes face to face with his familial neglect as seen in James Weldon Johnson's novel. After his Black mother who had provided a foundation for his musical abilities has died and after years of being on his own, the Ex-Colored Man attends a play by Faust in France and while sitting next to a young white girl, he sees his white father and his wife. The protagonist is so traumatized by this encounter that he feels the urge to scream out that "a tragedy, a real tragedy" is in the audience. As when he watched the white widow being shot in the throat by her Black lover, the Ex-Coloured Man's reaction is shock: "This impulse grew so strong that I became afraid of myself, and in the darkness of one the scenes I stumbled out of the theater. I walked aimlessly about for an hour or so, my feelings divided between a desire to weep and a desire to curse" (81). Here Johnson provides a synthesis of miscegenation and incestuous desire (the Ex-Coloured Man is attracted to the white girl, who he discovers to be his sister), but more important as it relates to Cross and his three sons is the issue of natal alienation. Natal alienation, born during the period of Black people's enslavement has continued into the Jim Crow period because their dire socioeconomic conditions make it difficult for Black males to be men. Having been also abandoned by his own father, Cross's stoic behavior reflects the transgenerational transgression of trauma. For Houston this is Cross's opportunity to redeem himself as he argues the significance of the father and son relationship: "You can redeem yourself with them.... Are you going to let them remember you all of their lives like this? Boys love to think of their fathers as strong, wise men.... To many a son the image of his father is what lifts him up in life. A father can make a boy feel that he has a sure foundation under him, can give him confidence" (521). Houston's discourse of redemption while admirable, does not take into consideration that America's white supremacist culture makes it extremely difficult for Black men to be husbands and fathers, especially to their sons. Damon did not even know his father, and his mother constantly demeaned his father as being the antithesis of strong and wise. Black men were then routinely being lynched for attempting to be strong and wise. Like his father, Damon abandoned his family for psychological and socioeconomic reasons. Wright suggests that as a single mother, Gladys will recreate in her three sons' future crosses that Black women will have to bear. Despite Houston's verbiage, America has always made it extremely difficult for Black men to stand tall and be a role models of strength for their children. Like the white priest on the train who refuses to be a witness for Bob Hunter in his conflict with the white woman, most white males do little to challenge the institutionalized system of white supremacy that requires that Black men acquiesce to its demands. For Damon, this white male supremacy was in the Post Office as well as in the Communist Party, and even here in his relationship with Houston, white male privilege is evident as Cross views him as a "little god." Like Cross's father who went off to war to fight for America's freedom overseas, many Black men fight an internal war with America's racism which left them with deep psychological scars—evident in the fact that Cross and his father both had problems with alcohol.

Like the Communist Party that puts Bob Hunter on trial and sentences him to a life in prison, where he would surely meet his death, Ely Houston places Cross Damon on trial. In both cases the arrogance of white males is on full display as they hold the fates of Black men in their hands. Houston's personal trial leaves him frustrated that Cross will not break from the psychological pressure that the district attorney places on him in order to obtain a confession to the three murders of the "little gods." Like Jack Hilton, Ely Houston believes that Cross killed so that he could have Eva to himself. Cross scorns this simplistic analysis: "Mr. Houston, I don't believe that you really believe that.... Before Gil died, I never touched his wife, never so much as looked at her with desire in my eyes" (524). The bond that Cross has with Eva is more psychological than physical. Having been deceived by Dot, Cross understands the betrayal that Eva experienced with Gil. However, the sexual relationship that Cross develops with Eva after the murder of Gil does represent his attempt to escape the blackness represented by his wife, his children, and his slave-like employment in the Post Office. It is Cross's unwillingness to be a slave that drives him out of his blackness and into a world of whiteness, where he encounters the 'little gods.' The concept of Black male and white female miscegenation advanced by Houston is also supported by the Communist Party, which also views Cross as a multiple murderer. This apprehension of miscegenation represents the lynchpin of white supremacy, which resulted in the extra-legal lynchings of Black men and the unjust incarceration of countless others like the Scottsboro boys.[6] Houston confesses that the police and the medical examiner have no physical evidence to connect Cross to the murders, and his investigation never connects the Joe Thomas murder to Damon. As we will discover in the other novels examined in this volume, the deaths of Black men become marginalized, and only the deaths of white males become important. Houston decides to release Cross from custody because he realizes that if Cross could stand there and deny his sons there is no possibility for redemption and to hold Damon over for a legal trial would be fruitless, especially with little concrete evidence. Eva is subjected to another trial-like experience with the Communist Party, who have finally discovered Cross Damon's past, that his real name is not Lionel Lane, and that he is from Chicago and married with three sons. Eva's confrontation with Cross leads to his confession, but he cannot be truthful with her when she asks why he killed her husband. Cross' deceptive response: "I don't know" is totally disingenuous, but he does confess that he does not "believe in anything" (532). Despite his earnest pleas for Eva's trust, Cross's enduring desire to embrace a life within whiteness has been undone by Eva's statement "*You've* deceived me too!" Cross becomes like the white men he murdered, Gil and Jack, two individuals who used deception to advance their personal objectives and the objectives of the Communist Party. Like the Ex-Colored Man whose white wife dies at the end of the novel, Eva, absolutely distraught by Cross's dishonesty and the full revelation that his earlier confession to the three murders was true, commits suicide by jumping out of the apartment window at Sarah's apartment in Harlem as two members of the Communist Party rush into the apartment.[7]

Death personifies Cross Damon's escape from blackness, and it personifies the end of his attempt to embrace whiteness. Yet too often Black individuals' embrace of whiteness provides only the illusion of freedom because they become trapped in the denial of racial betrayal. Eva came to represent Damon's only hope for a future with his new-found identity based on murder, arson, and deception. With the New York City Police Department, the district attorney, the Communist Party, and Eva all knowing his true identity and the depths of his deception, Cross's masquerade comes to an end. Cross had blood on his hands when he threw Joe Thomas out the hotel window in Chicago, and Wright provides a circular narrative of death when Eva jumps out the window in Harlem, leaving Cross with bloody hands again. Eva's jumping out of the widow was foreshadowed when, confronted by Damon's desire for an abortion, Dot stated: "If you ask me that again, I'll jump out of the window." Cross's fabricated death leads to Dot having the abortion; thus there is another death brought on by Cross's duplicitous actions. The irony here is the possibility of this child facing the same fate as Cross's three sons, absolute abandonment—the issue that for Houston put Cross beyond redemption.

As characterized by the actions of his father and Cross's own irresponsibility, absentee fathers imperil the survival of the Black family. Houston finally realizes that Eva was the person who knew the truth about Cross's crimes and comments on the paradoxical nature of her death:

> The only witness I could have put in the box against you was Eva Blount, and she's dead. If she hadn't leaped from that window, you'd be on your way to the electric chair.... If she had lived, she would have told me what you told her, and what you told her made her kill herself.... What made that girl kill herself was what made me unable to admit that you were guilty.... You depended upon the human heart rejecting a horror of that magnitude and you were almost right, almost successful. (557)

Eva's death frees herself from Damon and simultaneously ends his freedom from blackness. Often the escape from one's race represents an illusion as Ellis Cose offers in *The Rage of a Privileged Class*: "For most blacks in America, regardless of status, political persuasion, or accomplishments, the moment never arrives when race can be treated as a total irrelevancy. Instead too often it is the only relevant factor defining our existence" (28). Realizing the tragic impossibility of attempting to escape his blackness, Damon seeks to return to the home of Hattie, a Black woman that he had "left to fend for herself with her confidence men" (579). In their brief encounter, Cross Damon was passing himself off as Addison Jordan. When he calls, she informs him that she is losing her home. Hattie's loss of her home symbolizes the loss of one's identity as dramatically represented by Cross's tragic journey from Chicago to New York and the death of five individuals. The attempt to return to the home of this too-trusting Black woman represents a larger issue of redemption for Cross, who has coldly and cruelly abandoned his own Black family. Unlike Cross Damon, the Ex-Colored Man reverses the natal alienation associated with his white father but bemoans the loss of artistic endeavors when he states:

> My love for my children makes me glad that I am what I am, and keeps me from desiring to be otherwise, and yet, when I sometimes open a little box in which I still keep my fast yellowing manuscripts, the only tangible remnants of a vanished dream, a dead ambition, a sacrificed talent, I cannot repress the thought, that after all, I have chosen the lesser part, that I have sold my birthright for a mess of pottage. (125)

Here the Faustian bargain represents selling his Black soul to a white identity and the ensuing white privilege defined by the Ex-Colored Man as follows: "I had made up my mind that since I was not going to be a Negro, I would avail myself of every possible opportunity to make a white man's success, and that, if it can be summed up in any one word means 'money'" (115). Although economic reasons were never the primary catalyst for him, Cross' desperate attempt at racial redemption ends in his own death at the hands of Hank and Menti, members of the Communist Party. Thus like most narratives of light-skinned Black individuals abandoning their blackness to embrace whiteness such as Johnson's *The Autobiography of an Ex-Colored Man* and Charles Waddell Chesnutt's *The House Behind the Cedars* (1900), this narrative ends with Cross Damon's deathbed confession. Struggling to speak, Cross acknowledges to Ely Houston that his life: "It.... It was...horrible.... Because in my heart.... I'm...I felt...I'm innocent.... That's what made the horror...." (586). With each deception and with each calculated killing, Cross Damon became more and more of a stranger to himself and an outsider. There would be no going back to his past within the Black society, but there would no future for Cross in a world of whiteness with Eva Blount. In many ways he is dead before he is killed. Unlike the Ex-Colored Man, Cross wanted freedom from ideologies and responsibilities because of a deep-seated self-loathing as expressed by his statement: "Men hate themselves and it makes them hate others" (585). For the white legal authorities and some of the officials in the Communist Party, the desire for Eva represents Cross's objective in the killings of Gil Blount and Jack Hilton. Beginning with the film *Birth of a Nation* this racial stereotype is pervasive in the minds of many white males. Then and now for many white individuals miscegenation between a white woman and a Black man represents the most disturbing aspect of America's seemingly democratic and pluralistic society.

Like many of the philosophical writers that he read and studied such as Franz Kafka and Fyodor Dostoevsky, Richard Wright in *The Outsider* is compelled to characterize those Black men who exist at the margins of society. In African American literature, Cross Damon represents the most extreme urban outlaw not only because of the apocalyptic tragedy and trauma that he created, but because he somehow believes that his actions were righteous. However, Cross Damon also represents another dominant figure in African American literary discourse, the Bad Nigger, because while his behavior is mainly individualistic (the exception being his rage about the fate of Bob Hunter), it can never be disassociated from the oppressive nature of white supremacy and racism. Damon represents the Bad Nigger because, as his last words tell us, he views himself as a victim fighting for his freedom.

Notes

1 In America's patriarchal society one's manhood is determined by his ability to support and protect his family. Accordingly, with Black men in a constant battle to secure decent employment, that issue plays a critical role in the sustainability of Black families.

2 In Arnold Rampersad's *Ralph Ellison: A Biography* (New York: Vintage Books, 2008), Rampersad discusses the Communist Party's relationship with Black people: "Of the major institutions in American life, only the Communist Party officially defined blacks as socially equal to whites. 'I was a Communist because I was a Negro,' Wright later

pointed out. 'Indeed the Communist Party had been the only road out of the Black Belt for me.' Both men [Wright and Ellison] of course knew that this equality was only token. The white ex-Communist Ben Burns, later the first editor of John H. Johnson's *Ebony* magazine, recalled that most white Communists remained 'ignorant of black institutions and society, of black businesses and churches, of black universities and fraternal groups.' Instead, there was 'the contrived, fawning, tiptoe behavior of Party people in relationship to Negroes'" (117).

3   Richard Wright, *The Outsider* (New York: HarperCollins Publisher, 2003) 7. All further references to this text will be given parenthetically.

4   James Weldon Johnson, *The Autobiography of an Ex-Colored Man* (New York: Barnes & Noble, 2007) 1. All further references to this text will be given parenthetically.

5   In Toni Morrison's *Sula* (New York: Plume, 1982), Morrison's characterization of this Black male who served in World War I and who came home traumatized by war is based on negation. Describing Shadrack, Morrison states: "Twenty-two years old weak, hot frightened, not daring to acknowledge the fact that he didn't even know who or what he was... with no past, no language, no tribe, no source, no address book, no comb, no pencil, no clock, no pocket handkerchief, no rug, no bed, no can opener, no faded postcard, no soap, no key, no tobacco pouch, no soiled underwear and nothing nothing nothing to do... he was sure of only one thing; the unchecked monstrosity of his hands" (12). What is striking about Morrison's characterization of this war veteran who is traumatized by the "monstrosity of his hands" is that he is forced to kill in order to survive; similarly Cross Damon has to kill and continue his killing in order to maintain his freedom. Shadrack is an outsider in the Black community called the Bottom who becomes accepted whereas Cross never finds his place in either the segregated Black community or the integrated white community with the Communist Party. In both novels death is a constant theme during the period of Jim Crow. In Morrison's novel we witness the death of Chicken Little and Plum, one by drowning and one by fire. Eva, the mother of Plum, baptizes him with kerosene before setting him on fire. Her rationale is that she would rather see him dead than see him kill himself through the use of drugs; other Black men like Jude, Nel's husband experience a more metaphorical death by being psychologically beaten down by racism, and Ajax disappears after being confronted by a changed Sula, whom he perceives as preparing a nest for them.

6   Like many other Black men, Richard Wright is a paradox. As Arnold Rampersad reveals in *Ralph Ellison: A Biography* (New York: Vintage Books, 2008): "Many black men thought intermarriage asserted the ideas of radicalism; to marry black women, it was usually a gross betrayal. Ralph was not against mixed marriage but believed it was not for him. He knew how fond Wright, for one, was of white woman, despite his insistence that he would never marry one. In May, Wright would suddenly announce plans to marry a black woman. When she failed the mandatory Wassermann test for syphilis, he dumped her. He would soon marry a white woman, and then, when that union quickly failed, as quickly marry another" (110).

7   Eva's suicide is eerily suggestive of Nella Larsen's 1929 novel *Passing,* in which Clare Kendry, upon being discovered to be passing for white by her white husband, Jack Bellew, jumps or is pushed from the window of a Harlem apartment.

3. A Black Man's "Veil of Horror": Oedipal Trauma and Psyche Redemption in Chester Himes' The Third Generation

Chester Bomar Himes, born July 29, 1909, in Jefferson City, Missouri, a master craftsman, authored seventeen novels, numerous short stories, essays, screenplays for films, and two autobiographical volumes. Sentenced to twenty years in the Ohio State Penitentiary for an armed jewel robbery, Himes obtained his real "education" in the same informal manner as Malcolm X and George Jackson, two phenomenal Black men whose autobiographical writings on their harrowing journeys into manhood and subjectivity within America's prisons and white supremacist culture (*The Autobiography of Malcolm X* and *Soledad Brother*, respectively) continue to be read throughout the world.[1] Like Frederick Douglass in his *Narrative of the Life of Frederick Douglass, An American Slave Written by Himself* (1845), Chester Himes literally writes himself into existence with candor, complexity, and sophistication. We recall Douglass' statement in response to his physical confrontation with the slave-breaker, Covey: "You have seen how a man was made a slave; you shall now see how a slave was made a man" (294).[2] This statement represents the fundamental call of transformation to which many Black male writers have responded. While in prison, Himes witnessed the catastrophic fire of 1930 that killed 320 convicts and became the subtext of his 1934 first nationally circulated short story, "To What Red Hell?" During the seven and a half years he served, Himes would write the short stories that launched his literary career. Once released from prison, Himes was befriended by Langston Hughes; he was then engaged as a playwright for Karamu House, and later became a friend of the white novelist, Louis Bromfield. His fiction ranges widely from the prison story *Cast the First Stone* (1952) and detective novels *Cotton Comes to Harlem* (1965) and *A Rage in Harlem* (1965) to novels such as *If He Hollers Let Him*

Go (1945), *The Lonely Crusade* (1947), and *The Primitive* (1955), which address many of the racial and class dynamics in African American life and culture. As Darryl Dickerson-Carr relates, Chester Himes' works have influenced other African American writers such as Walter Mosley and are firmly connected to the socioeconomic realities of Black people:

> Concomitantly, Chester Himes published two semiautobiographical novels on the political and social conditions in Los Angeles and its factories during World War II: *If He Hollers Let Him Go* (1945) and *Lonely Crusade* (1947). They stand as two of the most richly detailed and poignant accounts of the black worker's life in the war years. Himes also observes the ironies of the new economic opportunities for African Americans during that time, most notably that none of these opportunities are given for purely altruistic reasons; war is the primary catalyst. (87)

Himes' two autobiographies are *The Quality of Hurt* (1972) and *My Life of Absurdity* (1977). Like Wright, Himes used writing as a form of therapy; he focused on Black male subjectivity, characters who ranged from pathetic losers or pathological victims destroyed by white supremacy to strong men who triumphed over social obstacles. Many know Himes by his detective stories about Coffin Ed Johnson and Gravedigger Jones, ostensibly pulp novels written for quick cash. Himes would argue at some point that these stories were his best work; the narratives combine surreal circumstances and strong characters. Always these protagonists are presented against the background of a fully realized social milieu. Just as Frederick Douglass documented the contemptible horrors of Black people's enslavement, Chester Himes chronicles white terrorism under Jim Crow segregation and Black people's response. After brilliantly paving the way for such African American writers such as Walter Mosley, Chester Bomar Himes died in Moravia, Spain, on November 12, 1984.

Like Richard Wright (*Native Son*, 1940), Ann Petry (*The Street*, 1946), William Attaway (*Blood on the Forge*, 1941), William Gardner Smith (*Last of the Conquerors*, 1948), Willard Savoy (*Alien Land*, 1949), Willard Motley (*Knock on Any Door*, 1947), John Oliver Killens (*Youngblood*, 1954), and other African American writers, Himes is grounded in the paradigm of naturalism that stresses that violence and pathological personalities result from racial oppression and systemic economic exploitation. Himes, I argue, goes further than the aforementioned writers and their respective texts with this paradigm in his psychological portrayal of the enduring intraracial conflicts within the African American family. Indeed, the level of violence in Himes' works, often brought on by Jim Crow segregation, pervasive racism, and socioeconomic exploitation by whites, tends to surpass that of his peers who were working in the realm of naturalism.

Chester Himes' *The Third Generation* (1954), an autobiographical novel, characterizes a troubled African American family, the Taylors. It is, as novelist John A. Williams sagaciously states in the foreword, a "chilling study of racism absorbed from whites and utilized by the Black victims to victimize other of their own race; it is the 'visiting the iniquity of the fathers upon the children unto the third and fourth generation.'"[3] Discussing this novel, Himes states, "*The Third Generation* is my most dishonest novel." After reading his first of two autobiographies, *The Quality of Hurt* (1972), which recounts the hostile, loveless family atmosphere of his youth and making a comparison, we can conclude that *The Third Generation* draws heavily if not exactly upon Himes' early life. Composed of a very light-skinned mother and a dark-skinned father along who were aggressively hostile to each other, Himes' middle-class parents mirror the marital conflicts of the Taylors in the novel. Accordingly, Himes' assessment of the disingenuous nature of his novel reveals that this work is more reality than fiction. The novel documents the saga of the Taylor family, which includes Professor William ("Fess") Taylor, his wife Lillian, and their three sons: Thomas, William, and Charles. The Taylors fight constantly, and Mrs. Taylor's erratic behavior forces them to move from one Black college to another, thus creating an unstable environment for their children. Thomas finally extricates himself from the conflict and after William is blinded by a chemical accident at school and sent off to various schools for the blind, Charles is left alone with his parents to referee the conflicts as an intense Oedipal relationship develops between Charles and his mother. According to Sigmund Freud's theory of the Oedipus complex, males feel the guilty tension of their feelings toward their mothers. They are aware of the threat of their father as a rival (representing the idea of castration) and are forced to repress their deeply embedded sexual feelings. Trepidation and repression are at the basis of masculine sexuality in Freud's theory. In *The Reproduction of Mothering* (1978), Nancy Chodorow discusses the dynamics of the Oedipal relationship:

> Compared to a girl's love for her father, a boy's Oedipal love for his mother, because it is an extreme of the intense mother—infant unity, is more overwhelming and threatening for his ego and sense of (masculine) independence....This mother-son love threatens her husband and causes him to resent his son. The intensity of the Oedipal mother-son bond (and the father-son rivalry) thus causes its repression in the son. (131)

In a symbolic manner Charles shares Lillian's body with his father, Fess. As a result of the Oedipal mother–son bond, Charles is unable to achieve any sustained kinship within or outside his family. Like Joe Christmas in William Faulkner's *Light in August* (1932), Charles is light skinned and thus becomes characterized within the realm of the tragic mulatto.

In *The Third Generation,* Chodorow's theory is complicated because Lillian Taylor seduces Charles and is also the "white" father figure who looms as the castrator, especially when Charles engages in intimate relationships with other symbolic "white" mother figures. On the other hand, Charles never views Fess Taylor as a threatening or castrating figure. Himes gives us evidence of Fess' powerlessness and Lillian's jealousy and its "castrating" effect. At the metaphoric level this marital relationship is analogous to the racial violence that exists between Blacks and racist whites. Williams argues:

> Himes is almost alone in examining this Black/"white" relationship and its horrendous effects. *The Third Generation* is a violent book, but Himes has always written violent work, many which have at their core the seething racism that so many Black people feel about each other. Himes was painfully aware of what he was writing about. In an essay, "The Dilemma of the Negro Novelist," he wrote: "The American Negro experiences two forms of hate. He hates first his oppressor [and Mrs. Taylor certainly does that] and then because he lives in constant fear of this hatred being discovered, he hates himself—because of this fear." (iv)

Himes "confessional" novel bears close resemblance to D. H. Lawrence's *Sons and Lovers* (1913), in which the protagonist, Paul Morel, struggles to free himself from his mother's obsessive grip and to find love with other women. Lawrence employs the *Bildungsroman* form to analyze the conflict between one plebeian male and one upper-class woman and their struggle for control of their sons; the struggle finally centers on one son, the most sensitive and the most loved. For example, Lawrence insinuates at the incestuous exchange of thoughts between mother and teenage Paul, riding a train together: "Suddenly their eyes met, and she smiled to him—a rare, intimate smile, beautiful with brightness and love. Then each looked out of the window" (92). Similarly, Himes distils the traumas generated within the African American community by the pressures of racism in the narrative of a single Black family, rent by the conflict between a Black-hating mother, who sees herself as "light-bright and damn-near white" and a generally absent and "ingratiating" Black father. Lillian Taylor's sins are those of passion for her son, Charles and extreme racial arrogance; Fess Taylor's sins are caused by coldness and remoteness concerning his relationships with his three sons. While the parents are engaged in conflict, the sons, especially the youngest, Charles, are caught in the middle of a cesspool of domestic violence.

The intraracial conflict within the novel has its matrix in the Oedipal Complex. Freud asserts that the complex is an erotic fantasy between a child and parent that goes back to Sophocles, who dealt with the subject in *Oedipus Rex.* Oedipus unknowingly kills his father and marries his mother, an action that brings further disaster to the troubled kingdom. The conflict between the Taylors is essentially a war that assumes some of the forms and the essence of a love triangle with both parents holding equally legitimate claims to love and loyalty. The coming to manhood of the protagonist, Charles Taylor, is encumbered by a legacy of slavery that is reenacted as a domestic drama. Professor Taylor is a shadow of a man who acts, but gives little direction or positive values to his son. On the other hand, Lillian Taylor, is a symbolic refiguration of an arrogantly racist white male in terms of her values, racial ideology, and her intense desire to dominate her family. Like Jocasta, Lillian is blind to her own part in this tragic family romance. She relates a story of a family romance of white supremacy through which she wishes to bring her sons, especially Charles, into manhood. *The Third Generation,* like Richard Wright's autobiography *Black Boy* (1945), is significant because the mother represents a critical factor in the Black man's achievement of subjectivity and self-worth. Whereas Wright's mother is a suffering absence, Lillian Taylor is a suffering presence in Charles' life. Himes deftly establishes that the mother is critical in the development of the African American male. Mrs. Taylor's role happens to be a negative influence, but in many aspects *Youngblood* (1954) by John Oliver Killens and *A Lesson Before Dying* (1993) by Ernest J. Gaines illustrate how many African American mothers have a profoundly positive effect on their sons. In *Youngblood,* Laurie Lee Youngblood whips her son Robbie in front of racist white police officers in order to save him from the more tragic fate of a reform school where Laurie Lee's brother had been sent; he returned to the community psychologically destroyed by that incarceration. Robbie was arrested after fighting off white boys who were attempting to rape his sister, Jenny Lee. And in *A Lesson Before Dying,* two older Black women, Miss Emma Glen and Tante Lou, are determined that the school teacher, Grant Wiggins, go to the jail and help the illiterate Jefferson to die with dignity after he was labeled "a poor dumb hog" by his white defense attorney, who was attempting to save his life after Jefferson's involvement in the killing of a white man, Alcee Grope. Jefferson did not slay Grope, but he was in the store when Bother and Bear initiated a confrontation that resulted in Brother, Bear, and Grope all being killed in a bloody shoot-out. Jefferson is sentenced to die in the electric chair, but his redemption in the face of death leads to Grant achieving his own subjectivity despite the enduring racism in Louisiana's Jim Crow culture during the 1940s. Like sturdy bridges, Black women continually support Black males, especially their sons, in the journey to self-respect and empowerment despite America's white supremacist cultural design to emasculate, symbolically castrate, and neutralize all Black males.

The major thesis for this reading of *The Third Generation* is drawn from Robert Con Davis's, "The Discourse of the Father." Davis argues that the paradigm of such unconscious processes as seduction, the primal scene, and castration (the operations of repression) constitute the substance of the text. These processes are instruments through which *The Third Generation* develops and means thereby the protagonist, Charles Taylor, achieves subjectivity or agency. In many ways *The Third Generation* as a text mirrors the archetypical ascent of the modern male subject. Davis assumes a "male" narrative that relies on the male point of view. Although the point of view is mainly female, I will argue that the text supports Davis' argument.

Much of *The Third Generation* narrative develops through a series of repetitions of two critical paradigms: a "rape" and a "family romance." Both paradigms entail the narrative displacement of the materiality (sexuality) of the Black male (castration). These repetitions follow the Freudian process of the original wound being obsessively although unconsciously re-enacted. Charles Taylor comes to a critical point where he "works through" and is motivated to move away from these paradigms as he achieves a clearer sense of his own identity despite the family drama.

The core of the novel is the relationship between mother and son: her struggle for domination and his struggle for freedom and personal identity. Himes' characterization of the erratic Lillian Taylor develops in a linear manner. Inexorably and tragically her arrogance and feelings of persecution that exist from the beginning become more and more dominant, until all flexibility in her relationship with her husband and sons is lost and she becomes almost deranged. The novel's original title— *The Cord*—has Freudian resonances for the entangled relationship between mother and son: "It was if the umbilical cord still held them joined together" (194). Himes acknowledges the filial relationship: "The theme of the story concerns itself mostly with her abnormal love for her youngest and most handsome son and what it does to him by the time he reaches nineteen" (Hughes 72). Charles continually strives for some sense of self; he is four years old when the narrative opens and is a very vulnerable young man when it closes. Himes, attempting to map African American history in *The Third Generation,* defines the protagonist—a new identity for Charles—through an inquiry into domestic life. Evaluating the complexity of self-definition in the African American family, Ralph Ellison in "Hidden Name and Complex Fate" argues: "We must learn to wear our names within all the noise and confusion in which we find ourselves. They must become our mask and our shields and the containers of all those values and traditions which we learn/or imagine as being the meaning of our familial past" (*Shadow and Act* 151). Ellison's analysis aptly describes how Charles Taylor experiences the world through "his veil of horror" (349) dictated by his family's tragic and traumatic history. With the permanence of white supremacy, the social evils that too many African Americans experience and internalize become an ongoing natural disaster with little relief from the punishing winds of injustice and racial violence.

Early in *The Third Generation,* Himes, metaphorically connecting Black life to nature, characterizes the yearly flooding of the Mississippi Delta in the following manner:

> Everything for miles around became bogged down in relentless mire. Old men who lived in houses along the river bank could count off fifty years by the high-water marks on their living room walls, like grains in a board of wood. Year after year it was the same. The natives stayed on as if chained inexorably to their fate, endured the same property damage, the loss of life . . . condemning their offspring to the same fate . . . .The mire drew all things down . . . .Then after the rains the sun grew hot. In the rich steaming soil, seeds germinated like magic . . . .The trees budded and leaved. . . . Brier patches where all winter long the rabbits had escaped the hunters' hounds miraculously became dark green jungles of Blackberry bushes, thick with copperheads and rattlesnakes. All day long the young black men, eager, earnest seekers of that vaunted education, could be seen plowing the tireless mules, turning long yellow furrows in the ceaseless race against the swift growing weeds . . . .All of nature ran wild. (72–75)

Individuals "chained inexorably to their fate" suggests the legacy of Black people's enslavement in America and the ominous reality that the past is always present. Without a doubt, Black people have been mired by slavery and its legacy, producing transgenerational transgressions of trauma. Despite this legacy and the ensuing trauma, there is the constant rebirth of Black people's desire to be one with America. In the repetitive images of captivity, victimization, and death yielding to images of fertility and growth, the central thematic significance of the novel develops. Old and young Black men are ensnared by this relentless mire and frame this description because they reinforce the cyclic nature of life. The Taylor family and especially Charles are trapped in the "mire" as they struggle against hardship, much of it of their own making (some not), and yet ultimately survive, transform and grow. This passage expresses symbolically the novel's fundamental theme as the inextricable relationship between psychological growth and psychological victimization and their racial metonymies. In language that suggests Joseph Conrad's 1902 *Heart of Darkness* (especially with regard to the repeated use of the word "natives"), Lillian Taylor views this southern Black college environment with trepidation and anxiety: "Yet Mrs. Taylor, in her own implacable way, sought to change all this and bring order to this chaos. She ordered packages of flower seeds and planted them in neat rows in her flower garden, and was startled when their sudden lush growth seemed to envelop her. She was exasperated" (75). As the novel is ultimately about Charles development and subjectivity, the passage foreshadows the triumph of the African American individual over forces which threaten to restrict or prevent growth. Accordingly, the overgrowth that Lillian Taylor views as "chaos" will become a metaphor for her problematic relationship with Charles, who finally becomes self-destructive and is propelled into criminal activity, and only through some resolution to the chaos can there be hope and redemption. Thus, the "relentless mire," a natural force to which Mississippi residents are bound, becomes a metaphor for the psychological forces which threaten to prevent but ultimately nourish one's development.

The Third Generation's title and central theme are derived from Exodus 20:5: "...For I the Lord thy God am a jealous God, visiting the iniquity of the fathers upon the children unto the third and fourth generations of them that hate me." Like the ironic structure of Ernest J. Gaines' novel, *A Lesson Before Dying*, where the teacher, Grant Wiggins, learns a profound lesson from his illiterate "student," Jefferson, this Biblical verse provides a paradoxical structure for the novel. First, Himes represents the results of a particular historical and interracial iniquity, the iniquity of Black people's enslavement by white slavers. African Americans victims of slavery are still paying, generations later, for the crime, not of their Black forefathers but of the white "fathers." White fathers of Black slaves such as Thomas Jefferson and other white Founding Fathers reveal the fundamental hypocrisy of America being founded by white males who were slave owners. Charles, the youngest male, is representative of the third generation since the freeing of the slaves. Second, although the quotation makes no mention of race, the novel explicates that slavery and racism are part of a larger iniquity, the malevolence of white supremacy and exploitative measures against African Americans purely on the basis of racial difference.

The relentless conflict between Professor (Fess) Taylor, who is short and dark, and his wife, Lillian, a small, proud, and light-skinned woman, opens the door of the novel with Lillian as white subject and Fess as a dark object. By using Lillian's taxonomic point of view, Himes establishes the mother as a critical influence on African American male subjectivity; Lillian is a subject because her point of view drives the narrative and provides the lens through which we most often view her husband. Fess becomes objectified by his stature and especially his blackness. Defined and marked by a blackness that goes beyond skin color, Lillian views him as a "short, Black man with a wiry, simian body, the bowed legs and pigeon-toed stance of great Negro athletes" (10). Lillian continuously taunts her husband with the discourse of despicable white racist epithets: "savage," "Black devil," "shanty nigger," and "cabin brood." Lillian's contemptuous words, which recall the psychological violence of slavery, illustrate her racial ideology and extreme enmity: "You Black devil! You're the most depraved, despicable liar that was ever born....Yes I hate you, you Black despicable nigger!"(41). Lillian and Fess exchange racial vituperations based on the very truths they know are most painful. Fess denigrates Lillian's pride and vainglory in her ancestry by calling her a "bastard" and a "white man's leavings" (40)—the irony is that the very refuge of her white ancestry—is in itself a historical result of illicit sexuality. Martha Nussbaum argues that "this stigma of racial hatred and shame" is "fundamentally deforming of human personality and community" (96–97). Accordingly, Lillian's racial hatred and shame affect her children and the Black community in which they live, bringing anguish to her husband. At one point, Lillian fervently admonishes Charles and his brother, William: "You mustn't think of yourself as colored. Your mother is as white as anyone. You both have white blood—fine white blood—in your veins. And never forget it" (99). Even at his lowest, his mother reminds Charles, "With your blood you should be able to do anything" (325). For Lillian her husband's blackness is a stigma and a Hamitic curse. By giving privilege to her light-skinned complexion, Lillian validates the non-consensual miscegenation (sexual violence) that produced mulattoes, quadroons, and octoroons. Equally significant, the obvious contradiction is that within white supremacist dogma and discourse Lillian, who views herself as white, would be characterized as a "nigger lover." As Randall Kennedy makes clear in *Nigger* (2002) the term has reflects the deep racial conflict between Blacks and whites:

> The term nigger lover continues to be heard amid the background noise that accompanies racial conflict. Whites who refrain from discriminating against blacks, whites who become intimate with blacks, whites who confront antiblack practices, whites who work on the electoral campaigns of black candidates, whites who nominate blacks for membership in clubs, whites who protect blacks in the course of their duties, and whites who merely socialize with blacks are all subject to being derided as 'nigger lover.' (27)

This provides us with the profound narrative paradox of a "white" nigger lover who hates the "nigger" that she has married and has children with. Subsequently, Lillian attempts to write her "master narrative"—the belief in the inherent white superiority in all aspects of human interaction including law, economics, politics, sports, entertainment, business, and the arts—into the lives and indeed the psyches of her three Black children: "Mrs. Taylor preferred to read in the living room because of the grand piano. Music had always been her sanctuary and the nearness of the piano gave her a sense of security. Besides, owning a grand piano had always seemed to her indicative of good breeding" (8). The term "good breeding" for Lillian means viewing herself a "white"; it means raising her Black children with white values. And her children's desire to be Indians and attack "palefaces" when they play is disturbing to Mrs. Taylor because it operated in opposition to her master narrative of whiteness: "She disliked this game [Cowboys and Indians] most of all. She was afraid it might encourage them to hate white people. She wanted them to grow up to love and respect fine white people as she did" (10). For Lillian, whiteness and her embrace of its culture represent the highest level of socioeconomic subjectivity. Lillian's personal narrative of white supremacy connects to America's long history racial and color hegemony that created intraracial conflict on the basis of skin color. As Khari Enaharo argues, there is the possibility of a narcissistic element to the internalization of these color-laden values:

> In the White supremacy mindset Whiteness of skin is considered one of the highest and most important standards of beauty. This factor combined with keen or straight facial features is a sure-fire recipe for victory. The closer one is to looking or being White, the better the chances of being classified as beautiful. The acceptability and classification of beauty of Black females have always been based on color. (296)

Lillian's "good breeding," along with her "love" and "respect" for white people, motivates her to rewrite her family history and create a white fable which she passes on to her children as fact: "She created the fiction of being only one-thirty-second part Negro" (18). The reality of Lillian's family history is that her parents were "body servants" to a Dr. Jessie Manning; her father was also his son from relations with a female slave, and her mother was the daughter of an Irish overseer and an Indian slave. The "family romance," Lillian creates represents a subversion and a repression of her true Black family's history:

> The resulting story was that her father was the son of Dr. Manning and a beautiful octoroon, the most beautiful woman in all the state, whose own father had been an English nobleman. Her mother was the daughter of a son a United States President and an octoroon who was the daughter of a Confederate Army general. (18)

This surreal "family romance" specifically fuels her extreme disdain for her Black husband and was generally the source of her feeling of superiority. Himes establishes this perception early in the novel:

> It was only after the disillusion of her marriage and the bitter conflict about color with her husband and the dark-complexioned faculty wives that she revived it. She never gave the story absolute credence, but it became conceivable. She certainly had a great percentage of white blood, she told herself. And it was quite reasonable it should be the blood of the type of persons who had been friends of the aristocratic Dr. Manning. She created the fiction of being only one thirty-second part Negro deliberately. It symbolized her contempt and disdain for all the Negroes she felt had tried to hurt her. It was her final rejection of all people who would not recognize her innate superiority. Because regardless of how much they hated her, or tried to hurt and belittle her, none of them could possibly be her superior, and but a very, very few her equal, because she possessed the very maximum of white blood a Negro can possess and remain a Negro. (18)

As we will discover with Matthew Antoine in *A Lesson Before Dying,* Lillian Taylor's racial fantasy represents the pathology of the preference by pigmentocracy philosophy. Her passionate hatred for Black people is mir-rored by Lillian's deeply ingrained sense of innate superiority based on skin color, the hypo descent rule. Here, Himes personalizes in Lillian the legacy of Black people's enslavement as it relates to color hegemony; this hege-mony developed on the slave plantations where the light-skinned slaves were often made to feel inherently superior to dark-skinned slaves. Mulattoes often received preferential treatment in terms of working in the house, obtaining literacy, and learning skilled trades such as carpentry, iron work, and husbandry. Lillian's fixation on skin color creates a line of demarcation and a periphery to protect her identity in this white supremacist culture. And as Andrea Dworkin explicates skin color is not only connected to one's identity, but to one's sexuality and worldview:

> The skin is our human mask; it is what one can touch of another person, what one sees, how one is seen. It is the formal limits of the body, a person, and the only bridge to human contact that is physical and direct. Especially, it is both identity and sex, what one is and what one feels in the realm of the sensual, being and passion, where the self meets the world—intercourse being, ultimately, the self in meeting the world. The other person embodies not only one's own privacy, but everything outside it. (22–23)

Obviously, the fundamental paradox is her marriage to a dark-skinned Black man, but this marriage with three sons represents a problematic psycholog-ical place to reinforce and reinscribe her delusions of white supremacy.

In contrast to Lillian as subject, Fess Taylor's point of view is almost non-existent. Fess' ingratiating or "condescending manner" represents his initial attraction for Lillian. She is only able to "give little of herself, and only to one she considered inferior, only in the manner of one bestowing a grace" (20). She desires an inferior and emasculated man who sees her as a white goddess and is willing to show his reverence: "But it [the initial attraction] had not been his position that had first attracted Lillian. It had been his homage. He had given the appearance of worshiping at her shrine even on occasions when she had acted ridiculously" (20). Lillian and Fess' erratic and confrontational relationship symbolizes the master and slave relation-ship in antebellum America with a reversal of gender. Along with the physical violence of the enslavement was the psychological violence by which the slave was socialized and manipulated to accept an inferior status and to view his or her white masters as physically and intellectually superior. Lillian with her delusions of grandeur represents a reconfiguration of the white slave master with Fess as her Black male slave.

Tragically, because of the psychological inequality of their relationship, Lillian and Fess decide to marry. Their wedding night foreshadows and is a prelude to the nightmare of their future life together. Additionally, this night reveals Lillian's father-fixation and her inability to give herself to Fess either physically or emotionally. Lillian's attitude towards her father and her belief in her white ancestry is further complicated by a distorted view of sexuality that she developed as a child. Lillian becomes traumatized. Like Laurie Lee Youngblood in *Youngblood,* who is physically and psychological assaulted on the street by a drunk white man when she is a young girl (when he succeeds in urinating on her thighs, Laurie Lee is so traumatized that she wants to cut off her legs), Lillian experiences psychological sexual violence. The narrator reveals:

> Once, as a little girl, when cutting through a vulgar street in niggertown, Atlanta, she heard an obscene reference to her vagina. She had not known then what it had meant, only that it was vulgar and dirty and had filled her with horrible shame. She had never told anyone, but the feeling of shame had lingered in her thoughts like a drop of pus, poisoning her conception of sex. As she had approached womanhood, she had resolved to make her marriage immaculate. And now it seemed dirtied at the very start by this cloying scent. (24)

As bell hooks argues, Lillian is shamefully reduced to her genitalia as the dirtiness of this incident will be connected to blackness: "Often post-slavery violence in African American life was an imitation of the patterns of abuse utilized by the dominating white master and mistress. It was one of the first indications that black folks had internalized habits of being learned from their oppressors" (26). Combined with her intense color complex Lillian's "cloying scent" significantly represents her perspective on sexuality, a symbolic decapitation. As Howard Eilberg-Schwartz and Wendy Doniger argue in *Off with Her Head!: The Denial of Women's Identity in Myth, Religion, and Culture* (1995), women come under attack in ways that seek to erode their subjectivity, agency, and voice reducing them to mere sexual and reproductive bodies because their identity threatens to unmake and disrupt the classic gender distinctions that have linked men to speech, power, identity, and the mind. The transformative act of female decapitation seeks to maintain male privilege:

> Decapitation is one way of solving the dilemma. Removing the female head relieves woman of both identity and voice and reduces her to a mere sexual and reproductive body. But there are other, less obvious forms of beheading. The eroticization of the female head extends to the body, turning the head into an alluring and sexually provocative organ. In this way, the female head becomes part of a woman's genitalia. To see a woman's face to look at her hair, to hear her voice, is imagined as an erotic experience. Eroticization of the head is thus a form of beheading, since it depicts women as nothing more than a sexual and erotic body. Magritte's painting *The Rape* illustrates just how the eroticization of the female head can lead to its submersion and disappearance into the body. The eyes become breasts, the nose a navel, the mouth a vagina. What women speak, eat, and see is nothing but desire. Speaking to a woman is a form of sex, seeing her hair is a violation of modesty. (1)

Lillian's shame-filled and philosophically poisoned view of her sexuality combined with Fess' very gentle behavior which grew somewhat aggressive result in a consummation which Himes describes in brutal and violent terms. On the way to the hotel, Lillian feels lonely, homesick, and frightened; also that that her husband is a stranger and that "this seemed a monstrously wrong thing they were doing" (22), Lillian attempts to accept the reality that she is married. In the darkness of their hotel room she is terrified by her husband's naked black body and has a traumatic psychological experience that suggests incestuous displacement as her Black husband

> had gone out of himself and was panting uncontrollably, unaware, unhearing, his head filled with the roaring fire of his lust. He mounted her like a stud. The penetration chilled her body like death. For an instant the vision of her father's kindly white face with its long silky beard flickered through her consciousness. Then her mind closed against reality as it filled with the sense of outrage; her organs tightened as she stiffened to the pain and degradation. (25)

However this is only the beginning of her traumatic experience as her husband, lost and uncontrollable in his lustful penetration continues:

> He struggled brutally and savagely and blindly and then desperately to overcome her, conquer her, win her. She fought to hold herself back. He could not control himself; his muscles jerked with frenzy, the vague pallor of her face floating through the red haze of his vision. When she felt her virginity go bleeding to this vile and bestial man she hated him. (25–26)

For a long time afterward, Lillian lies, arms extended, gripping the sheets in the figure of the crucifixion. Subsequently, Lillian, feeling debased by an animal, calls him a "beast" and associates the consummation of the marriage with her rape and victimization and accordingly associates her husband's blackness with debasement and depravity:

> Each time, she received him with horror and revulsion. Although a child was conceived, she never got over that first night. She was never able to separate the blackness of his skin from the brutality of his act; the two were irrevocably bound together in all her thoughts of him. (26)

In Lillian's psyche, this "rape" scene reinscribes the stereotypical racial discourse of lusty Black men seeking to rape white women. Simply put, Lillian in her mind becomes the white virgin (victim) and Fess becomes the Black rapist (buck). Of course, the historical response to a rape of a white female is the castration of the Black male, often done before he was lynched. In terms of genital space, Lillian's perspective reinforces the idea that white women's genital space is a sacred and protected space principally for white males, whereas Black women's vaginal space is a thoroughfare to which all males regardless of race have access. Equally important, this scene destroys Lillian's desire to have an "immaculate" marriage in which the notion of her innate superiority would remain intact. Lillian has internalized the myth of "sacred white womanhood." Fundamental to the philosophy of white supremacy is that the white woman is a pure and sacred individual who must be protected from Black males who were lecherous and sexually out of control.

This notion of the Black male as sexual beast as well as racist white people's apprehensions concerning miscegenation (this fear was mainly centered around Black males having sexual relations with white females because white males having sexual relations with Black females was of little concern) became ingrained in American culture by D. W. Griffith's *Birth of a Nation* (1915). Here a virginal white woman throws herself off a cliff when pursued by a Black male who seeks to talk with her; this explosive incident in the film was critical in the rise of the Ku Klux Klan. This episode of "rape" drives Lillian and Fess away from each other and attempts to resolve the hostilities fail. Lillian's view of the consummation of her marriage as a "rape" and primal scene (she sees her father's kindly white face) combined with her obsessive racial beliefs, are the source of their marital problems and undermine her relationship with her children. Unknown to Fess, he is in the middle of an incestuous triangle of sexual desire involving Lillian and her imagined white father. It is in her fantasy, too, that we see the source of the racial conflict in her family; not only is Lillian in love with the image of her father but she is married to a Black man who is the antithesis of that pristine image, a white father figure she at times represents along with the white supremacist values she has internalized. While married to Lillian, Fess unknowingly becomes displaced to the sacrosanct image of the kindly white father. From the night of consummation until Lillian divorces him twenty-six years later, she detests Fess Taylor. The objectification of Fess reveals the process of his displacement from the South and his craft of blacksmithing— two elements which define his existence as a Black man. Blacksmithing was one of the trades that enslaved Africans were allowed to learn on the planta-tions, and this skill gave them some autonomy while enslaved and some subjectivity after Emancipation. Although Fess is described as being extremely entertaining and having a "strong and bitter pride," the most conspicuous characteristic remains his being "disarmingly ingratiating, not only toward his superiors but toward most persons" (11). Fess is emascu-lated and symbolically castrated in that he fails to exercise any power, pro-tection, or authority over his children other than providing the essential requirements of life—food, clothing, and shelter. The racist and hostile environment of the South is compounded by Fess' hostile and sexually frus-trating relationship with Lillian (they sleep in separate bedrooms). Equally significant, Lillian's resistance to the demeaning aspects of Jim Crow segregation causes Fess to be displaced from both the South and his craft. One incident involved Lillian being arrested in Natchez, Mississippi, for patronizing a white dentist, and another involved her registering in a white hotel in Vicksburg and then letting it be known that she was Black. This later incident results in the governor calling Fess and informing him that he has forty-eight hours to get his wife out of Mississippi. Many other such incidents function to beat Fess down both psychologically and spiritually:

> Deep in his heart he wanted to be a rebel. Had he ever become a hero in the eyes of his wife he might have been a leader. He had the physical courage. Often he trashed grown students half again his size. But his wife and the circumstances of his life had put out much of his fire. (11)

In a real sense, Fess represents, to use Toni Morrison's naming strategy in *Sula* (1973), a "Boy Boy" in that he becomes symbolically emasculated by both external social forces and internal psychological forces. This is most evident in his relationship with President Burton who forbids the Black teachers in his college to read W. E. B. Du Bois' NAACP materials from the North. Himes characterizes Fess Taylor as sly and obsequious, wanting to be viewed by those white southerners in power as a good Negro:

> Professor Taylor always held a deep, secret fondness for those white southerners in authority. He knew instinctively how to get along with them, just how far to go and when to be ingratiating. As a consequence, he seemed far more audacious than the other professors. His interviews with the governor always gave President Burton a nervous stomach. And yet the governor liked him best of all the faculty members. (66)

Himes' juxtaposition of Lillian's internalization of white supremacy and Fess' internalization of some innate inferiority (especially when he is around white people in authority) combined with his occasional lack of fatherly guidance create a chaotic household where the three sons are in a perpetual state of turmoil with their parents, especially Charles who becomes self-destructive.

Under white supremacy, some light-skinned Black individuals seek to obtain the privileges associated with whiteness. Lillian does this by occasionally passing for white, but this leads to domestic tragedy. Lillian's overall antipathy for Black people leads her to search for the services of white professionals or accommodations reserved for whites. Using her whiteness as a badge of pristine privilege, Lillian goes to Natchez to see a dentist. When the white dentist views her in familiar conversation with a Black woman from the college, he discovers her duplicity. "The dentist charged her with breaking the law which prohibited Negroes from patronizing white places" (96). Lillian's arrest eventually involves the chief of police and the president of the college. The governor issues Fess Taylor a harsh directive: "You get that yallah woman of yo's outta Natchez an' keep her home....You know better'n tuh let her run 'round trna pass herself off" (97). On another occasion, "She went to Vicksburg and registered in a white hotel. When she came down next the manager confronted her" (130). Here Lillian is exposed not by her association with another Black person but by the college address that she gives upon registration. Again the governor is informed: "Willie, Ah'll give you forty-eight hours to get that woman out of Mississippi" (130). A change in geographic location furthers Lillian's masquerade of passing for white yet it reflects a deep-seated unhappiness with her life married to a Black man: "Now she took to coating her face thickly with white powder and rouging her cheeks. She looked white as a corpse. On those days she ate in the white restaurants. Her desire to talk was overpowering. She got into long, involved conversations with strangers. Most times it ended in unpleasantness" (170). It is during these episodes in racial misrepresentation that Lillian makes outrageous statements that are antithetical to her sense of racial superiority. In her conversation with these white strangers, Lillian says: "I destroyed my life by marrying a Negro" (170). Lillian's racial contempt and hostility extend to her husband's family when they are forced to move to Cleveland; Fess' sister Beatrice confronts her on her prejudice: "You don't like black people but soon's you get down and out you come running to us" (172). Despite being forced to have Charles stay with her Black in-laws, Lillian's response represents unreserved contempt: "I married a black man who happens to be your brother" (172). Lillian's passing for white and overall hostility to Black people lead to the entire family having to leave the state of Mississippi, and the displacement is most profound for the two remaining sons, William and, most evidently, Charles:

> It was the end of something; the beginning of change. Charles never liked change; he was more sensitive to it than most. He was affected by its imminence and again by its actuality. It required the readjustment of his two worlds; sometimes he made the one without the other, never both, often none. For all its unpleasantness, his life in Mississippi had been simply wonderful. It was the end. He hated the end of anything. He cried for Mississippi. (130)

Here Lillian's racial arrogance leads to collective and personal trauma within her family. Despite segregation, in Mississippi life for Charles in his Black community is relatively secure and predictable. The "two worlds" suggests the parental divide where Charles is often at odds with both Lillian and Fess. The larger issue of Lillian's racial passing is that it represents her extreme selfishness because she can only pass when she is not with her husband or her children. Although Lillian only passes temporarily, she denies her blackness, her family, and her culture. This becomes a problem when her children become conscious of racial difference, and Charles reminds his mother that she called Fess a "shanty nigger." A color-struck, Lillian acknowledges her fault but emphasizes the whiteness inside her Black children. By emphasizing "white blood" Lillian supports a system of white supremacy designed to permanently keep Black people in an inferior socioeconomic position. In James Weldon Johnson's *The Autobiography of an Ex-Colored Man* (1912), the protagonist's mulatto mother gives her son, who has been allowed to think he is white, a similar message when he is exposed as Black at school: his mother says that she is not white but that he has "the best blood of the South." This statement will lead eventually lead to the protagonist's total denial of his blackness and his marriage to a white woman; his children will never know his or their blackness. Like the Ex-Colored Man's mulatto mother, Lillian causes extreme conflict within the family and confusion for her children. In both of these novels whiteness becomes a vehicle to class privilege and a key to survival in a white supremacist culture.

Although there is a progressive dissolution of family life, Himes does not subscribe to conventional and stereotypical notions of the matriarchal African American family. Lillian represents the dominant figure, but Fess has his sphere of influence—he enjoys a middle-class occupation and often owns property. Early in the novel, the children benefit from a double-headed household, and find a way to transcend the increasingly virulent family strife. Thomas, the eldest son, is sent North to Cleveland to stay with Fess' relatives and becomes a peripheral figure in the novel. William is blinded in a chemistry explosion, yet enjoys a special status as he achieves academic success. Notwithstanding Fess' sphere of influence, Lillian, emotionally and psychologically, takes control of the marriage and the lives of their children, and as a result Fess, a sturdy, energetic, and talented Black man, suffers defeat both in his confidence and sense of direction:

> Only his wife could make him feel inferior. In the presence of most people he felt a wonderful assurance. But she was so conscious of her white blood she kept him constantly on the defensive. He could never be natural with her. He was either indulgent or resentful. She seemed destined to bring out the worst in him. Now, added to her contempt for himself [sic], was her attitude toward the children. She wanted to rear them in the belief that they were in large part white; that their best traits came from this white inheritance. (35–6)

After numerous predicaments associated with and caused by Lillian's racial ideology, we view the anguish and afflictions of a broken Fess, forced from the rural South into the urban life of the North. After William's blindness Fess becomes a waiter and is defeated: "It was in his home that he'd been defeated. He was a pathetic figure coming home from work; a small black man hunched over and frowning, shambling in a tired-footed walk, crushed old cap pulled down over his tired, glazed eyes, a cigarette dangling from loose lips" (159). Then later the novel reveals:

> ...Professor Taylor had been without a teaching post for four long years, he had still felt he belonged. Deep down he had still considered himself a teacher. Now he didn't. It broke him inside where it counted. He gave up. He lost his will to try. In many ways, the effect on this little man born in a Georgia cabin, who'd tried hard to be someone of consequence in this world, to live a responsible life, rear his children to be good, and teach his backward people, was the greatest tragedy of all. (245)

Unlike his father, Caleb Taylor, who possessed a "truly ungovernable temper," and similar to Booker T. Washington, Fess Taylor had visions of greatness and service to his people. In his own manner, Washington represented a challenge to white cultural assumptions when he states in *Up From Slavery* (1901): "No white American ever thinks that any other race is wholly civilized until he wears the white man's clothes, eats the white man's food, speaks the white man's language, and professes the white man's religion" (81). At one point, Fess Taylor had the spirit and will to be Washington-like, but those visions and altruistic desires were ground into dust never to rise again.

Fess Taylor's relationship with Charles also reveals his fall from greatness and service to Black people. When Charles is a young man, he challenges Fess and triumphs. Charles goes against his father's order to stop playing tennis after he has a seizure, and when his father picks up a stick to beat him, Charles defies him:

> He grappled with his father and they tussled about the court, digging deep holes in the packed clay surface. Finally Charles got the stick and threw it over the fence. His father looked astonished. Without another word he turned and went back to his shop....His father never referred to the incident in all his life. He never tried again to whip Charles. (151)

Fueled by his mother's constant disrespect of Fess, Charles is motivated to fight his father by his fury over the mortification of being beaten in front of the woman he plays tennis with. The next day, Fess takes Charles downtown to buy him "new long pants." If we consider the woman as representative of the mother and the "rotten stick" (150) as Fess' manhood, this scene underscores Charles' absence of any trepidation of his Black father and his intense desire to fight in order to be respected by the mother. It also strongly suggests that Charles views his father as lacking manhood and the defeat of his father meant that "Now the older women looked at him" (151). Older women tend to become mirror images of Lillian for Charles. Charles is (in a negative manner) the "rebel" that Fess wanted to be before Lillian and life with her robbed him of that desire. Charles is similar to the rebellious

Lillian, who assumes the protective role of the "white father." For example, a white racist farmer interrupts and humiliates Lillian, Charles, and William along with their driver as they try to pass him and his mules, causing Lillian to become enraged when he places a rifle to the head of the driver. As the man walks away, Lillian pulls a gun. Although William cries and pleads with his mother not to shoot, "Charles hated the uncouth, bestial man and hoped his mother would shoot him" (100). What is truly significant here is the absolute rage that both Lillian and Charles feel and their desires to act on that rage.

Lillian's passion for Charles and her racial beliefs combined with Fess' general absence lead to Charles' self-destructive behavior. There are numerous examples of Charles' deleterious behavior as he attempts to develop a sense of manhood: "Charles drank a glass of his urine to show how brave he was" (128). What's more, Charles engages in jumping freight trains: "He landed turning from his own momentum, his outstretched legs across the rail. The onrushing heavy steel wheel struck them as they turned, knocked them away from the rail as it sped on. He kept rolling down the steep embankment, came up skinned and breathless in the gulley" (133). Despite being whipped by his father, Charles continues jumping trains. His self-destructive behavior continues to escalate: "Once Charles exploded a dynamite cap on the front porch. Luckily the charge went down instead of up and blew a hole through the floor. The only injuries to himself were tiny cuts all over his face and hands, as if his skin had burst in a hundred different places" (139). Among his peers, both in high school and college, Charles feels estranged and inadequate: "More than all others he yearned to cut a dashing figure" (193). Charles' actions are mirrored by his insolence, defiance, and disrespect to his mother. During this time of rebellion, his brother is blinded in a chemistry experiment and the language of the explosion conveys Lillian's trauma at the consummation of her marriage: "William stood there for an instant in the center of the stage, the silence deafening about him, holding his face in his hands. There was something of the crucifixion in his posture, a stone of rigid tragedy in a field of barren loneliness" (143). A profound sense of loss encompasses Charles as he reflects on the lost of Mississippi, William, and the loss of his mother's love. While there is some temporary relief, Charles is always hurt; sensing rejection, Charles covers these feelings with a veneer of bravado. This self-destructive behavior foreshadows Charles experiences as an adult, especially with women. His first romantic attempt with an older woman leads to rejection when she tells him: "You find a girl your own age. Ah like you, honey, but you're jes' too young" (153). Traumatized Charles cries and then escapes to his world of fantasy. "He tried to play at making out that he was great and famous and that she would come seeking his attention" (153). At this point, a distraught Charles has no one to confide in (Tom has gone to live with his father's relatives and William becomes sightless), and he continues to be alienated from his parents. Indeed, with Tom gone (Lillian had viewed him as her savior from her failing marriage); Lillian believes that she must make a choice between William and Charles: "Now she was faced with a terrible choice. Both sons needed her desperately. Whichever one she tried to save, the other would be surely lost. Should it be the seeing or the blind?"(147) Shame and guilt plague his consciousness, but Charles is relentless in his defiance and becomes even more self-destructive.

Lillian and Fess' enduring conflict ultimately centers on Charles, whose defiance and self-destructive behavior lead to criminal activities. Even before he comes to Cleveland, Charles is caught stealing. Working for a German druggist he "stole a package of cigarettes, two packages of chewing gum and a chocolate" (164) and "three weeks later he was fired from another job for stealing. All that day he'd stolen things to carry home—a camera, a nickel-plated watch, a carton of cigarettes and two quarts of ice cream—and had stored them in an empty barrel in the basement" (166). In the first incident, Charles is in a daze not knowing why he stole, and in the second incident he is in total denial of stealing. While in Cleveland, Charles feels alienated and all the normal feelings of adolescence as he attempts to fit into a new environment. "He wanted so desperately to be important, to stand out; if not that, at least to belong to something" (196). Paradoxically, before being involved in an automobile accident that causes damage to several persons and property, Charles achieves popularity and acceptance with those in the Black community who either ignored him or treated him with contempt. Here Charles' Aunt Bee allows him to drive even though he did not have a license and it makes him feel "big and important again." Obviously the connection between Charles' sense of manhood and the automobile is evident, but the significance is that because his mother never knew that he was allowed to drive, this accident and its aftermath cause added hostility between Lillian and Fess as well as between Lillian and her husband's relatives. Again the husband and wife conflict centers on Charles and the issue of racial hostility in Lillian's reaction to the automobile accident: "You contemptible sneak. God curse the day you ever became the father of my children" (199). Again, Lillian curses her marriage to Fess and curses every time that they have sexual relations. Lillian's curse connects us back to the title of the novel and the Hamitic curse, and in her God-like posture she blames Fess's iniquities for the damage that they have done to her children. The court reprimands Charles, but Fess's relatives lose their house and life's savings because of the legal liabilities. For Lillian the focus of this tragedy is on her beloved Charles and saving him from "some dreadful kind of horror" (203). Fess' emasculation is heightened when Lillian (with salvation of Charles as her focus) uses the money from the sale of their house in St. Louis to buy another house instead of giving some of the money to Fess's relatives. The larger concern here is Lillian's eagerness to protect Charles from any social or legal responsibility, in Charles' mind placing him outside of society's legal stipulations. A deep and cutting pain is never healed.

"Castration" for Charles represents his emotional, psychological, and physical inability to function as a normal, healthy male in his relationships with women and his overall behavior. Fess's insecurities and inabilities to impart positive values for himself and his family and help Charles develop a healthy self-esteem and personal identity lead Charles to numerous painful and superficial relationships. In his frustrating failed relationship with a young woman, Della, Charles experiences rejection over his inability to dance as well as another man. His traumatic response here (as with William's blinding) is denial: "He had developed a credo: *No matter how hurt you are, if you don't think about it, it can't hurt.* Some-times it worked; sometimes it didn't. The hurt was always there, big and deep. But sometimes the hard quality of his rejection refused it recognition" (217; author's emphasis). After failed attempts with girls his age, these shallow relationships are mainly with prostitutes—refigurations of his mother, who does little to instill posi-tive values or assist Charles to mature. The processes of seduction, the primal scene, and castration combined with Charles' "romance" produce pathological behavior in Charles as he attempts to formulate his identity. Charles' delusions of grandeur connected to his "romance" are innocent enough when he is young, but they become serious acts of negligence as he matures. For instance, Charles sees the automobile as a powerful object that enables him to be important:

> He wanted so desperately to be important, to stand out; if not that, at least belong to something. It was mainly because of that, because he had to be different, to be seen, that he accepted his Aunt Bee's offer to drive their car, although he knew his mother wouldn't like it. (196)

The offer of the automobile leads to an accident when Charles is distracted as he waves to a young girl. Among the many people hurt, two persons are seriously injured. The sense of importance that Charles could not effect in any other way is found behind the wheels of another automobile: "...feeling invincible, as if he could drive his goddamn car right straight down through the solid goddamn earth, daring earth" (283). Driving becomes for Charles the ultimate assertion of manhood and power. Symbolically, Charles experi-ences the dominance that he cannot assert over his mother or other women. Essentially, the automobile defines Charles' troubled sense of masculinity:

> He knew with that car he could outspeed all his fears and trepidations, his shames and humiliations, the gnawing self-consciousness imposed by his injury, the terrible depression that had settled on his thoughts. With the car he could

defy everyone. He could take that goddamn car and drive off the edge of the world...he was driving slowly down Cedar Avenue, looking at the passing girls, he knew somehow without actually thinking it, he could also rescue damsels in distress. (277)

Charles also receives a similar feeling of power when he tries to collect money on a damaged car that he and a friend stole: "It was a strange sensation, as might be experienced by standing on a ledge fourteen stories high and looking down. At the time he had no intention of jumping. But it gave him a wonderful feeling of power to know he had a choice" (305). It is this power that he lacked with his first sexual experience with a prostitute named Margaret:

> Shame and fear combined in excruciating agony. He'd never be a man, he thought. And the shame of having revealed it to a senseless whore. How could he have done this to himself, gone to that den and bared his naked soul to a brutal prostitute? How could he have so debased himself? (256)

Himes' use of the automobile as a symbol of phallic subjectivity reinforces the problems that Charles has with women, especially his lost of control in intimate interactions. Even the power of the automobile and Charles' subjectivity become displaced because he cannot take the automobile home, knowing his mother would disapprove and force him to return the vehicle. An automobile gives Charles power, influence over his friends, and the mobility in his relationships with women. For Lillian the red roadster that Charles obtains represents a key to his self-destruction, and she goes as far to charge her son with the felony of forging a check. "She feared any day they'd bring him home dead, or that she'd be notified he was in jail for some terrible crime" (283). Even in front of the judge she reveals her concerns: "Its not only the check. He's wasting his life. Sooner or later if he isn't controlled he's going to wind up in the penitentiary or the gallows" (286). Lillian's reference to the "gallows" suggests that Charles is capable of murder or some other felony; indeed, she fears that Charles is involved with a white woman. "The gallows" suggest lynching, a possibility that is suggested when Charles has his first automobile accident. One person informs the incredulous Charles that "The white people were going to lynch you if the colored people hadn't stopped them" (203). Himes uses the issue of the forged check to foreshadow Charles actually forging a number of checks and being arrested. Lillian's obsessions result in the leasing company repossessing the car, but she is unaware of how strongly Charles' identity is connected to the automobile. Forcing him to give the automobile back leads to an unsuccessful suicide attempt: "So he stepped on the accelerator and pulled head-on into the concrete abutment beneath the railroad line" (289). Breaking a young man's nose at a high school party and throwing a girl across the room at college are only inconsequential precursors to this act of destruction designed to wound his mother. There is little doubt that his father's lack of guidance and overall weakness along with his mother's obsessive controlling behavior make Charles not just violently self-destructive but suicidal. In jail for forging checks, Charles escalates his descent to an outlaw, and it is now that the divorce between his parents becomes finalized. Even in the legal arena of the divorce, Charles is absent yet present as both parents testify that the other's behavior with respect to Charles was a critical factor in the dissolution of their marriage. Fess is characterized as irresponsible and Lillian is characterized as nagging. For Lillian the choice is clear: "She would rather get rid of her husband than lose her son. For in the final analysis, even though she no longer admitted it to herself, he was still her own lovely baby, and deep down she loved him in the same intense, passionate manner she always had" (298). In the traditional narrative the son attempts to kill off the father and have the mother to himself; here we have a twist to the Oedipal Complex in which the mother is willing to kill off her relationship with her husband in order to have her son for herself.

Lillian has a passion for Charles that exists at the boundary of physical and psychological seduction. The sublimations of Lillian's affection, the love and passion that should have been devoted to her husband, are lavished on Charles, thus developing and heightening his Oedipus Complex: "Mrs. Taylor rarely kissed her youngest son. All of his intense emotion poured out through his kiss and she was shocked by her own passionate response" (80). Lillian tries to make real the family romance; she tries to keep Charles' hair straight by massaging his scalp with olive oil and giving it one hundred strokes daily and frequently pinching the bridge of his nose to keep it from flatting out (12). Constantly, Lillian reminds Charles of his white ancestry on her side of the family as if it, not the African heritage of his father's side, is what he must live up to. Interestingly, Himes states that his own mother nagged, scolded, punished, and pushed her sons because of her desire for them to live up to their "white heritage" (*Quality of Hurt* 5). Essentially, Lillian tries to make Charles "white" in the same manner that she creates her white romance fantasy. In response, Fess "whiningly" accuses her of trying to make a girl out of her son. Fess' confession suggests the possibility that Lillian represents the phallic woman with subliminal sexual desires for her own son. And there is some veracity to this accusation because Lillian acknowledges that she wanted a girl when Charles was born. Charles as a consequence, grows up with a double burden—the destructive racially snobbish attitudes of his mother and the disturbing problem of personal and sexual identification she imposes on him.

Charles begins to realize that he loves and hates his mother at the same time, and he is both attracted and repelled when she allows him to groom her. Grooming represents a mother's fundamental affection for her child, but the duration and intensity of Lillian's grooming of Charles allows her to connect to her father.

> She longed for him to resemble her father, after whom he had been named. From his birth she had taken great pains with his hair, nursing it along as if his life depended on it being straight. Every night she massaged his scalp with warm olive oil and gave his hair a hundred strokes with an imported brush; and several times each day she gently pinched the bridge of his nose to keep it from flattening out. At times Professor Taylor complained, 'What are you trying to do make a girl out of him?' But she ignored him and continued to do all within her power to cultivate her son's white features. (12)

Within the Black community, the politics of skin color mirrors the politics of skin color. "Good hair" becomes defined as straight and European whereas nappy or kinky hair is "bad hair."[4] Indeed, there is the sense that Lillian is metaphorically attempting to comb and brush white culture into her son:

> She had been reared in the tradition that Negroes with straight hair and light complexions were superior to dark complexioned Negroes with kinky hair. This conviction was supported by the fact that light-complexioned skin and straight hair did give Negroes a certain prestige within their race. (12)

The later grooming that he does for her becomes an equally disturbing aspect of a mother and son relationship. Himes relates the interactions that foreshadow those difficulties that Charles will have in his future relationships with women:

> Sometimes she let Charles brush her long silky hair. He loved the feel of it on his hands and face. He brushed with long hard strokes until it cracked and sparked....Sometimes she let him file her nails. He fashioned gently rounded points of which he was inordinately proud....Then Charles sat before on the floor and taking each foot in turn, massaged them with a strange tenderness. He was infinitely patient with her and slowly, gently rubbed in the ointment until the pain disappeared. (80)

These acts on intimacy on Charles' part are a sharp contrast to the unambiguous "sexual" scene between Fess and Lillian. The "rape" is described in a brutal and violent manner, and the scenes with Lillian and Charles are pregnant with such tenderness and affection that makes Lillian's love "so intense she was afraid to look at him" (80). Consequently, the natural affinity between mother and son becomes distorted because Lillian induces deeper and inappropriate sensuous feelings. On the other hand, when Lillian has to discipline Charles (which is quite often), she becomes unreasonably vicious: "There was a fury and jealousy and strong frustrations in her punishment of him. It resembled some horrible, silent ritual. At moments in her passion she felt she would kill him. She received a vicarious pleasure, hating herself" (92). Accordingly, Lillian develops intense feelings of guilt concerning her passion: "She became obsessed with the fear that God was going to punish her for the strange passion she had for him. She brooded for weeks, worrying and fretting between moments of intense anguish" (135). Charles' seduction leads to his Oedipal Complex, which operates concomitantly with the intraracial conflict (being Black but hating blackness). When Charles' father and mother quarrel, as they often do, he has the urge to decapitate his father with an ax. "He felt violently protective toward his mother" (81). On one occasion when he finds his parents fighting, Charles knocks his father senseless even though it is his mother who started the squabble. Throughout the narrative, Charles states he hates his father, and on one occasion, he implies that he wishes his father was dead.

The Third Generation suggests a repetitive nature to the primal scene; indeed two scenes suggest Charles' primal scenes—a child first observance or awareness of sexual intercourse between the parents. Charles' reactions in these two traumatic experiences function to frame his attempts to come to manhood. The first primal scene echoes Lillian's "rape," Charles observes a young woman brutally crushed by a wagon:

> In the excitement a woman fell and before the laughing, straining crew could be halted she was run over by the wagon. Charles was standing near enough to see her ribs flatten beneath the heavy iron-tired wheels and the blood start surging from her mouth and nose....He saw her hands grope desperately for the spokes of the first wheel, and then fall limply, jerking spasmodically in the dust as the hurt down in his throat and chest, and he felt as if his ribs were crushed by the heavy wheels also. The sharp brackish sensation of ruptured blood vessels filled his head as if blood was spurting from his own mouth and nose. His mind could not contain it, and could not throw it off. He couldn't cry or scream or breathe. He felt himself going down-down-down with the dying woman into the cool dark valley of death....Now, in the cool, dark deep, away from the shock and horror, it was no longer terrifying. (60)

The body of the light-complexioned girl is described as "thin and undernourished" (60). Himes' description recalls Lillian who is also thin, light-skinned, and "had never completely recovered her health since the birth of Charles..." (9). On the other hand, Fess symbolizes the "heavy iron-tired wheel" that crushes the young woman. Lillian in the "rape" scene is similarly crushed under the weight of the blacksmith, Fess, and like the woman who is ruptured and bleeds through her mouth, Lillian bleeds vaginally. The language that Himes uses to describe the girl being crushed is wild yet sensuous:

> When the wagon finally came into the college grounds, pandemonium broke loose. The men climbed aboard and kissed the women at random....Their [the women's] Black and yellow faces gleamed with sweat and their faces to be kissed. The big rough country men milled about the wagon, hanging on the sideboards and jumping to the hubs to get a kiss and see what girl was new. (59)

Charles becomes engrossed in the excitement, and the subsequent crushing of the young woman has a traumatic effect on him. This "primal scene" suggests Charles is a victim in the same manner that his mother, Lillian felt victimized by her marital "rape." Himes' language in the primal scenes of both mother and son is almost identical; the ensuing repression—Charles cannot talk about the experience or express his feelings to his mother—leave Charles with a deep wound. In a manner that suggests her own experience, Lillian's statement appropriately sums up the effect of this scene: "His soul is hurt," she says in a condemning manner to Fess. There is a continuous sense of a profound wound in Charles, and his sense of "falling" in his relationships and a feeling of being "castrated" (the physical and emotional disruption of his manhood) throughout the remainder of the novel are both physical and symbolic, all involving women. Like Lillian and her fantasy of her kindly white father, Charles constructs a "romance" for himself to displace his loneliness and trauma:

> In the cold dimly lit attic he fought a thousand duels and saved as many damsels in distress. He was Ivanhoe and Richard the Lionhearted, Alexander the Great and the Count of Monte Cristo, Genghis Khan and the Scarlet Pimpernel. It was often his face in the iron mask, and his strong back, instead of Jean Valjean, lifting the carriage from the mud. Most often he was Achilles chasing Hector around the wall of Troy. (129)

Here the "iron mask" denotes Charles' deep-seated feeling of shame associated with his body. As we will see in the characterizations of his brothers, Charles has his own unique response to the trauma of psychological abuse and abandonment.

In Charles' involvements with women, similar traumatic patterns emerge, patterns which link sexuality, darkness, hurt, and death, which contrast with his idealistic wish to experience pure, selfless love. In his fantasies, Charles becomes the victorious savior; he especially sees himself as the gallant savior of womankind, and when rejected in this role, Charles experiences immense pain. Himes connects Charles' "castration" with his being deeply hurt; his senses of falling and drowning are mainly associated with women. Hurt becomes a prevailing motif in *The Third Generation* as Himes focuses the reader's attention on the particular "quality of hurt," the hurt Charles receives and the hurt he inflicts on others. Tragically it is this hurt which makes all men and women victims as Charles eventually comes to believe that, "No matter how hurt you are, if you don't think about it, it can't hurt. It helped him over many a painful situation. Sometimes it worked; sometimes it didn't. The hurt was always there, big and deep. But sometimes the hard quality of his rejection refused it recognition" (217). An example of this cavernous hurt occurs when Charles as a young boy is rejected by a young mulatto woman, whom I argue is a mother figure. Himes tells us that Charles is drawn to the woman with an "...affinity deeper than kin [his mother]. He went toward her timidly, filled with the great flaming desire to serve her with his life" (119). The words "affinity deeper than kin" suggest the relationship between Charles and his mother, where skin color brings them together in intimate ways that make normal family relations insignificant. Although economic oppression and racial discrimination are documented throughout the novel, skin color remains a dominant theme. Skin color or the preference by pigmentocracy philosophy is the determining factor for Lillian, and Charles becomes like her in this regard (all of the women Charles has relationships with are light-complexioned). The young woman's response to Charles is "utter viciousness." She bellows: "Git der hell away from heah an' mind yo' own bizness" (119). By using this common discourse, Himes suggests that while this young woman has a similar phenotype; she is antithetical to the prim and proper Lillian. For a boy who has never been rejected by his mother, the woman's words are painfully shocking: "...deep inside he was badly hurt, first opened by the suffering of the people (the scene is a house on fire), then poisoned by the strange woman's scorn. He couldn't understand her viciousness; her rejection cut him to the heart" (119). As Charles grows older, he learns to repress the hurt he feels, but this particular incident is hard to resolve: "...he never forgot the utter loneliness of the woman standing in the darkened doorway, watching the misery of her people, nor the utter viciousness of her rejection" (120). This rejection is mirrored by his mother's rejection when Charles' father dies in the hospital. "He [Charles] felt a strange sense of rejection, as if he didn't belong there, as if he were intruding on an intimate scene between the two of them (348). Here we have a clear description of the Freudian primal scene with Charles experiencing the rejection and shame associated with it. These feeling are repeated in Charles' other relationships with other women.

Himes has foreshadowed Charles' physical fall down an elevator shaft in a hotel by his psychological distress with his mother and other women. Two attractive young white women at the hotel where Charles works intrude into his thoughts and effect his fall down an elevator shaft. "Looking back at the young women" and feeling that "he was already loving them," Charles walks into a darkened elevator. This "fall" is symbolic of the lack of control in Charles' relationships with women: "He clutched spasmodically with both hands, finding nothing. For a brief tight instant he was filled with the sense of falling. He was fully conscious of falling. He felt the sensation of his body going swiftly down through the darkness with nothing to stop it" (228). Subsequent to his actual fall, Charles dreams of falling: "Finally he slept and dreamed that he was falling. Three nights in a row he dreamed that he was falling" (242). The fall and the dreams associated with it foreshadow Charles' sexual fall and failure with women. There is a similar spasmodic nature and sense of death that Charles sustains when he becomes tumescent. His sexual experience with Margaret, a prostitute, occurs soon after he comes out of the hospital. Charles' sexual failure is a debilitating experience:

> His body sealed against his velvet skin. At the instant of contact it was all over. He was done, spent, finished. His face burned like frostbite; his blood congealed....He felt miserably ashamed, mortified, unutterably chagrined. He wished he could die on the spot. (252)

Charles' normal socialization combined with his immaturity lead him to define himself primarily through his flesh, which at this point and others is inoperative. Similar to Lillian's "family romance," Charles develops a "romance" of his body, and his premature eruption reveals how much his self-image and existence depend on his flesh:

> Everything he'd ever dreamed of doing depended on his body. How could he be brave, noble, gallant, without physical perfection? He might never be in love, because it was the flesh also; might never know what it was like to be with a woman. That was the bitterest thought of all. He pulled the covers over his head to muffle his sobbing. (240)

It could be argued that Charles never truly experiences what it is like to be with a woman because of Lillian's suffocating affections and her overbearing presence.

Lillian's imperious presence intrudes into Charles' relationship with his girlfriend, Peggy, thus forming a triangle of desire. The descriptions of sexual intimacy in the novel all have a violent nature to them. Charles' manhood seems to be overwhelmed by the Black women he becomes intimate with. In his relationship with Peggy, she is in control: "And she'd take him, enfold him in her soft hot body so that he drowned in ecstasy....Once she screamed and bit his shoulder. Instantly he was flooding, overflowing, all of himself gushing into her" (278). Peggy takes Charles in the same manner Lillian was taken by Fess. Both Charles and Lillian are sexual objects in act of intimacy. Lillian's passions of jealousy are most prominent in Charles' relationship with Peggy, a "soft, voluptuous woman with reddish hair and fair skin." Although Lillian never sees Peggy, she knows Charles is involved with a woman and she assumes that she is white. Lillian's reaction approaches madness: "She was overcome with a fierce unreasonable jealousy....She was shocked. That he would take up with a white woman was unendurable. She couldn't realize that she wanted to be the only white woman in his life. And she was certain the woman was mature" (279). Lillian's presence also comes into play when Peggy raises the question of marriage: "To marry her was beyond his comprehension...He just couldn't marry a common ordinary colored woman like herself. What would his mother think? She'd feel betrayed after all the things she'd told him about his white forebears... He knew at that moment, he could never leave his mother" (280). Charles runs from Peggy, who is pregnant "as if demons were chasing him" (280). Although Charles says he loves her and realizes how wounded Peggy must feel, his love and psychological bond to his mother "castrate" any possibility of sincere and committed relationship with other women.

Charles' relationship with Veeny, a prostitute, who is a refiguration of Lillian, again reflects Charles' "castration" and falling, causing him to re-experience a deep hurt. Although Veeny is a prostitute for his criminally-minded friend, Dave, Charles becomes "revolted and entranced." His first sexual encounter with her is similar to his first sexual encounter with Margaret. Here Charles is physically and emotionally out of control in her presence: "He let her force him and gave in. The touch of her skin was like death. He spent himself uncontrollably over her legs and the bed" (330). As a recast of previous encounters with prostitutes, this symbolic "castration" is most evident in Charles' relationship with Veeny because Lillian's presence is so overwhelmingly strong:

> He hadn't visited his mother since the night he first met Veeny. He couldn't understand why he felt such an intense fear whenever he thought of her. There was a period each night just before he became unconscious, when his mind seemed sharp and clear. Quite often, during this period, which sometimes lasted no longer than a fleeting moment, he thought of his mother. (332)

Charles' feeling of horror intensifies to the point where there is a strong feeling of falling into Veeny's womb: "Finally he gave up and let his will go. He closed his eyes and felt himself sinking down into her womb" (334). Thus in the protection of the womb there would be no longer the fear of death—"castration."

There is a striking similarity in Charles' scenes of sexual intimacy and Fess' "rape" of Lillian. Himes describes both characters as being sexually out of control. Additionally, Lillian can be seen as out of control concerning her passion for Charles and her racial beliefs that eventually play a major role in her move to madness and the demise of the Taylor family. Charles, like Lillian, comes to associate sexuality with images of sordidness and ultimately with death. For example, before visiting a prostitute, Charles is strangely moved by the "thick Black slime in the gutters" (275). He experiences a strong desire to wade in it and get "his clean white shoes filthy" (275). Not surprisingly, Charles develops a preference for older women, which links his feelings toward his mother and his relegation of sex to illicit behavior. In one particular incident, when he boards for a brief time with Mrs. Robinson and her son (that mother-son relationship is similar to that of Charles and Lillian), he feels sexually attracted to this woman. Feelings of guilt and shame are the results of this attraction: "He couldn't stay in her presence without having an erection. It shamed him and he was afraid she might discover it" (183). Having sexual relations with Mrs. Robinson would act as mirror and sublimation of Charles' ultimate desire to sexually usurp Fess and embrace his mother.

In Charles Taylor's other primal and Oedipal scene near the conclusion of the novel, his Oedipal Complex is fully revealed and Charles becomes extremely emotional, indeed enraged. Standing in his mother's rented room, his gaze turns to the ash tray, where he sees "the butt of two cork tipped cigarettes marked with lipstick, and the butt of a homemade cigarette stained brown with spittle" (337). Charles becomes frozen with the shock of his mother and father being in her room together. He vigorously believes that at this point his mother's love and affection belong only to him. The possibility that his estranged parents might have been sexually intimate and that Lillian has finally accepted her husband's sexuality (this acceptance also implies an acceptance of his blackness), stunningly reveals Charles' life of deep-seated hurt and repression:

> Suddenly, uncomprehendingly, his senses were stunned in the manner of a lover's discovery of his loved one's infidelity. Then he was caught up and hurled into a sea of bitter torment. Everything he tried to forget, to push from his consciousness, to drown in drink and dissolution—the despair over the loss of his home, the breaking up of his family, his parent's divorce, his failure in school; the open sores of sorrow in his father's face, the unread blood-and-thunder stories, the vacant stare, the pile of smoldering cigarette butts; the bitter hurt living in his mother's eyes, the brittle laugh and hennaed hair; and his own remorse for all the things he had done to bring them to such an end—all of it dug up and brought alive in the picture presented by those three cigarette butts. (337–38)

Although this long and complex reflection brings to the surface many of the issues Charles has been repressing, resolution is not the result. Here we see the triangulation of the Oedipus scenario. Charles asks: "Why couldn't his father leave her alone and let everything rest?" (338)

Charles projects most of the pain and frustration of his family on his father. Unable to acknowledge his and Lillian's impact on the family's devastation, Charles blames the victim—Fess—whereas the "white" father figure—Lillian—goes unblamed and still deeply loved. For Charles the love of his mother and the sexual overtones of that love establish a link between sex, guilt, and death—the ultimate state of victimization. During a dream involving his mother, he experiences a sexual discharge and is subsequently consumed with feeling of guilt: "He felt utterly debased, he wanted to die" (274). At one point, Charles tragically refers to his mother's kiss as the "kiss of death" (235). Here Himes intersects incestuous desire with infanticide as this "family romance" spins out of control.

In the final chapter of *The Third Generation,* we experience the closure of the Oedipal mother-son relationship as an inebriated and rebellious Charles is in Veeny's bed when Lillian and Fess track him down. Here Lillian understands that she needs her husband to help Charles. Veeny's pimp gets rough with Lillian, and when Fess defends his wife, he is mortally wounded. Charles drunkenly attempts to aid his father but is unable to do so amid images of passivity and falling: "He felt himself going down-down-down into the cool dark valley of oblivion" (345). The violent end, although symbolically appropriate, fails to achieve a climatic effect because it is essentially no different from the tenor of the rest of the novel. And yet despite this, this is a novel that includes jubilation as well as sorrow. Neither the fact of racism nor the fact of the neuroses of Lillian and Charles prevents Himes from describing the joyous, positive aspects of life, elements which co-exist with the pain in the Taylor family and in the lives of other Blacks. In fact, the presence of such positive aspects is crucial to Himes' fundamental theme that the "mire," no matter how destructive, contains within it the source of rejuvenation and resurrection. Like Ernest J. Gaines' *A Lesson Before Dying, The Third Generation* illustrates the fundamental humanity evidenced by whites attempting to help Charles: the grocery store owner tries to help him; the college dean offers him a second chance; and the judge gives him a suspended sentence after his arrest for passing bad checks. Consequently, there is hope and possibility in the mist of trauma and despair. It is also here in this final chapter that Fess dies so that Charles might live a productive life. At the hospital, the Oedipal phase comes to a conclusion when Lillian decides to stay at the hospital with her dead husband instead of going home with Charles, making the gesture (the sacrifice of her son) that allows him to mature. Charles realizes the significance of his mother's action: "He knew then, in that instant, that she had gone back to his father; that she would belong to his father now forever. He felt as if he had been cut in two; as if a part of himself had been severed from himself forever. But at that moment it did not hurt; and the hurt had not come" (348). This psychic division reminds us of the Du Boisian double consciousness that creates an internal warfare within the Black individual whose eternal determination keeps him or her from being torn asunder. With the psychologically diseased part gone, that part which had bound him to his mother, Charles can begin the process of creating a new adult self. The "veil of horror" has concluded and Charles must accept the responsibility of being a man. Alone in his father's room Charles decides to look up Peggy and his child; he feels as if a cycle has come to completion, as if whatever punishment has been due him and his family is now over:

> Finally he thought about himself. He wondered what would become of himself now. Maybe he'd look up Mr. Small and become a waiter. He'd look up Peggy too.

> She had his child somewhere. He'd find out where she was and write her. He'd tell
> her everything. Maybe she'd understand. If she would have him after that he would
> marry her. If she wouldn't maybe she'd let him help the child. (350)

At this point, Charles is willing to face those individuals that he has been running away from and willing to accept the responsibility of being a father to his child. Charles' last words to himself as he goes to sleep are "Good-bye Mama." Thus Charles finally accepts the existential notion of responsibility for his own freedom and subjectivity; the Oedipus complex is finally resolved, and the tragic cycle of victimization and self-destruction concludes.

Through the series of traumatic events—the conflict between Lillian and Fess, the young woman being crushed by the wagon, William's accident, Charles' fall down an elevator shaft and the stabbing of his father—all connected to the "rape" and the "family romances," Himes strings together a chain of images that explicates the theme of double guilt through intraracial oppression and an unresolved Oedipal complex. And in the process Charles removes himself for the mire and learns the cause of his own self-destructive urges; redemption occurs. This raises the critical question: is nature or nurturing ultimately the determining factor in child development? Like any skilled writer, Chester Himes furnishes us no simple answer to this question because although the parental issues are salient, a plethora of environmental issues such as racism and segregation also have a significant impact on Charles Taylor. On the issue of segregation the novel reveals its personal and societal impact on Charles:

> So much that he liked was negated by its [college] pattern of segregation. The city
> itself was segregated in much the same manner as St. Louis had been. But in St.
> Louis he'd attended a segregated school; he'd been a part, he'd belonged. While
> in the university he had no part in any life outside the cold and formal classes.
> Negro students were barred from all the fraternities and sororities whose houses
> bordered the university grounds, nor were they invited to join any of the student
> clubs and honorary societies of the university itself. Nor could they patronize any
> of the privately owned restaurants, cafes and theaters of the neighborhood, which
> seemed so essential to a sense of ease. From the very first he knew he didn't really
> belong, and that he never would. (259)

In all the novels under consideration here, Jim Crow segregation has an enormous impact of the quality of Black life. And this enduring issue of segregation is behind the some of the apprehensions that Lillian Taylor has for her sons, especially Charles. Segregation of restaurants, cafes, and theaters seems designed to eliminate or prevent miscegenation, especially between Black males and white females. While the Black students developed lives of their own, segregation will surely impact on their futures once they graduate from the university. Perhaps the most dramatic and demeaning representation of the impact of Jim Crow segregation is Fess Taylor, the former college professor, being reduced to a waiter and doing menial jobs to survive, losing the respect and admiration of his three sons. His personal loss in the novel is directly connected to Tom abandoning his family, William being blind, and the ongoing self-destructive behavior of Charles. With Charles Taylor as the focus in this novel, *The Third Generation* contains both the history and the confession of Fess Taylor, one of the "talented tenth" (that class of college-bred black Americans in whom W. E. B. Du Bois placed so much faith) and his offspring while highlighting the internal conflict around color bias. Like the Ex-Colored Man in James Weldon Johnson's *The Autobiography of an Ex-Colored Man* (1912), Fess Taylor longed to be like the heroic Booker T. Washington; indeed Himes' professional characterizations of Fess suggest this possibility.

The Third Generation through the processes of seduction, primal scenes, and symbolic castration, resonates the theme of intraracial victimization, a theme also treated by other African American writers such as Richard Wright in *Uncle Tom's Children,* James Baldwin in *Go Tell It on the Mountain,* Toni Morrison in *Sula,* and Gayl Jones in *Corregidora.* The novel renders a rather candid psychological treatise and portrait of a Black family, especially Black males—all affected by the ensnarling winds of racial injustice which attempt to create a perpetual winter in the lives of Black people. However, Himes illustrates that redemption is always a possibility because the human spirit has no limitations and the possibility of change is always present. The trauma-filled processes of self-discovery lead to healing and a new self-direction. Thus although Chester Bomar Himes' *Third Generation* is relentlessly bursting with violence and intraracial conflict, this impressive Black writer may be justly described as a warm-hearted moralist who protests America's enduring white supremacist culture and all aspects of inhumanity.

Notes

1   Chester Himes, *The Third Generation* foreword by John A. Williams (New York: Thunder Mouth Press, 1989): iii. All further references to this text will be given parenthetically.

2   For Lillian Taylor's behavior and Fess Taylor's response, see Kathy Russell, Midge Wilson, and Ronald Hall's *The Color Complex: The Politics of Skin Color Among African Americans* (New York: Doubleday, 1992) in which they argue: "Clearly, hair is less an issue for men than for women. Beginning in childhood, boys conventionally wear short hair while girls grow their hair long" (83). Because of America's white supremacist culture, hair texture, like skin color, carries much more social and historical significance to Blacks.

3   While both Malcolm X and George Jackson were both incarcerated, Jackson was assassinated while in prison. On August 7, 1970 George Jackson's seventeen year-old brother Jonathan was killed in an attempt to break his brother out of prison. A year

later in August 1971 at San Quentin prison and three days before he was to go on trial, George Jackson was killed during an alleged prison escape. During the twenty-three hours of solitary confinement, Jackson would write *Blood in My Eye* and *Soledad Brother*. Malcolm X would also be assassinated while making a speech.

4   In Frederick Douglass' *My Bondage and My Freedom* (Chicago: University of Illinois Press, 1987), Douglass reflecting on his horrific experience with this demonic white individual states: "I shall never be able to narrate the mental experience through which it was my lot to pass during my stay at Covey's. I was completely wrecked, changed and bewildered; goaded almost to madness at one time, and at another reconciling myself to my wretched condition. Everything in the way of kindness, which I had experienced at Baltimore; all my former hopes and aspirations for usefulness in the world, and my then present lot, but increased my anguish. I suffered bodily as well as mentally. I had neither sufficient time in which to eat or to sleep, except on Sundays. The over work, and the brutal chastisements of which I was the victim, combined with that ever-gnawing and soul-devouring thought—'*I am a slave—a slave for life—a slave with no rational ground for hope of freedom*'—rendered me a living embodiment of mental and physical wretchedness" (137). Like David Walker's appeal, Douglas converys the absolute wretchedness that Black experienced and the psychological trauma that would be passed on to future generations.

4. *Black Male Subjectivity and the American Dream: Working Outside the Law in Walter Mosley's* Devil in a Blue Dress

> We Black folks, our history and our present being, are a mirror of all the manifold experiences of America. What we want, what we represent, what we endure is what America is. If we black folks perish, America will perish. If America has forgotten her past, then let her look in the mirror of our consciousness and she will see the living past living in the present, for our memories go back, through our black folk of today, through the recollection of our black parents, and through the tales of slavery told by our black grandparents, to the time when none of us, black or white, lived in this fertile land. The differences between black folk and white folk are not blood or color, and the ties that bind us are deeper than those that separate us. The common road of hope which we all traveled has brought us into a stronger kinship than any words, law or legal claims

> Richard Wright, *12 Million Black Voices* (1941)

The issue of identity formation represents a critical aspect of African American history and literature from the slave narratives to the present, and when this issue resides in the lives of Black male characters it has nuances that involve not only race, but culture, economics, politics, and psychology. In America, the practice and philosophy of white supremacy involves all of these factors and much more, and like a persistent storm African Americans seem to be always at the epicenter of this enduring tempest. As James Baldwin explains in *The Fire Next Time*:

> At the center of this dreadful storm, this vast confusion, stand the Black people of this nation, who must now share the fate of a nation that has never accepted them, to which they were brought in chains. Well, if this is so one has no choice but to do all in one's power to change that fate, and at no matter what risk— eviction, imprisonment, torture, death. For the sake of one's children, in order to

minimize the bill that they must pay, one must be careful not to take refuge in any delusion—and the value placed on the color of the skin is always and everywhere and forever a delusion. (104)

This delusion associated with the philosophy of preference pigmentocracy finds no better expression or representation than in the paradoxical phenomenon of racial passing, of light-skinned African Americans assuming a white identity and being accepted as white by the white society. As argued in *The Tragic Black Buck: Racial Masquerading in the American Literary Imagination* (2004) this particular phenomenon of performance

> is a kind of Faustian paradigm that represents a profound paradox which both challenges the doctrine of white supremacy (the essentialism of whiteness) and requires a denial of one's blackness at the same time that it reaffirms the existing racial hierarchy, white power, and white privilege. Personhood is whiteness, and whiteness means possibility and privilege. Paradoxically, within racist constructions, whiteness defines blackness and whiteness is defined by blackness. (8)

This phenomenon of racial passing originating in the slave narratives such as William and Ellen Craft's narrative *Running a Thousand Miles to Freedom* (1848), continuing with Frances Harper' *Iola Leroy or Shadow Uplifted* (1892), Mark Twain's *The Tragedy of Pudd'nhead Wilson* (1894), Charles Waddell Chesnutt's *The House Behind the Cedars* (1900), and James Weldon Johnson's *The Autobiography of an Ex-Coloured Man* (1912) and evident in many Black novels written during the Harlem Renaissance such as Jessie Redmon Fauset's *Plum Bun* (1928), Nella Larsen's *Passing* (1929), George Schuyler's *Black No More* (1931), and Langston Hughes' *The Ways of White Folks* (1934) can be found in present-day African American literature. Passing as a strategy for socioeconomic subjectivity mirrors the quintessential rags-to-riches narratives of the American Dream such as Theodore Dreiser's *American Tragedy* (1925), where the "passing" resonates around ethnicity and class status. And like Danny Senna's *Caucasia* (1991) and Philip Roth's *Human Stain* (2000), which combine the theme of family romance with the theme of racial passing, Walter Mosley's *Devil in a Blue Dress* (1990) combines a postwar detective mystery with the theme of racial passing; implicit in these two genres is the issue that complicated secrets will be revealed often with tragically violent outcomes. The novels *The Sweeter the Juice: A Family Memoir in Black and White* by Shirlee Taylor Hazlip, *Life on the Color Line: The True Story of a White Boy Who Discovered He Was Black* by Gregory Howard Williams and *Love on Trial: An American Scandal in Black and White* by Earl Lewis and Heidi Ardizzone represent passing narratives. One of the most fascinating true narratives of racial passing is that of the writer and *New York Times* critic Anatole Broyard, a Louisiana Creole, who chose to pass for white in his life in New York City and Connecticut and married a woman of European descent. In 2007, his daughter, Bliss Broyard, published a memoir about her father and her exploration of family mysteries entitled *One Drop: My Father's Hidden Life—A Story of Race and Family Secrets*. Like the fictive detective novels, these authentic modern-day narratives are suspenseful and rich with individual and family secrets.

Walter Mosley's *Devil in a Blue Dress*, the first volume in Mosley's Easy Rawlins mystery series,[1] set in Los Angeles in 1948 chronicles the adventures and misadventures of Ezekiel (Easy) Rawlins, a Black World War II veteran just dismissed from his job at a defense plant.[2] Attempting to drown his financial woes with alcohol at a friend's bar (Joppy's) and wondering how he will pay the mortgage on his small house, Rawlins the hard-boiled hero,[3] meets DeWitt Albright, a menacing white gangster and lawyer who will plunge him into danger, romance, and murder in his mission to locate the enigmatic Daphne Monet,[4] a blonde beauty known to frequent Black jazz clubs. Here class status becomes racialized and central to the novel, as Albright cannot go into Black clubs with the ease of Rawlins. By combining the genre of detective fiction and the theme of racial passing , Mosley constructs a compelling narrative with a plethora of twists and turns along with narrative surprises. Like Chester Bomar Himes, who wrote numerous detective novels, Walter Mosley writes about racial relationships in an intensely race-charged atmosphere. Equally significant is the characterization of Easy Rawlins as a Black private investigator, a position that places him inside a quasi-legal framework and outside of a legal authority more often than not defined by white male privilege and power. Like other Black writers, Mosley encapsulates his narrative within the duality of Black life in America. As Helen Lock argues in "Invisible Detection: The Case of Mosley," the author's narratives offer a plethora of duality:

> The ambivalence and duality necessarily inherent in such a detective's perception of both society and of himself take on a more profound significance in Walter Mosley's novels, where they become a powerful metaphor for the African American experience of 'double consciousness' (in W. E. B. Du Bois' phrase), especially in the urban America of the period. The changing implications of the investigative process become infinitely more complex, and painful to negotiate, when a black detective finds himself haunting an additional borderland, that where the interests of his own community and those of the broader, predominantly white society uneasily co-exist and frequently collide. Mosley's protagonist, Easy Rawlins, is in fact characterized and motivated most centrally by his experience of duality and by a resultant ambiguity of attitude toward the cases he investigates, often reluctantly. At the same time, however, it is this very duality that facilitates the functional invisibility that he exploits to his advantage, making his detective work possible. (78–79)

Accordingly, the novel represents Easy Rawlins' journey to self-discovery, especially with regard to his masculinity and America's legal matters. It is this paradoxical framework that encapsulates my critical analysis of this novel.

One is immediately struck by the subtle yet rich historical context that Mosley constructs in recreating this era, evoking the edgy combination of freedom and disillusion in this postwar Black community. Like World War I, World War II was a period of opportunity and frustration for many Black soldiers specifically and Black people in general as it relates to their enduring desire for the American Dream, a dream full of promise and laden with pain. Black soldiers who fought for democracy in Europe returned home seeking inclusion into American society but experienced domestic warfare, especially in the areas of housing, education, and employment along with physical violence.[5] As Kareem Abdul-Jabbar and Alan Steinberg argue in *Black Profiles in Courage* (2000), Black service in the military represents a paradox:

> Historically, all the way back to the Revolutionary War, Blacks understood they earn respect in the military that they were denied in society. There was an element of self-esteem involved in joining the armed forces; it represented an oasis of escape from repression and discrimination. But Black service in the military also underlined a major contradiction in our attitude toward equality. Here was a people that always volunteered to serve the country in times of war only to have the country deny them the equality that was their birthright. (155–56)

Indeed, America can fundamentally be defined as a paradox: a country founded by white male slaveholders who wanted freedom for themselves. Accordingly, Black soldiers fighting in Europe for democracy would encounter life-threatening conditions in America in their quest for socio-economic equality. History reveals a plethora of incidents where returning Black soldiers were harassed, beaten, and in some cases lynched in their uniforms; at a minimum they encountered the same disenfranchisement and racial violence that their fathers experienced when they returned from World War I. W. E. B. Du Bois sums up the significance of Black soldiers' commitment to democracy when he states that: "Perhaps their greatest credit is from the fact that they withstood so bravely and uncomplainingly the barrage of hatred and offensive prejudice aimed against them....Thus the black man defended America from the beginning to the World War. To him our independence from Europe and slavery is in no small degree due" (*The Gift of Black Folk,* 64). Without a doubt, war and conflict are Walter Mosley's dominant themes.

Somewhat late in *Devil in a Blue Dress,* Easy Rawlins, our protagonist and Black sleuth, makes a profound judgment on justice, race, and money in America: "But I didn't believe that there was justice for Negroes. I thought that in there might be some justice for a Black man if he had the money to grease it. Money isn't a sure bet but it's the closest to God that

I've ever seen in this world."[6] As a veteran of World War II, Rawlins' candid statement comes in the face of his own calamitous personal and economic circumstances and the overall reality of life for Black people in the 1940s. Just fired from his job at a defense plant and desperate to pay his mortgage, Rawlins becomes enmeshed in the seemingly straightforward task of finding the blond beauty, Daphne Monet. DeWitt Albright's view of fast and easy money becomes a mysterious and deadly encounter laden with sexuality and intrigue as the contradictions and perplexities of race abound. Equally important, the novel is about Rawlins' desire for independence as argued by Marilyn C. Wesley: "Through the adventure and the ambivalence of the black detective, *Devil in a Blue* Dress and subsequent works in the Rawlins series enact a Foucauldian structure which teaches that power, like law, is not an order to be retrieved but the contingent result of specific circumstances that black men may understand through violence and adapt to their own need for respect and freedom" (104). In this richly atmospheric *noir* novel, Walter Mosley continues a long-standing tradition of Black detective fiction, especially that of Chester Bomar Himes, but adds some nuances that create his own authorial signature.

Keeping and maintaining the American Dream become central to Mosley's novel through the characterizations and desires of Easy Rawlins. Like F. Scott Fitzgerald's Jay Gatsby, the character most often associated with the American Dream (symbolized by Daisy Buchanan), Easy Rawlins becomes a desperately desiring individual willing to take enormous personal risks. However, unlike Gatsby's over "forty acres of lawn and garden" surrounding his towering mansion in West Egg, the unemployed Rawlins has a sublimated love affair with his diminutive house:

> The house itself was small. Just living room, a bedroom, and a kitchen. The bathroom didn't even have a shower and the backyard was no larger than a child's rubber pool. But that house meant more to me than any woman I ever knew. I loved her and I was jealous of her and if the bank sent the county marshal to take her from me I might come at him with a rifle rather than give her up. (56–57)

As a descendant of sharecroppers who had never owned anything until he brought that house, Rawlins' desire to "protect and defend" his small portion of the American Dream becomes particularly significant. On this issue, Eric Foner makes the point that African Americans emancipated from the dungeon of enslavement got "nothing but freedom."[7] The concept of property ownership lies at the heart of the American Dream, especially for African Americans who have never been compensated for over four hundred years of slave labor and quasi-slavery under Jim Crow, the Black Codes,[8] and sharecropping, a systematic form of economic slavery in the South that benefited white landowners.[9] Indeed, the United States is based on the lofty premise that everyone should be a homeowner; however, this theory and regulations by the government have supported segregation in housing, creating Sundown communities.[10] Segregation in the defense of democracy becomes connected to segregation at home. Black people's response to segregation was to migrate to those places that they believed held more opportunity, such as Chicago, New York, and, in this case, California. Describing other Black people who migrated, Rawlins relates: "All of them...and half the people in that room had migrated from Houston after the war, and some before that. California was like heaven for the Southern Negro. People told stories of how you could eat fruit off the trees and get enough work to retire one day. The stories were true for the most part but the truth wasn't like the dream" (72). A fundamental part of this dream is homeownership. Of course, the paradox of owning a home is that it ties workers like Easy Rawlins down and intensifies his desire to save his house by finding Daphne Monet. As aptly suggested by Daphne's last name (sounds like money), she represents the answer to Easy Rawlins keeping his home and providing for himself just as it powerfully recalls Nick Carraway's observation that Daisy Buchanan's voice "was full of money—that was the inexhaustible charm that rose and fell in it, the jingle in it, the cymbals' song in it..." (120). Sexuality and desire become intermingled with power here. Accordingly, property and money become the two cornerstones to the fundamental concept of the American Dream and suggest the possibility for personal freedom and power, especially for some Black men who tend to define themselves by patriarchy and capitalism.

Walter Mosley begins the novel with deficiencies and complex desires that must be fulfilled if Easy Rawlins is to maintain the lifestyle that he has become accustomed to and even his single status resonates with the charge to find Daphne Monet. This deficiency becomes enhanced by the juxtaposition of Rawlins and Albright. Mosley's begins his novel with racial conflict and a racial challenge: "I was surprised to see a white man walk into Joppy's bar....When he looked at me I felt a thrill of fear, but that went away quickly because I was used to white people by 1948" (45) announces Easy Rawlins. Rawlins' masculinity comes into play here as he has been transformed by his World War II experiences; having killed white males in battle, he knows this white man is to be respected but not feared. It is Rawlins's friend, Joppy Shag, who gives him the "slave tip," a lead on a job by introducing Easy to Albright. Beyond the obvious racial and class distinctions between them, character and morality become evident. Despite Rawlins' hyperbole of defending his home with a weapon, we admire his willingness and tenacity to sacrifice his freedom and indeed perhaps his life for a noble yet capitalistic idea, a man becomes defined by what he owns. Like the hard-working and upright Silas in Richard Wright's short story "Long Black Song" in *Uncle Tom's Children* (1938), who decides to die in his burning home fighting off racist white males, Rawlins' character is that of rugged individualism.

Betrayed by his wife, Sarah, Silas engages in a shootout with white males who come to lynch him after he destroys a musical instrument used by a white man to seduce his wife. We discover Rawlins' strength of character in his conversation with Albright; Rawlins instinctually knows that the snake-like Albright is speaking half-truths. Rawlins immediately becomes on guard despite (or because of) how Albright identifies himself: "I used to be a law-yer when I lived in Georgia. But now I'm just another fella who does favors for friends, and for friends of friends" (49). There are two things interest-ing about Albright's statement. First, he "used to be a lawyer," which means that he quit practicing or that he was disbarred from practicing. Second, by mentioning that he does favors for friends and friends of friends, he indi-cates that he is a middleman who may or may not be telling Rawlins the real reasons he needs to find Daphne Monet, and as Rawlins will discover Albright has some ulterior motives. Furthermore, for most Black people white lawyers have been a critical component in maintaining the quasi-slav-ery of sharecropping and the theft of thousands of acres of Black people's land in the South. Making a comparison between DeWitt Albright and his friend Raymond Alexander (Mouse) has the effect of setting Easy Rawlins' "teeth on edge." Rawlins' paradoxical state of desire has an added psycho-logical component as he engages in a Du Boisian conversation with himself over Albright's enigmatic offer. For most Black men, the issue of the law is ever present because of America's long history of legal and extra-legal ter-rorism. Violent racial hatred has been and continues to be a fundamental part of American society. Discussing racial hatred in *100 Years of Lynchings* (1962) Ralph Ginzburg states: "The reason is that the race-hater is inwardly a man who hates himself. He finds it necessary to shift to others his own unconscious feelings of guilt. Hence he chooses as his victim a member of a minority group who is less able to defend himself than the average person. To his victim he unconsciously shifts his own shortcomings and guilt-laden desires."[11] Drawing on his mother wit or street smarts, Rawlins states: "Working for Joppy's friend was the only way I saw to keep my house. But there was something wrong. I could feel it in my fingertips. DeWitt Albright made me uneasy....I knew I was going to take Albright's money and do whatever he wanted me to, providing it was legal, because that little house of mine needed me and I wasn't about to let her down" (57). The central stipulation is the legality of this investigation. An added psychological-phys-ical element based on Rawlins' time spent fighting and killing white men in World War II is also evident is his decision to take the proposition:

> DeWitt made me a little nervous. He was a big man, and powerful by the look of him. You could tell by the way he held his shoulders that he was full of violence. But I was a big man too. And like most young men, I never liked to admit that I could be dissuaded by fear. Whether he knew it or not DeWitt Albright had me

caught by my own pride. The more I was afraid of him, I was that much more
certain to take the job he offered. (57)

With a paradoxical mixture of apprehension and desire, Rawlins' pride
compels him to seriously consider the offer; the possibility of violence
between Albright and Rawlins is also evident. Walter Mosley's foreshadowing
of future violence is within a description of DeWitt Albright that is eerily
suggestive of F. Scott Fitzgerald's characterization of Tom Buchanan in *The
Great Gatsby*. Tom is described as having "arrogant eyes" and the narrator
notes that "not even the effeminate swank of his riding clothes could hide
the enormous power of that body...you could see a great pack of muscle
shifting when his shoulder moved under his thin coat. It was a body capable
of enormous leverage—a cruel body" (11). Later in the novel, the married
Tom Buchanan punches Myrtle Wilson (his married lower-class lover) in
the face, breaking her nose. An aggressive, short-tempered man, Tom sparks
continual disorder by abusing —physically or emotionally—Daisy Buchanan,
Myrtle Wilson, George Wilson, and Jay Gatsby throughout the novel. Like
Jay Gatsby and Tom Buchanan and their conflicting desires for the seemingly white Daisy Buchanan,[12] a fundamental conflict between Easy Rawlins
and DeWitt Albright is announced, a conflict centered on the beautiful
blonde and seemingly white, Daphne Monet.

Easy Rawlins' diminished subjectivity because of his financial troubles is
on display when he goes to meet Dewitt Albright; here we also view the indi-
vidual and institutional manifestations of ingrained white male supremacy.
Being challenged by a "little white man" at Albright's building conjures up
Rawlins traumatic past as a child as well as violent reflections of the war;
Rawlins assumes the role of the Black slave, feigning ignorance:

> It was a habit I developed in Texas when I was a boy. Sometimes, when a white
> man of authority would catch me off guard, I'd empty my head of everything so
> I was unable to say anything. 'The less you know, the less trouble you find,' they
> used to say. I hated myself for it but I also hated white people and colored people
> too for making me that way. (58)

Rawlins' statement reflects the overall trauma of the belief of racial inferiority that many Black people have internalized and passed on. Beyond this
general trauma, Rawlins's trauma is specific to his parents. In a symbolic discourse that reflects severe natal alienation, he laments: "I often think of
how so many people have walked into my life for just a few minutes and
kicked up some dust, then they're gone away. My father was like that; my
mother wasn't much better" (60). Indeed this is the only reference in the
novel to his family; we get the sense that Rawlins is alone in the world. With
a clear issue of familial abandonment, Rawlins carries the burdens of his

personal past and especially the burdens of Black people as a result of ongoing segregation. As delineated in Richard Wright's "The Ethics of Jim Crow" in *Black Boy* (1945), during segregation there were strict regulations for interactions between Blacks and whites . Most southern white Americans who grew up prior to 1954 expected Black Americans to conduct themselves according to well-understood rituals of obsequious behavior. This racial etiquette governed the actions, manners, attitudes, and words of all Black people when in the presence of whites. To violate this racial etiquette placed one's very life, and the lives of one's family, at risk. Blacks were expected to refer to white males in positions of authority as "Boss" or "Cap'n"—a title of respect that replaced "Master" or "Marster" used in slave times. Sometimes, the white children of one's white employer or a prominent white person might be called "Massa," to show special respect. If a white person was well known, a Black servant, hired hand, or tenant might address the white person as "Mr. John" or "Miss Mary." A Black male who violated these rules risked a violent reaction by whites, and the worse possible result of the "trouble" could be a lynching. Not saying "sir" to a white man, not stepping off the sidewalk to allow a white person to pass, not taking your hat off in the presence of a white woman, looking a white person in the eyes—these were just some of things that could cause Black individuals to be beaten, jailed, or lynched. All Black males were referred to as "Boy," "Uncle," or "Old Man" regardless of their age, and all Black females were referred to as "Girl," "Auntie," or "Wench."

This practice of addressing Blacks by words that denoted contempt or inadequacy reduced the Black individual to a non-person, especially in newspaper accounts. In reporting incidents involving Blacks, the press usually adopted the gender-neutral term "Negro," thus designating Blacks as lifeless and unknown persons. For example, an accident report might read: "Rescuers discovered that two women, three men, four children, and five Negroes were killed by the explosion." " 'We only take deliveries between nine and six' " (58), is the assumption articulated by the "little white man" when Rawlins arrives after 8:30 PM. Rawlins' deliberate hesitation in giving the name "Albright" combined with the white man's benign bigotry causes racial conflict. Contemptuously, the little white man asks Rawlins: "Did he give you a note saying you're to come in here after hours" (59). Rawlins continues to play the role of ignorant darkie by shaking his head, but his thoughts are far from benign as Easy's warfare mindset takes hold: "I would have liked to rip the skin from his face like I'd done once to another white boy" (59). Racism and blatant disrespect become explicit when the white man asks: "Well how am I to know that you aren't just a thief? You can't even remember his name and you want me to take you somewhere in there. Why you could have a partner waiting for me to let you in…" (59). His remark illustrates that Black males as criminals represent one of the fundamental

stereotypes in American society, and the reference to the note recalls the
written permission needed by Black slaves as they moved from one plantation to another and the absolute necessity for indigenous Black South
Africans to have a "pass" in apartheid South Africa. As a homeowner and
veteran, Rawlins' sense of manhood and rage become apparent: "You just
tell him when you see him that Mr. Rawlins was here. You tell him that the
next time he better give me a note because you cain't be lettin' no street
niggahs comin' in yo' place wit no notes" (59). No longer willing to accept
this psychological castration, Rawlins becomes absolutely defiant with his
sarcasm by informing this little white man that he is "Mr. Rawlins" and not
some nigger thief or some nigger pickanny needing a note from his white
master. As a hardworking homeowner and a veteran, Rawlins reveals his
complex persona as his tolerance for this white man's bigotry disappears,
and he makes it clear that he does not desire to be treated like some "shift-
less nigger" or criminal. Like Shadrack in Toni Morrison's *Sula* and other
Black veterans of World War II, Easy Rawlins' subjectivity has been inalter-
ably defined by the psychological trauma of war:

> I signed up to fight in the war to prove to myself that I was a man. Before we
> launched the attack on D-Day I was frightened but I fought. I fought despite
> the fear. The first time I fought a German hand-to-hand I screamed for help the
> whole time I was killing him. His dead eyes stared at me a full five minutes before
> I let go of his throat. (94)

Thus this racial conflict at Albright's office emphasizes the objective of
Jim Crow etiquette, which came down to one concern: Blacks must display
their innate inferiority to whites by actions, words, and manners. Laws
constructed to benefit white males supported this racist code of behavior
whenever racial customs started to deteriorate or break down in
practice—as they did during the Reconstruction period. When the laws
were weakly or slowly applied, whites resorted to extra-legal violence
against Blacks to reinforce the Jim Crow culture. Indeed, whites commonly
justified lynchings and the horrible murders of Blacks during the Jim
Crow era as defensive actions taken in response to Black violations of the
color line and rules of racial etiquette. This racial conflict further foreshadows Rawlins' conflicts with white males inside and outside the legal
system. Like ghosts dragging their weighty chains, many Blacks carry with
them the psychological legacies of slavery and segregation. With Rawlins'
rage being both external and internal, his defensive behavior yet juvenile
demeanor is produced by this white male's internalized racism. For this
little white man, Rawlins is the wrong race in the wrong neighborhood. In
light of this demeaning confrontation, Rawlins' second meeting with
Albright initially exacerbates the racial tension when Albright's men,
Shariff and Mandy, try to search a protesting Rawlins. Showing Rawlins a

picture of Daphne Monet makes the desire to find her and obtain the money to pay his mortgage real:

> It was a picture of the head and shoulders of a pretty young white woman. The picture had been black-and-white originally but it was touched up for color like the photos of jazz singer that they put out in nightclubs. She had light hair coming down over her bare shoulders and high cheekbones and eyes that might have been blue if the artist got it right. After staring at her for a full minute I decided that she'd be worth looking for if you could get her to smile at you that way. (63)[13]

As we shall discover this description and statement suggest a plethora of issues concerning race, but the most important aspects here are Daphne's sexuality and Rawlins' sexual desire. Here we have the typical taxonomic male gaze and the objectified female. Looking at Daphne's picture creates a desire to look for her in order to obtain the gaze the picture represents. As Suzanne Moore relates: "Women as erotic spectacle bring both pleasure and pain. The anxiety induced by seeing the image of women supposedly reminds the male spectator of the threat of castration and is therefore displaced by the fetishisation of the image. Through this process...the image of woman is once more made perfect or visually complete" (52). For Rawlins this "castration" is more symbolic and tied to his emasculation by white males. Further, Rawlins' taxonomic gaze constructs a triangle of sexual desire between the two men and the woman, and looking for Daphne in order to save his little house becomes sublimated by his desire to have her "smile." The apparent racial ambiguity or racial paradox is revealed by Albright's statement that: "Daphne has a predilection for the company of Negroes. She likes jazz and pig's feet and dark meat, if you know what I mean" (63). Like Toni Morrison's use of "pig meat" in *Sula* in reference to Sula Peace and Nel Wright, who become symbolically decapitated, by Black men, Daphne is also symbolically decapitated because only her head and shoulders are visible. As Howard Eilberg Schwartz and Wendy Doniger argue "the display of the female face can be another form of decapitation, turning the female head into a symbol of desire, rather than a symbol of identity and of the capacity for speech and language" (2). Equally important is Rawlins' silent response: "I knew but I didn't like to hear it" (63). For Albright, Daphne is a white girl who likes Black culture, food, and Black men, but Rawlins' response is confusing: Does he dislike white women who like Black men sexually? Or does he loathe Albright mentioning this fact about Daphne in light of the "full minute" that he took looking at her picture? Nevertheless, Daphne's culturally subversive sexuality as a "nigger lover" becomes established and Rawlins' sexual desire is also affirmed. Mosley's description of Daphne Monet recalls a similar characterization of Clare Kendry in Nella Larsen's *Passing* (1929). In this novel a light-skinned Black woman who is permanently passing for white reveals to her friend,

Irene Redfield, that, " 'You don't know, you can't realize how I want to see Negroes, to be with them again, to talk with them, to hear them laugh' " (239).[14] Clare's intense desire to be with Black people leads to her abandonment of her white husband, Jack Bellew, and daughter, Margery, culminating in a tragic death in Harlem, where she is either pushed or falls out a window. Like Clare who uses her white looking Black body to make herself available for consumption by white males, there is the suggestion that Daphne has also blurred the boundaries of race and reduced herself to commodity status through her associations with white males. As Meredith Goldsmith states,"African American women must constantly vaccillate between the role of consumer and that of object of consumption"(99). Like race, sexual desire represents a complex issue considering America's long-standing history of miscegenation. Now it becomes understandable why Albright needs Rawlins; Easy can venture into certain parts of Black communities without the skepticism or hostility that a white man would receive, especially if he is looking for a blonde woman who likes Black men. As Albright sarcastically states, he is "not the right persuasion." This speaks to the issue of knowledge; Easy Rawlins' "education" and his ability to persuade other Black people are beyond Albright's realm. Power and knowledge become enmeshed in race. On this point, Marilyn C. Wesley writes: "The historical placement of the novel speaks to the complex inscription of power and knowledge around political altered issues of black manhood during the post-war years" (105). For Rawlins the legality of this investigation is a persistent issue despite the hundred dollars for a week's work. "I don't know Mr. Albright, I mean, how do I know what I'm getting mixed up in....I don't want to get mixed up with the law is what I mean" (64). Like most Black men, Rawlins has morbid apprehensions of the law. Again, it could be argued that the law in America was made to benefit white men, especially wealthy white men. This analysis is partly confirmed by Albright's revealing comment that "The law is made by the rich people so that the poor people can't get ahead. You don't want to get mixed up with the law and neither do I" (64). Obviously, this is an ironic statement for a white man who was a lawyer when he lived in Georgia and obscures the racial element. As Gloria J. Browne-Marshall argues in *Race, Law, and American Society: 1607 to Present* (2007): "By 1836, Africans had provided two hundred years of slave labor to the United States. Their legal rights were subject to the whim of Whites. Forbidden to defend themselves or their loved ones, Blacks were in a constant battle against the rule of law" (6). Finding Daphne Monet will lead Rawlins into a complex and deadly battle inside and outside the law.

With Albright's sincere pledge of a "bonus mortgage payment," future employment, or even the possibility of helping Rawlins get back his job at Champion Aircraft, Rawlins' return to his part of the American Dream becomes possible. This second meeting concludes with an ominous note as Albright tells Rawlins that he must "have a sense of balance when it comes to the law" and asks him about the war. "You ever kill someone up close? I mean so close that you could see it when his eyes went out of focus and he let go? When you kill a man it's the shit and piss that's worse. You boys did that in the war and I bet it was bad. I bet you couldn't dream about your mother anymore, or anything nice" (67).[15] Although Rawlins does not respond, he vividly recalls "the wide-eyed corpses of German soldiers" that he "once saw stacked up on a road to Berlin" (67). Beyond his experiences that infer that he has killed, Albright's provocative question eerily suggests that Rawlins should be prepared to take life and protect his life during this adventure of tracking down Daphne Monet. Exchanging the money for this investigation closes and foreshadows the deadly deal, and Albright suggests that Rawlins instigate his search for Daphne at an illegal club in the Black community.

The search for Daphne Monet mirrors Easy Rawlins' search for knowledge. From the beginning of the novel, Rawlins is always questioning and seeking to know what he is mixed up in. Like a Black Sherlock Holmes, Easy Rawlins uses his experiences in the Second World War and his mother wit to survive. Later, when the two white police officers question him, he demands, "I wanna know what's goin on" (75). Rawlins consistently takes this approach with DeWitt Albright and Todd Carter; his experiences have empowered him to confront white males. He asks Carter: "What I need is for you to help me understand what's happening" (116). Highlighting a quality that transforms the blue-collar factory worker into a detective, Rawlins muses: "It was a simple ranch-style house, not large. There were no outside lights on, except on the front porch, so I couldn't make out the color. I wanted to know what color the house was. I wanted to know what made jets fly and how long sharks lived. There was a lot I wanted to know before I died" (196). Rawlins' inquisitive spirit along with the assistance of Mouse allows him to survive the realm of violence. In fact, it could be argued that Mouse is Rawlins' alter ego. As we see, there are a number of incidents during which Rawlins thinks about killing certain individuals, but it is Mouse who easily kills people regardless of the legal consequences.

Black men's relationship with the American legal system has always been problematic, and there is a great deal of historical evidence to show white law enforcement's complicity in racial violence and the continued failure of the federal and state courts to render justice. Mosley makes a point of highlighting the injustices that Black people face. At the illegal club we are introduced to a number of Blacks who are at odds with the legal system. Indeed, as Mosley relates, the club was founded on illegality:

> John's Place was a speakeasy before they repealed Prohibition...John liked the
> speakeasy business though, and he had been in so much trouble with the law
> that City Hall wouldn't have given him a license to drive, much less to sell liquor.
> So John kept paying off the police and running an illegal nightclub through the
> back door of a little market at the corner of Central Avenue and Eighty-ninth
> Place. (69)

Like many other Americans. especially immigrants or migrants, Blacks have
done many things outside of the law in order to survive; Rawlins' search for
Daphne cannot be characterized as legal, because he has no legal authority. While at the club, he asks about a white girl, but he does not give her
real name so that there can be no connection to him if Albright has misled
him. Here Rawlins hears about a Black man named Howard Green who
was killed after being beaten so viciously that "his wife, Esther, said the only
way she could identify the body was because of his ring" (72). Through
Rawlins' conversation with Junior Fornay, we learn that Rawlins was fired
from his job at Champion Aircraft because of conflict with his Italian supervisor. Again race is at the center of this conflict when the supervisor informs
Rawlins that his "people have to learn to give a little extra if we want to
advance" (73). Rawlins' response that leads to his firing was that his people
"been givin' a little extra since before Italy was even a country" (74).
Rawlins' signifying response is interesting in light of his own service in
World War II and the more profound fact that the number of Black soldiers
swelled from a few thousand to over two hundred thousand; examples such
as the absolutely heroic actions of the Tuskegee Airmen could also be what
Rawlins is suggesting. The Tuskegee Airmen were enthusiastic, strong-
minded young men who enlisted to become America's first Black military
pilots, at a time when there were many people who thought that Black men
lacked intelligence, skill, courage, and patriotism. They came from every
section of the country, with large numbers coming from New York City,
Washington, Los Angeles, Chicago, Philadelphia, and Detroit. Each one
possessed a strong personal desire to serve the United States of America at
the best of his ability. The exceptional record of Black airmen in World
War II was accomplished by men whose names will forever live in hallowed
memory. Each one accepted the challenge and proudly displayed his skill
and determination while suppressing internal rage from humiliation and
indignation caused by frequent experiences of racism and bigotry, at home
and overseas. These courageous airmen fought two wars—one against a
military force overseas and the other against white supremacy at home and
abroad.

Mosley seems to be connecting the issue of criminality and Black men
returning from the war. If hard-working Black men like Rawlins can find difficult conditions, then we can understand how other Black men such as

Frank Green can become career criminals. Rawlins describes him: "We called him Knifehand because he was so fast to pull a knife that it seemed he always had one in his hand. I stayed away from Frank because he was a gangster. He hijacked liquor trucks and cigarette shipments all over California, and Nevada too. He was serious about everything and just about ready to cut any man he met" (75). Frank Green is notably in all-dark clothes, which for Rawlins means "he was about to go out to work—hijacking or worse" (75). This characterization of Frank Green pales in connection to that of another Black man, Raymond Alexander, referred to as Mouse. Mouse has been Rawlins' best friend back in Houston, Texas, but he is one dangerous and deadly individual capable of extreme violence. Rawlins' connection to Mouse involves a murder; in fact, Easy going off to war is connected to Mouse's irresponsible violence. While in a stolen car, Easy accompanies Mouse to his stepfather's house to ask for an inheritance his mother had promised him before she died. Later, Mouse returns to the house with Clifton and the stepfather, Daddy Reese, and Clifton wind up dead. Easy relates that "He told me that Clifton held up Daddy Reese because the old man wouldn't relent to Mouse's claim. He told me that when Reese got to a gun Clifton was cut down, and then Mouse killed Reese. He said all that in complete innocence as he counted out three hundred dollars, bloody money, for me" (93). At some point, Navrochet, Reese's son comes looking for Easy and Mouse; Mouse with a braggadocios and contemptuous tone relates: "I shot him four times 'fore he hit the floor. Same amount' a lead I put in his fuckin' son-of-a-whore-daddy" (78). Rawlins' reflects that "He had killed his stepfather five years earlier and blamed it on another man. But if the law ever found out the true circumstances he'd have been hanging in a week" (77). Rawlins' realization that Mouse "could put a knife in a man's stomach and ten minutes later sit down to a plate of spaghetti" (94) and his acknowledgment of the possibility that Mouse might kill him because of what he knows cause Easy to run. "I ran away from Mouse and Texas to go to the army and then later to L.A. I hated myself. I signed up to fight in the war to prove to myself that I was a man" (93). Mosley's omnipresent theme of Black male subjectivity and violence becomes inescapable; both Easy and Mouse are linked by bloody violence and Easy's experiences in the war inculcate in him the necessity for violence with sexual rewards as a byproduct of the violence. For Easy and all Black men fighting oversees the sexual reward that can be defined as "white pussy." When Mouse and Easy were back in Texas, Mouse asks: "You get any white pussy in the war?" Rawlins responds: "All they got is white girls. What you think?" (78). Along with Black men fighting and killing white men, Black men having sexual relationships with white women was another factor that would forever change America's culture of white supremacy. Dewitt Albright having Easy Rawlins search for Daphne Monet suggests a racial shift in racial relations and the possible birth of a new nation. Accordingly,

Daphne becomes a site of transfiguration and a symbol of transgression of the historical boundaries of race and sexuality. Hence, Mosley extends the theme of Black male subjectivity and violence and connects it to the issue of miscegenation.

Easy Rawlins' search for Daphne Monet and the ensuing violence can be literally and symbolically defined as this Black man's search for "white pussy," the historic racial taboo that fueled countless lynchings of Black males and racial riots after World War I (the Red Summer of 1919) such as the riots in Rosewood, Florida and Wallstreet, Oklahoma.[16] At John's Club and acutely aware of the racial dynamics of a Black man looking for a white woman in a Black club, Rawlins cavalierly asks a number of individuals if they have seen white girl named "Delia" or "Dahlia" who has blonde hair and blue eyes and " 'that she was worth looking at' " (79). Rawlins states that his rationale for not using her real name is: "I didn't want anybody to connect me with her if Albright turned out to be wrong and there was trouble" (82). During this period of nationwide Jim Crow segregation, any connection between a Black man and a white woman was trouble, often lethal trouble, as in the brutal murder of fourteen-year-old Emmett Till in Money, Mississippi, in 1955. Till allegedly gave a wolf whistle and touched or squeezed the arm of a white woman, Carolyn Bryant, and said "Bye, baby" on his way out the local store. To the naïve Till, visiting from Chicago, this was a joke to impress his young male friends and relatives. However, to her white husband, Roy Bryant and his brother-in-law, J. W. Milam, it was a crude and crass violation of the etiquette of Jim Crow, an insult that required severe punishment, lest other Blacks try to cross the color line in such a fashion.[17] Some legal scholars view the murder of Till as connected to the Supreme Court's *Brown vs. Board of Education* decision of 1954, in which the Court ruled that separate but equal was unconstitutional. For some whites this ruling was seen in purely sexual terms; for example, Walter C. Givhan, an Alabama state senator, had this to say about the decision, "What is the real purpose of this? To open the bedroom doors of our white women to Negro men." It should be noted that the only way his mother could identify Emmett Till's battered body was his father's ring. Mamie Till-Mobley remembers that "Emmett had looked at the ring a couple of days before he was to leave for Mississippi, he pulled it out again. With a little tape, it might fit his ring finger" (*Death of Innocence,* 103). She told Emmett then that his father was a soldier in World War II and that he was killed overseas. The cause of death she explained was "willful misconduct." Never having been told the meaning of this term, she was only informed that there would be no benefits to her because of the willful misconduct. The "willful misconduct" that resulted in the death of Emmett Till's father suggests some behavior not associated with warfare, and, considering that many Black soldiers had sexual relationships with white women, the issue of miscegenation comes to mind. Of course, "willful misconduct" would be one way to describe Emmett Till's behavior in Money, Mississippi.

It can be argued that the fundamental issue for most white supremacists about segregation in education, housing, and, to a lesser degree employment, then and now is the apprehension concerning miscegenation between Black males and white females. Most white parents fanatically desire to protect their white females from any social contact with Black males.[18] On the other hand, there is little concern over the consensual or non-consensual (rape) miscegenation between Black females and white males; many white males define their subjectivity by having sexual relations with Black females and thus eradicating Black males. As Rawlins has been socialized by Blacks to perform in an inferior manner around whites, it is accurate to conclude that Rawlins was also socialized to view all white females as "trouble." Of course, the striking contradiction here is that Rawlins did have sexual adventures with white women while fighting in Europe; this could lead some adventurous young Black males to consider the possibility of miscegenation at home. While no one else at John's Club has any information on Daphne, the cheery, brown-skinned, Coretta James reveals to Rawlins that she knows Daphne. While helping Coretta bring her lover, Dupree Bouchard, home after he becomes intoxicated to the point of unconsciousness, Coretta seduces Rawlins by unbuttoning her blouse and saying: "Daphne be sleep now...You cain't get none'a that [white pussy]right now" (87). Implicit in Coretta's blundering statement is that Rawlins has some sexual interest in finding Daphne Monet and that he should have sexual relations with her instead of chasing after some "white pussy." This statement reveals the historic tension between some Black men and women over the issue of miscegenation. Given the significant disproportion of available Black males, some Black women are troubled by those Black men who seem to prefer whites, especially considering America's long history of lynching Blacks for the alleged rape of white women. Under segregation there was the absurd notion among some Black consumers that the white man's ice was colder than the Black man's ice; accordingly, "white pussy" was better than "Black pussy." Coretta reveals: "Daphne. Ain't that right? You said Delia but that ain't her real name. We got real tight last week when her date an' my date was at the Playroom" (87). Coretta has held onto this information to seduce Rawlins. With the cool scent of jasmine coming from outdoors and the hot smell of jasmine coming from Coretta's abundant breasts, Rawlins, perhaps out of gratitude for the information about Daphne Monet, decides to have sexual relations with Coretta, with his friend Dupree asleep in the next room. As with DeWitt Albright, the connection between sexuality and economics comes into play when Coretta asks an agreeable Easy" "Don't ole Coretta get a little ten dollars if you fines that girl, Easy? I *was* the one said about it" (89). A true opportunist, Coretta wants to get paid for helping Easy locate Daphne Monet.

Meeting Albright with the information from Coretta brings Rawlins additional racial conflict. Rawlins' common sense makes him uncomfortable about meeting Albright in a white community like Santa Monica. "I never loitered anywhere except among my own people, in my own neighborhood" states Rawlins. Rawlins statement echoes the historical reality of segregation. As James E. Loewen notes in *Sundown Towns: A Hidden Dimension of American Racism* (2005): "In Redwood City 22 miles south of San Francisco, the newly built home of John J. Walker, Black war veteran, was burned in December 1946 'after he had received threats to move out,' according to a news story in *Pacific Citizen*" (393). But the possibility of paying the mortgage and dreaming of the day when he would "be able to buy more houses, maybe a duplex...to own enough land that it would pay for itself out of the rent it generated" (97) propels Rawlins into foreign and potentially hostile territory.

Sure enough, an innocent conversation with a seventeen-year-old white girl, Barbara Moskowitz, leads to a racial confrontation between Rawlins and a twenty-year-old white boy named Herman and five of his friends. Again miscegenation is the issue when like the proverbial white supremacist, Herman states: "We don't need ya talking to our women" (99). Like a well-trained soldier in battle, Rawlins contemplates how he "could have broken his neck...put out his eyes or broken all of his fingers" and considers a more purely lethal response: "Five of his friends were headed toward us. While they were coming on, not yet organized or together, I could have killed all of them too. What did they know about violence? I could have crushed their windpipes one by one and they couldn't have done anything to stop me. They couldn't even run fast enough to escape me. I was still a killing machine" (99). For Herman, Rawlins' conversation with Barbara equals only one possibility: "Nigger's trying to pick up Barbara" (99) he informs his white friends. Despite Barbara's unwavering protests of his innocence, a couple of the white boys had picked up sticks and began moving in on Rawlins. With Rawlins not wanting to kill or be killed, suddenly DeWitt Albright appears and pulls out a pistol "which looked somewhat like a rifle" and levels the barrel at the large white boy's eye and says: "I want to see your brains scattered all over your friends' clothes, son. I want you to die for me" (100). Sadistically enjoying this moment, the smiling Albright, cocking the hammer of the .44-caliber pistol, tells the young man: "I wouldn't move if I were you son. I mean, if you were to breathe too heavily I'd just kill you. And if any of you other boys move I'll kill him and then shoot off all of your nuts" (101). Considering that Black men were generally castrated when they were accused of raping white women, Albright's statement of shooting off the "nuts" of these white boys represents racial mockery. Albright adds his own paradoxical statement of miscegenation to this encounter by introducing Rawlins to the crowd as his friend and says that he would be "proud and happy if he [Rawlins] was to lower himself to fuck my sister and my mother" (101). Rawlins introduced as "Mr. Jones" and Albright referred to as "Mr. Smith" harass these crying young men until they plead for forgiveness for their bullying. The psychic harassment, mainly by Albright, leads to sexual perversion when he tells Herman to "get down on your knees and suck his [Rawlins'] peter. I want you to suck it good now" (102). Understanding that this is a malicious joke, Rawlins is still repelled by this suggestion which places a truly incongruous twist to miscegenation between a Black man and a white woman. Attempting to prevent some perceived miscegenation between the Black Rawlins and the white Barbara, the white Herman is ordered by the white Albright to suck Rawlins' black penis. This confrontation ends when Albright slams the pistol into Herman's head and his terrorized friends run off. Threatened with death if he informs the police, Herman is let go. Ironically this is a scene that seeks to emasculate both Herman and Rawlins because it is pistol-menacing Albright who is in total control, reinforcing white violent male hegemony. Through this racial encounter Rawlins understands the true violent and sadistic nature of Albright and realizes that: "[I]f Albright could do something like this to one of his own then I knew he could do the same and much worse to me. But if he wanted to shoot me he'd just have to do it because I wasn't going down on my knees for him or for anybody else" (103). Like a soldier in battle who discovers that a fellow soldier savors killing, an infuriated Rawlins finds Albright absolutely repulsive.

The hegemonic relationship between Easy Rawlins and DeWitt Albright reinforces the contemptuous interaction between a white master and a Black slave. Alone in Albright's white Cadillac, Rawlins reveals that Daphne Monet associates with a dangerous criminal named Frank Green and they were at a bar called the Playroom; he also gives Albright Green's address at the Skyer Arms apartments. Replying to Albright's questions, Rawlins informs him that Frank Green is a very dangerous individual, especially with a knife. Through their conversation we understand that Easy Rawlins has become fixated on Daphne Monet; he wants to be sure that neither she nor anyone else will be harmed so he lies about not having her picture with him. Rawlins explains: "I don't know why I wanted to keep her picture. It's just that the way she looked out at me made me feel good" (105).[19] Like Jay Gatsby who has become obsessed with the married Daisy Buchanan, Easy Rawlins has become visually attached to the sensual Daphne Monet, believing that she is looking only at him. Daphne's penetrating gaze and Easy's emotional response to her gaze create the subliminal miscegenation that causes Coretta to want to have sexual relations with Easy. By keeping the seductive picture of Daphne Monet with him, it suggests the strong possibility that this subliminal attraction can someday become real.

Mosley reinforces and reinscribes the racist hegemony between white males and Black males when Rawlins goes back to Champion Aircraft to see if he can get his job back. After encountering Dupree who asks if Rawlins has seen the missing Coretta, Easy confronts his boss, Benny Giacomo. Easy cannot keep but making a comparison between two powerful white males, Benny and Albright.

> I tried to think about what Benny wanted. I tried to think of how I could save face and still kiss his ass. But all I could really think about was that other office and that other white man. DeWitt Albright had his bottle and his gun right out there in plain view...Benny didn't care about what I had to say. He needed all his children to kneel down and let him be the boss. He wasn't a businessman, he was a plantation boss, a slaver. (111)

Like Albright, Rawlins knows that Benny wants him to kneel and either "kiss his ass" or symbolically suck his peter in order to get his job back.[20] Not willing to prostrate or humiliate himself, Rawlins is straightforward in articulating his desire: "I want my job back, Mr. Giacomo. I need to work and I do a good job....I need money so that I can pay my mortgage and eat. I need a house to live in and a place to raise children. I need to buy clothes so I can go to the pool hall and to church..." (112). Not hearing the obsequious response that he wants and Rawlins' unwillingness to "kiss his ass," Benny dismisses him by saying: " 'I have to get back to my job, Easy" (112). Knowing that he will not get his job back, Rawlins attempts to leave with dignity by challenging Benny to call him Mr. Rawlins. "I said you have to treat me with respect. Now I call you Mr. Giacomo because that's your name. You're no friend to me and I got no reason to be disrespectful and call you by your first name...My name is Mr. Rawlins" (112). Suppressing a desire to strike this impudent nigger, Benny relaxes and with contempt states: "I'm sorry, Mr. Rawlins...But there are no openings right now. Maybe you could come back in a few months, when production on the new fighter line begins" (112). Essentially, this means "get lost nigger" before I call the police to beat you and drag you out of here. Rawlins understands the dismissal and yet like Frederick Douglass after his physical encounter with slavebreaker Edward Covey, he feels empowered: "My chest was heaving and I felt as if I wanted to laugh out loud. My bills were paid and it felt good to have stood up for myself. I had a notion of freedom when I walked out to my car" (112). Unlike Dupree and other Black men who work under this quasi-slave plantation system, Rawlins through his own ingenuity has found some temporary freedom working with Albright. The continual battle of Black men like Easy Rawlins is to survive and prosper while maintaining a sense of manhood and dignity. However, Rawlins understands that the factory job represents safety and stability whereas working for Albright represents a dangerous freedom.

As with Albright's two henchmen, Rawlins' manhood and dignity became tested with his encounter with two white male police officers. Paradoxically, the encounter begins when Rawlins comes home and two white males (waiting outside his house in a car) approach him; one of these men respectfully asking if he is "Mr. Rawlins." Respect quickly disappears when Mason and Miller ask Easy to come with them and he verbally resists. After Easy makes a statement about his "rights," the sadistic response by one of the detective is: "You got a right to fall down and break your face, nigger. You got a right to die" (114). For these white detectives, Rawlins is a guilty "nigger" with no "rights" who must prove to them that he is innocent. Rawlins is then punched in the stomach, handcuffed, and dragged into their car; he is told not to vomit in the car. The portly detective named Mason says to the gagging Rawlins: "You vomit on my carpet and I'll feed it to ya" (114). Taken to Seventy-seventh Street station, the sagging and bowed Rawlins is dragged inside and dropped on his knees in an unpainted and piss-smelling room. Whether Easy Rawlins is dealing with white male police officers like Miller and Mason or dealing with Benny at Champion Aircraft, he is pushed into a subservient position on his knees and suffers the consequences of physical, psychological, or economic violence. Confrontations with the police are not new to Rawlins and he defines it as the "game of 'niggers and cop'":

> The cops pick you up, take your name and fingerprints, then they throw you into a holding tank with other 'suspects' and drunks. After you were sick from the vomit and foul language they'd take you to another room and ask why you robbed that liquor store or what did you do with the money....They figure that you did something because that's just the way cops think, and you telling them that you're innocent just proves to them that you have something to hide. But that wasn't the game that we were playing that day. (115)

This game of "nigger and cops" suggests a fundamental and stereotypical manner in which Black individuals are forced to deal with regardless of economic status. And one's guilt is always predetermined regardless of one's protestations of innocence. It also suggests that Black cops play this game of "niggers and cops" in the same manner, perhaps even harder. Because the cops knew Rawlins' name and address, he knows that this game will be somewhat different. In the corner of the room was a dead mouse and based on its dryness, Rawlins makes a comparison to the mouse and his present condition, cornered. Soon the interrogation of the "smart nigger" begins with questions and physical violence when Rawlins' responses are not satisfactory. Mason kicks Easy in the chest and knocks him upside his head along with another deadly threat: "Means we can take your Black ass out behind the station and put a bullet in your head" (117). This deadly threat represents extra-legal authority within the legal arena in which white police officers become judges and executioners. Like white slave masters who enjoyed the process of "seasoning" (the psychological and physical conditioning of slaves), these racist white police officers can be considered "nigger breakers." Questions concerning Rawlins' whereabouts and the legal violence continue until Rawlins has had enough of the violence:

> He [Mason] knocked me to the floor but I grabbed onto his wrist. I swung around and twisted so that I was straddling his back, sitting on his fat ass. I could have killed him the way I'd killed other white men in uniforms, but I could feel Miller behind me so I stood straight up and moved to the corner....I imagined that I was the convict and the mouse was Officer Mason. I crushed him so that his whole suit was soiled and shapeless in the corner; his eyes came out of his head. (119)

Like Frederick Douglass who aggressively chokes the white slave master Edward Covey, Rawlins temporarily turns the tables on chubby Mason, letting him understand that he will not be physically abused without retaliation. This represents the fundamental mindset of many Black soldiers returning from the war; they were no longer willing to take the mistreatment associated with Jim Crow segregation and white supremacy. Later, these racist cops inform Rawlins that he is free to go and that they will be in touch with him if they have additional questions—typical treatment by arrogant white male police officers. Rawlins leaves not knowing why he was picked up and viciously beaten; also, he has no way to get back home because the buses stopped running.

Easy Rawlins relationship with Matthew Teran reveals a rather perverse aspect to this sexually-laden narrative. While Rawlins is walking home from the police station, he is stopped by Teran; this encounter brings Easy some answers to why the police have picked him up. Matthew was running for mayor and then dropped out and he is now looking for Daphne Monet. In the chauffeur-driven car Teran states: "Daphne is a white girl, Easy. Young and pretty. It means an awful lot to me if I can find her" (125). Teran's revelation suggests that he is the individual who hired Albright to employ Rawlins to locate Daphne Monet. Beyond the discomfort that Teran gives Rawlins, Easy is also repelled by a small Mexican boy wearing "soiled briefs and dirty socks" who was in the car. The close physical relationship between Teran and the small boy suggests pedophilia. Teran asks numerous questions and Rawlins responds with numerous fabrications and half-truths, the way he deals with white men: Albright, Benny, Miller, and Mason. While Teran never reveals to Easy why he was picked up by the police, once Easy is dropped off at John's Club, Hattie informs him that Coretta James has been murdered in the same manner that Howard Green was killed, beaten beyond clear recognition. Back home, a drunken Rawlins is awakened by Junior, who tells him that he has seen Daphne Monet with Frank Green. A few hours later, the mysterious and sought-after Daphne Monet calls Easy. "My name is Daphne Monet. Daphne Monet...Your friend, Coretta no? She came to see me and asked for money. She said that you were looking for me and if I don't give it to her she goes to tell you. Easy no?" (131). Daphne and Easy's conversation goes back and forth with questions and responses that reveal that the knife-slashing Frank Green is her friend and to her surprise Coretta has been murdered. When she asks Easy to be of assistance to her and he refuses, Daphne threatens to go to the police. Daphne warns Easy that: "But if you do not help I will 'ave to go to the police to find my friend. I will 'ave to tell them about you and this woman, this Coretta" (132). Daphne has no idea how disturbing this threat is and Rawlins finally relents to help her find her friend (not her lover), Frank Green. Rawlins divulges his basic trepidation; "I was afraid of the police too. Afraid that the next time I went down to the police station I wouldn't be getting out" (133). Twice Miller and Mason have threatened to execute Rawlins and like the white police officers who kill Fred Daniels in Richard Wright's "The Man Who Lived Underground", there is little doubt that they could murder him and not be held accountable. At this point in time police brutality and police malfeasance were extreme, especially in the Black community. Nevertheless, Rawlins still is at a lost to understanding the situation that he has been brought into by Joppy and Albright, but the number of dead bodies (Howard Green and Coretta James) is building and he is in the middle of this deadly and violent situation.

Easy's meeting with Daphne raises some issues concerning race, sexuality, and representation along with bringing back Easy's memories of women in France, and looking at her arouses him:

> Her face was beautiful. More beautiful than the photograph. Wavy hair so light brown that you might have called it blonde from a distance, and eyes that were either green or blue depending on how she held her head. Her cheekbones were high but her face was full enough that it didn't make her seem severe. Her eyes were just a little closer than most women's eyes; it made her seem vulnerable, made me feel I wanted to put my arms around her—to protect her. (135)

Carrying Daphne Monet's picture has created an emotional bond, and Rawlins' desire to protect her is analogous to protecting his home. Of course, the author is again making the connection to miscegenation which for Rawlins originated while fighting in Europe. Even during warfare there was the opportunity for Black men to have sexual relations with white women, perhaps to the disgust of some white male soldiers who viewed this as Black men raping white women. Indeed, Rawlins reflecting on his war experiences makes this point concerning hatred and respect:

> There were Blacks, whites, and even a handful of Japanese-Americans in our platoon. And the major things we had to worry about was killing Germans. There was always trouble between the races especially when it came to the women, but we learned to respect each other out there. I never minded that those white boys hated me, but if they didn't respect me I was ready to fight....I was trained to kill to kill men but white men weren't anxious to see a gun in my hands. They didn't want to see me spill white blood. They said we didn't have the discipline or the minds for a war effort, but they were really scared that we might get to like the kind of freedom that death-dealing brings. (144, 143)

Although Rawlins has not killed anyone at this point in the narrative, he has acquired a stronger sense of freedom in his dealing with white men such as Benny Giacomo, the white detectives, and DeWitt Albright. Rawlins' dealings with Daphne will offer additional transitions and challenges. Another aspect of this woman is her use of language; Rawlins notes that she has a French accent, even "her dress was the simple blue kind the French girls wore when I was a GI in Paris" (135). Convinced to help Daphne find her friend, Rawlins is concerned about traveling in public with her because "the police have white slavery on the brain when it comes to colored men and white women" (137). When they arrive at Daphne's friend's house the door is open, and they discover Richard McGee dead with a butcher's knife buried deep in his chest. Ironically, Rawlins remembers this white man from John's Club when he offered Easy twenty dollars to help him get into the Club because he was looking for some girl (Daphne). Violence and sexuality mesh when Daphne kisses Easy slowly and deliberately. Dropping the French accent, Daphne tells Easy: "Too bad we won't have a chance to get to know each other, Easy. Otherwise I'd let you eat this little white girl up" (141). Like the white women in Europe, Daphne provocatively suggests cunnilingus. As Rawlins previously stated in the adventure of killing Germans there was always the issue of white women who are often the spoils of war. Daphne's blatant discourse of sexual consumption echoes back to Rawlins first looking at her black-and-white picture with a consumptive gaze. With this sexually provocative statement lingering in his consciousness, Daphne places a suitcase in his care at Richard's house and escapes the murder scene. Mosley's analogy of the war in Europe and warfare in the streets of Los Angeles holds true: intimate relationships between Black men and white women in Europe were generally passionate but temporary and we witness this with Daphne Monet and Easy Rawlins, especially when dead bodies and the atmosphere of death are all around. Even in a conversation with himself Rawlins acknowledges his predicament: "You gotta stand up man.

Lettin' these people step on you ain't right. Messin' with French white girls, who ain't French; working fo' a white man kill his own kind if they don't smell right. You gotta find out what happened and set it straight" (142). Daphne's deception in language suggests other deceptions, especially when we understand that her "friend" Richard McGee was "a Blackmailer and a homosexual pimp. He worked for rich men with sick appetites" (164). Richard McGee's sordid and criminal activities connect him to Matthew Teran who is later found dead with a "nice little bullet hole through his heart" (206). With both Matthew Teran and Richard McGee violently killed, Rawlins explains the nature of the law as it relates to race:

> The police didn't care about crime among Negroes. I mean, some softhearted cops got upset if a man killed his wife or did harm to a child. But the kind of violence that Frank Green dished out, the business kind of violence, didn't get anybody worried. The papers hardly ever even reported a colored murder. And when they did it was in the back pages....The difference was that two white men had died also. To kill a white man was a real crime. (208)

Although this is accurate what is missing from this description is the fact that white supremacy and the enduring disenfranchisement of Black people create a higher level of crime because Black unemployment and underemployment are always high. Indeed, Easy Rawlins has been thrust into this arena of criminality and death because of his unemployment and because of the racism at Champion Aircraft. If Rawlins had relented to kissing Benny Giacomo's ass he would still have his job but very little dignity. During the period of enslavement and especially during the earlier period of Jim Crow segregation it was extremely clear that Black people's lives had little value or no value compared to a white person, and the law was designed to protect white people and their property.

An escalation in the racial tension between Rawlins and Albright occurs over the issue of property. Returning home from seeing Daphne fleeing the bloody murder scene, Rawlins discovers that Albright and his two henchmen, Manny and Shariff, have broken into his house; in fact, Albright is in Easy's kitchen making coffee. Rawlins is initially outraged over this home invasion but relaxes when he considers the truly violent nature of Albright and the fact that he is outnumbered three to one. Rawlins does challenge him by asking Albright how he would feel if he broke into his place. Like the white police officers who threaten to put a bullet in Rawlins' head, Albright's unsmiling response ("I'd tear your nigger head out by its root") (147) is racist and contemptible. Not finding Daphne with the information that Rawlins has provided, Albright explains racial economics to him: "You take my money and you belong to me....We all owe out something, Easy. When you owe out then you're in debt and when you're in debt then you can't be your own man. That's capitalism" (148). Despite Rawlins' response that he does not "belong to anybody," he does realize that he has made a proverbial deal with the devil. As in most conflicts, money is involved and this situation is no different; Rawlins learns that Daphne has taken thirty thousand dollars and Albright wants that money. Although Albright tells Rawlins that if he finds Frank Green their business is done, Rawlins suspects that Albright will murder him at some point. As Rawlins puts it: "I was ready to die but I was going to go down fighting" (150). Realizing that he is in a different type of warfare, but a war nonetheless, Rawlins calls Etta looking for his ruthless friend, Mouse.

Rawlins' relationship with Mouse in the past has been often centered on money and violence as when Mouse killed his stepfather for his inheritance and gave Easy three hundred dollars in blood money. Not surprisingly, when Frank Green has a knife pressed to Easy Rawlins' throat, Mouse appears and announces his problem to Frank: "You see, Frank , I got this here long-barreled forty-one caliber pistol pointed at the back' a yo' head. But I can't shoot it 'cause I'm afraid that if you fall you gonna cut my partner's throat" (195). Once back in power, Rawlins asks Frank about Daphne, but he obtains no response. Mouse's violent nature and bloodlust erupt: "Without warning Mouse pistol-whipped Frank three times; every blow made a sickening thud. Frank fell to his knees with the dark blood coming down his dark clothes" (197). Not wanting Frank killed in his house, Rawlins comes between Mouse and Frank, and this allows Frank to bolt out the door. Although Mouse is upset that Rawlins's cut throat has gotten blood on his coat, he views Rawlins as a changed individual. "You use' t'be kinda scared of everything. Take them little nigger jobs like gardenin' and cleanin' up. Now you got this nice house and you fuckin' some white man's girl" (198). Although Rawlins denies that he has "touched" Daphne, in a perverse way this symbolizes the American Dream for some Black men: property and "white pussy." While Rawlins is thankful to Mouse for saving his life, he understands that Mouse is vicious and violent when money is involved. Mouse audaciously announces his desire: "First thing I want to figure out is how I can get that money you told Frank about" (199). Mouse hears the reservation in Rawlins's voice about needing his assistance, and he crudely makes his point in a manner that articulates his modern-day version of the American Dream: "Nigger cain't pull his way out the swamp wit out no help, Easy. You wanna hole on t'this house and git some money and have some white girls callin' on the phone?... But Easy you gotta have somebody at yo' back man" (200). Rawlins does not tell him everything (especially the exact amount of money that Daphne has taken), Mouse may not be who he wants, but Mouse is defiantly who he needs, especially against Albright and his two henchmen. Using the language of warfare, "It felt good to be fighting back. Mouse was a good soldier though I worried about him following orders. And if I had the whole thing scammed out right we'd both come out on top; I'd still be alive and have my house too" (202), Rawlins declares his new approach and his ultimate desire, keeping his house.

There is little doubt that whites such as the insensitive factory foremen, the two sadistic police officers, violent criminals like Albright, crafty politicians, or wealthy businessmen with their white supremacist perspectives are the ones that a Black man like Rawlins has to deal with if he is going to survive and keep his property. With the murder of Richard McGee who is discovered to be connected to John's Club, the police pay Rawlins another visit. Taken back to the police station for fingerprinting, Rawlins is bombarded with questions concerning the murders of Howard Green and Richard McGee. When the detectives Miller and Mason discover that the fingerprints on the butcher knife that killed McGee do not match Rawlins, he is released without being beaten this time but with an ominous threat. "You can go, Mr. Rawlins....But we're going to get you again. We're going to bring you down for something, Ezekiel, you can bank on that" (209). This threat is typical of racist white male police officers who view Black men as innate criminals. Here the white police with the assistance of the courts become the judge, the jury, and the executioner devoted to the protection of white wealth and property. A business card from Albright leads Rawlins to the offices of Lion Investments and to the president Todd Carter, the name Daphne Monet mentioned to Easy Rawlins. After some time, Rawlins meets with Carter and discovers that he is the one looking for Daphne because he wants to marry her, and he also discovers that she took thirty thousand dollars from him, to Carter an insignificant sum. More importantly, Rawlins finds out about Daphne and her relationship with Carter:

> He told me that she was from New Orleans and that her family was an old French family that traced their heritage to Napoleon. We talked about her eyes for a half hour. And then he started to tell me things that men should never say about their women. Not sex, but he talked about how she'd hold him to her breast when he was afraid and how she'd stand up for him when a shopkeeper or waiter tried to walk over him. (165)

There are two things that are significant about this statement. Knowing that Daphne Monet is from New Orleans suggests miscegenation, quadroon balls, racial passing, and the light-skinned Black elite and their private clubs. Second, we understand that despite Todd Carter's wealth he is extremely insecure and needs a woman like Daphne to psychologically support him. Here Carter comes off as rather juvenile and perhaps that is why Daphne fervently tongue kissed Rawlins, "she lunged so deep into my throat that once our teeth collided and my canine chipped" (141) and suggested that Easy could "eat" her someday. Daphne's metaphoric statement of consumption reflects her own lack of subjectivity and how she commodifies depending on the relationship. However, the racial discrimination that Rawlins encounters here is more benign than the overt racism of the white detectives:

> It was a strange experience but I had seen it before. Mr. Todd Carter was so rich that he didn't even consider me in human terms. He could tell me anything. I could have been a prized dog that he knelt to and hugged when he felt low. It was the worse kind of racism. The fact that he didn't recognize our differences showed that he didn't care one damn about me. But I didn't have the time to worry about it. I just watched him move his lips about love until, finally, I began to see him as some strange being. Like a baby who grows to man-size and terrorizes his poor parents with his strength and his stupidity. (166)

Rawlins sees a profound example of benign white supremacy whereby his fundamental humanity is lost. Carter just views Rawlins as a "prized dog" commanded to fetch a lost bone, in this case Daphne. Like the Ex-Colored Man in James Weldon Johnson's 1912 novel, in which the protagonist plays the piano for the white millionaire, Rawlins' value is defined by what he can produce. In both incidents we see the Hegelian master and slave dialectic illustrated and the subsequent loss of subjectivity; indeed the subjectivity of the Ex-Coloured Man and Easy becomes dependent on white male power and wealth. Rawlins is further objectified when Carter announces that he is a very wealthy man and that the "mayor and the chief of police" eat at his house regularly. Ironically, Carter has all this wealth and power but he cannot find Daphne Monet. Rawlins challenges him on this point and Carter just says: "Find her for me" (166). Like the phonetics of Daphne's last name, Rawlins realizes that life in America's white supremacist culture comes down to one simple element:

> Somewhere along the way I had developed the feeling that I wasn't going to outlive the adventure I was having. There was no way out but to run, and I couldn't run, so I decided to milk all those white people for all the money they'd let go of. Money brought everything. Money paid the rent [or mortgage] and fed the kitty. Money was why Coretta was dead and why DeWitt Albright was going to kill me. I got the idea, somehow, that if I got enough money then maybe I could buy my own life back. (167)

As tragic as it sounds this represents Rawlins' reality in dealing with these white males who view him as a commodity to be used and discarded. Since the days of enslavement the commodification of Black bodies has been a fundamental aspect of using Black labor to create white wealth. So like the Ex-Colored Man,[21] Rawlins is willing to sell his very soul in order to buy back his life, epitomized by his little home.

It is through this process of looking for Daphne Monet that Easy creates or calls himself into existence; he becomes a Black private detective. Having picked up something at the scene of Richard McGee's murder, he directs Mouse to take him to the home of Junior Fornay, the nephew of Hattie Parsons. Now beginning to put some of pieces of the puzzle together, Rawlins asks Fornay why he killed Richard McGee. Realizing that Hattie told Junior to take Richard home and that Junior told him about seeing Daphne with Coretta, Rawlins senses that something happened that night that led to murder. Junior is still in denial until Rawlins tells him that "Mouse is gonna waste" his ass if he does not tell the truth. Junior finally confesses that he took Richard home because he promised him twenty dollars, then increased it to a hundred, if he drove him home and told him how to find Daphne; once they got there Richard pressed him to give Frank Green a message about having something on Daphne Monet. Junior says he got angry because Richard reneged on his promise about the extra money and told him he could walk home with the twenty dollars; thinking that Richard was going to get a gun, Junior got a knife from the sink and stabbed him to death. For Junior Fornay to kill Richard McGee over this small amount of money is a poignant commentary, but it provides Rawlins with additional information on Daphne Monet—she is hiding some unfathomable secret.

The search for Daphne Monet brings Easy into a dangerous adventure, but there are some sexual satisfactions and surprises. When Daphne eventually calls Rawlins for his help, he comes running. Alone with Daphne, Easy's frustrations explode. Pointing to the bruises on his eye inflicted by the police, he says: "Look at that....I been arrested twice, blamed for four murders, threatened by people I wished I never met" (227). Rawlins' mother wit in not trusting Albright and asking him what he was getting "mixed up" in with regard to Daphne bring Easy problems inside and outside the law. Also, all the suggestions concerning miscegenation become manifest when Daphne and Easy make love until Rawlins is physically sore. Like a WWII Black soldier with a white woman, Rawlins finds some temporary relief in this intimate embrace that has a sadistic element. She tells him: "If my pussy was like a man's thing it'd be a big as you head, Easy" (229). A bold and beautiful Daphne seduces Rawlins by "whispering obscene suggestions" in his ear as they "yelled and screamed and wrestled all night" (229). The more Rawlins hurts, the more enjoyment for Daphne; however, Rawlins is left bewildered:

> When I look back on that night I feel confused. I could say that Daphne was crazy but that would mean that I was sane enough to say, and I wasn't. If she wanted me to hurt, I loved to hurt, and if she wanted me to bleed, I would have been happy to open a vein. Daphne was like a door that had been closed all my life; a

door that all of a sudden flung open and let me in. My heart and chest opened as wide as the sky for that woman. (230)

Rawlins' metaphor of the "door" suggests miscegenation and the taboo associated with Black men having sexual relations with white women. More specifically, the "door" represents Daphne's genitals within the context of America's white supremacist culture. Having sexual relationships with white women in Europe as a soldier was very different from having sexual relations with white women in America during Jim Crow segregation in the 1940s. And Rawlins's complex description goes completely beyond some sexual fixation and speaks to some deep fulfillment of desires, creating a completely vulnerable individual. Further there seems to a sadistic and masochistic element here that derives from all the abuse and death that Easy Rawlins has been exposed over the last few days. Finally, Daphne and Rawlins have a conversation; she reveals that Richard McGee, Matthew Teran, Howard Green got together with some information on her to cause trouble so they could get at Todd Carter. She also reveals that Joppy killed Howard and Coretta. Considering the absolutely brutality of these murders, Joppy as the murderer makes sense as he is a former boxer who epitomizes meaningless violence and brute force: "His big draw was the violence he brought to the ring" (52). Indeed, Mosley hints at Joppy's being a human butcher by the location of the bar "on the second floor of a butcher's warehouse" and by his description:

Joppy was a heavy-framed man, almost fifty years old. His hands were like black catchers' mitts and I never saw him in shirtsleeves that didn't strain at the seams from bulging muscle. His face was scarred from all the punishment he had taken in the ring; the flesh around his big lips were jagged and there was a knot over his right eye that always looked red and raw. (51–52)

As an agent of DeWitt, Joppy is the person to beat someone to the point of unrecognizability. More so, it emphasizes the ruthless nature of DeWitt, who uses both Joppy and Rawlins to find Daphne, and the theme of Black men as consumable commodities is reinforced. Mosley's juxtaposition of these two men reinforces the idea that many Black men have been or placed themselves in positions where they have to fight and kill to survive. While Joppy's scars are visible, Rawlins' scars are psychological.

Because of her own psychological scars, Daphne, "the chameleon lizard" (230) never reveals her emotional relationship to Frank Green and somehow believes that even with white men looking for her and people coming up dead, she and Rawlins can stay in this house. Rawlins' fixation with Daphne's picture combines with the sexual encounter to convince him that they are in love. Despite the desire and death looming around them, Rawlins unconvincingly states: "We don't have to listen to them. If we love each other we can be together. Ain't no one can stop that" (234). Now Rawlins becomes frustrated and confronts her: "You mean all you want from me is a roll in the hay. Get a little nigger-love out back and then straighten your clothes and put on your lipstick like you didn't ever feel it" (234). Conflicted by his relationship to Todd Carter who has paid him to find Daphne and who wants to marry her, Rawlins asks her why she called him. Daphne's simple response is: "I love you, Easy. I knew it from the first moment we met" (235). While Rawlins may be flattered by this revelation, it makes his responsibility to DeWitt Albright and Todd Carter extremely complicated because Albright wants the money and Carter wants Daphne; neither one of them has any use for Rawlins beyond what he can produce by giving up Daphne. This further complicates Daphne's offer of doubling the money that Rawlins would receive from Albright if he gave her to Frank. Then through a meandering narrative of her father taking her to the zoo where she views two zebras engaged in coitus, Daphne divulges that she has been a victim of incest and parental abandonment:

> From then on, my whole fourteenth year, he'd take me to the zoo and the park. Always at first he'd kiss me like a father and his little girl by then we'd get alone someplace and act like real lovers. And always, always after he'd cry so sweet and beg me to forgive him. He bought me presents and gave me money, but Id've loved him anyway....My daddy never took me anywhere again after that year. He left Momma and me in the spring and I never saw him again. Nobody ever knew about him and me and what had happened. But I knew that that was why he left. He just loved me so much that day at the zoo and he knew me, the real me, and whenever you know somebody that well you just have to leave. (239)

Rawlins is so sickened by this revelation that he "wanted to run away from her," but his own troubles compel him to stay. Daphne reveals that her relationship with Carter is similar to that with her father because he knows her better than any other man. Rawlins hates Carter for that reason. Having established the theme of miscegenation early in the novel and having reinforced it throughout the text, Mosley links it with the themes of incest and abandonment. Considering the troubled history of Black people during enslavement, miscegenation between white males and Black females was pervasive through both non-consensual and consensual sexual relations. The rape of Black females by their white slave masters was quite common, and the disconnection between them could lead to white slave masters having sexual relations with their own daughters from these relationships. Often these children would be sold because of the conflict caused by the close resemblance of the Black slave children to the white masters' children. Natal alienation, a disconnection between the parent and the child, would be the result and Daphne's disturbing sexual revelation of the family romance conjures up these historical aspects and helps us understand her relationship with Rawlins; she can only love someone who does not know her. As Rawlins states: "I hated Carter then. I wanted to know Daphne like he did. I wanted her, even if knowing her meant that I couldn't have her" (239–40). Rawlins' desire for her is a complex paradox; Daphne represents a racial riddle. Like Jay Gatsby, Rawlins' consistent desire to know things centers on a woman who is beyond his reach.

When Easy and Daphne return to Primo's house, they encounter Albright inside the house and their trouble escalates. Knocked unconscious, Rawlins begins to hallucinate about being in a ferocious battle:

> I was on a great battleship in the middle of the largest firefight in the history of war. The cannons were red hot and the crew and I were loading those shells. Airplanes strafed the deck with machine-gun fire that stung my arms and chest but I kept on hefting shells to the man in front of me. It was dusk or early dawn and I was exhilarated by the power of war. (241)

Rawlins is still hallucinating, and it is Mouse who tells him "Easy! We gotta get outta here, man. Ain't no reason t'die in no white man's war" (241).[22] Mouse plays a dual role in this hallucination: the logical voice that tells Rawlins that he is in a battle that he cannot win as well as the only individual who can help him get Daphne back from Albright. Rawlins come to after Primo pours water over his face and he finds out that Joppy and Albright have taken Daphne. Rawlins' inner voice compels him to right this wrong: "You gotta find that girl, man. You gotta make this shit right" (243). Having finally tasted this "white pussy," Rawlins takes on the mission to save Daphne; essentially, he declares a private war on DeWitt Albright and his henchmen.

Like most suspenseful novels in this Black detective genre, the novel concludes with dead bodies and a resolution to the many conflicts. Tracing Albright to an address in Malibu Hills, Rawlins discovers a naked Daphne tied to a chair with Albright and Joppy stripped to the waist; they were choking her and screaming at her about the money. The naked and tied-up woman suggests a reconfiguration of the Black female on the slave auction block. Instead of a white master and a sadistic Black overseer inspecting the Black slave for her reproductive or money-making potential, here Albright and Joppy seek to elicit the location of the money she took from Todd Carter. Typical of the hard-boiled detective genre the hero must save the captured female, and the battle begins once Rawlins climbs through a window and shots are fired. Suddenly, Mouse appears and hog- ties Joppy in the kitchen and then shoots Albright who crashes through a window and escapes in his white Cadillac. A closer analysis of this scene where Easy Rawlins is a voyeur suggests a primal scene in which Joppy represents the father (he is also a property owner and attempts to help Easy pay his mortgage) and Daphne symbolizes the mother. Easy states: "She'd whisper a sweet word and I was brought back to the first time I felt love and loss. I was remembering my mother's death, back when I was only eight, by the time Daphne got to my belly. With Joppy subsequently being castrated and killed, Easy Rawlins has full sexual access to Daphne Monet.[23] With scant mention of a father, Joppy and Easy's friend, Odell symbolize Easy's father figure, but it is only Joppy who represents the sexual threat and the castrating figure who must be killed.

Mosley's description of Joppy being murder by Mouse suggests the inversion of power, and Rawlins' reaction suggests abhorrence and acceptance of the violence associated with a war. Diminutive in name, Mouse's actions in the novel loom large; and Joppy's name suggests some massive unidentifiable and grotesque creature. This juxtaposition culminates in a Mouse's bloody castration and execution of Joppy:

> He turned casually to his right and shot Joppy in the groin. Joppy's eyes opened wide and he started crying like a seal. He rocked back and forth trying to grab the wound but the wires held him to the chair. After a few seconds Mouse leveled the pistol and shot him in the head. One moment Joppy had two bulging eyes, then his left eye was just a bloody ragged hole. The force of the second shot threw him to the floor; spasms went through his legs and feet for minutes afterward. I felt cold then. Joppy had been my friend but I'd seen too many men die and I cared for Coretta too. (249)

For Black people who had heard stories and seen the remains of Black people who were lynched, Mouse's actions reflect a modern-day lynching. Like the lynchings in which Black males were mutilated, castrated, and burned alive, Mouse's actions are clearly sadistic. Joppy being reduced to an animal reflects a double decapitation: a shot to the groin and a shot to the head. Despite Rawlins' expressed sympathy for Coretta, perhaps he is satisfied that Mouse has killed Joppy for his physical abuse of Daphne. It is interesting to note that the most violent individuals in the novel are two Black men, Mouse and Joppy, with Easy often having violent thoughts associated with his experiences in war. This suggests that violence defines certain aspects of Black masculinity in a white supremacist culture in which violence was the main means to control Black people's socioeconomic advancement. Years of lynchings and, more currently, Black men fighting and killing in America's wars have produced a more violent defense reaction to white male domination. White male violence characterized by the white police officers and Albright are very much connected to their power, be it legal or economic. This clash of violence between Black men and white men is most evident in the numerous bloody race riots, especially those occurring after World War I. Here Black cities were literally and metaphorically raped by white males. Before the final violent scene, Rawlins hears loud male voices and a woman's pleading and looks through the window of a simple ranch-style house:

> Over the sill I saw a large room with a darkwood floor and a high ceiling. Before the blazing hearth sat a large couch covered with something like bearskin. Daphne was on the couch naked, and the men De Witt and Joppy, stood over her. Albright was wearing his linen suit but Joppy was stripped to the waist. His big gut looked obscene hanging over her like that and it took everything I had not to shoot him right then. (244–45)

With Joppy half naked and Daphne totally naked, there is the suggestion of a rape and the symbolism associated with consumption. Recalling Daphne's statement to Easy about eating her, the half-naked Joppy is poised to consume her or throw her into the blazing hearth. A fundamental aspect of enslavement was the inability of Black men to protect Black women from lusty white slave masters or hearty Black male overseers; here Easy's violent desire to shoot Joppy suggests a myriad of possibilities beyond his infatuation. One obvious possibility is that the grotesque-looking Joppy with his obscene stomach is in a position to eat Daphne's "white pussy." However, here, as we have seen throughout the novel, it is Mouse who does the violence that Easy thinks about doing. Rawlins is so happy to see Mouse that he hugs him, especially since Albright was about to shoot him. Discussing Frank Green, Mouse informs Daphne who he calls "Ruby" that "Your brother is dead," that Joppy killed him. Because Frank is a Black man, this is a shock to Rawlins: "I had only been in an earthquake once but the feeling was the same: The ground under me seemed to shift. I looked at her to see the truth. But it wasn't there. Her nose, cheek, her skin color—they were white. Daphne was a white woman. Even her pubic hair was barely bushy, almost flat" (248). Like some white supremacist, Rawlins' racial essentialism conveys all of the stereotypical ideas associated with physical attributes and recalls Irene's discourse in Nella Larsen's *Passing* when she believes that she has been exposed as passing for white while vacationing in Chicago:

> Absurd! Impossible! White people were so stupid about such things for all that they usually asserted that they were able to tell; and by the most ridiculous means: fingernails, palms of hands, shapes of ears, teeth, and other equally silly rot. They always took her for an Italian, a Spaniard, a Mexican, or a Gypsy. Never, when she was alone, had they even remotely seemed to suspect that she was a Negro. (178)

Daphne's secret is now exposed: she is a Black woman passing for white and Frank Green is her half-brother. Mosley's characterizations of Daphne recall the tragic mulatto passing for white.[24] Daphne symbolizes the tragic mulatto because of her acceptance into the white world and because of her sexual relationship with Todd Carter and the metaphorical slave hunter, DeWitt Albright; the revelation of her racial status creates the tragedy. Of course, this is the reason that Howard Green, Richard McGee, and Mathew Teran were trying to blackmail her to get money from Todd Carter, who, they assumed, did not know her true race. Mouse's focus is on the money. With Rawlins in his car as Mouse follows in Dupree's car, Daphne tells Rawlins that she killed Teran and brought the little Mexican boy to her place. Obtaining a bag from the YMCA locker, Mouse counts out ten thousand dollars for each person. Like the blood-money that Mouse gave Rawlins when he killed his stepfather, this money is also soaked with blood from the deaths of numerous individuals. While waiting for a cab, Daphne adamantly tells Rawlins why she cannot stay with him and why she does not even want him to touch her:

> I'm not Daphne. My given name is Ruby Hanks and I was born in Lake Charles, Louisiana. I'm different than you because I'm two people. I'm her and I'm me. I never went to that zoo, she did. She was there and that's where she lost her father. I had a different father. He came home and fell in my bed about as many times as he fell in my mother's. He did that until one night Frank killed him. (251)

Daphne revelations suggest how she has internalized the stereotypical discourse of the tragic mulatto that makes her attractive to white males and problematic to Black males. There is the clear sense that Daphne has used her body and her white appearance to get ahead in life and how discreetly the currency terms are bargained and whether the price is high enough to purchase her sense of respectability are part of the bargain—these factors will determine the length of the relationship. Daphne is not just selling her sexuality and beauty, she is selling her mixed race status. As Carol Camper argues:

> The other stereotype of mixed race women is that of moral and sexual degeneracy. It is as if our basic degeneracy as women of color is magnified by White ancestry. Our so called 'Whiteness' increases our 'beauty' along with our awareness of it, driving us to a frenzy of bitter abandon so disagreeable and piquant to our White male pursuers. (xxi)

Daphne's whiteness allows her to pass and develop her relationships with white men, and her brief sexual relationship with Rawlins is contingent on his thinking that she is white. Passing gives her access to the power of the white phallus. Black male subjectivity is often connected to Black female subjectivity. For Easy Rawlins his agency becomes connected to his home. Daphne Monet's subjectivity resides in her body as a text and as a site for desire. There is the clear suggestion that Daphne makes herself available to wealthy white males for consumption, transforming her body into a marketable product for the pleasure of white men for a hefty price. Discussing the "rules" of racial passing, Lawrence Otis Graham lists in *Our Kind of People: Inside America's Black Upper Class* (1999), a number of actions that appear to resonate with Daphne Monet's behavior:

Change your last name to one that is not associated with Black family names....Relocate to a new community that insulates you from interacting with Blacks and that is a few hundred miles from your family's home. Avoid cities like New Orleans and Charleston, South Carolina, where whites are adept at spotting light-skinned Blacks who are passing. (380–83)

In typical Du Boisian terms, Daphne announces her dual identity: a Black female and a white female and caught up in the paradoxical phenomenon of passing. Daphne/Ruby has two names and two places of birth. This explains her false French accent and her deceptions around her half-brother, Frank Green. Like most light-skinned Blacks who pass for white, Daphne moves from her place of birth to a location (California) where she believes no one knows her real identity. It is by selling her racialized body that others view her as an opportunity to exploit her relationship with the wealthy Todd Carter. Mosley never reveals how Richard McGee, Matthew Teran, and Howard Green discover her Black identity but with Mouse knowing her and her half-brother she can never have a relationship with someone who knows that she is Black. Moreover, the main idea that Daphne articulates here is the trauma she encountered as a child; this trauma of ongoing sexual molestation and the death of her father have shaped her adult identity. Discussing the nature of trauma, Judith Lewis Herman argues:

The conflict between the will to deny horrible events and the will to proclaim them aloud is the central dialectic of psychological trauma. People who have survived atrocities often tell their stories in a highly emotional, contradictory, and fragmented manner which undermines their credibility and thereby serves the twin imperatives of truth-telling and secrecy. When the truth is finally recognized, survivors can begin their recovery. But far too often secrecy prevails, and the story of the traumatic event surfaces not as a verbal narrative but as a symptom. The psychological distress symptoms of traumatized people simultaneously call attention to the existence of an unspeakable secret and deflect attention from it. This is most apparent in the way traumatized people alternate between feeling numb and reliving the event. The dialectic of trauma gives rise to complicated, sometimes uncanny alterations of consciousness, which George Orwell, one of the committed truth-tellers of our century, called "doublethink," and which mental health professionals, searching for a calm, precise language, call "dissociation." It results in the protean, dramatic, and often bizarre symptoms of hysteria which Freud recognized a century ago as disguised communications about sexual abuse in childhood. Witnesses as well as victims are subject to the dialectic of trauma. It is difficult for an observer to remain clearheaded and calm, to see more than a few fragments of the picture at one time, to retain all the pieces, and to fit them together. It is even more difficult to find a language that conveys fully and persuasively what one has seen. Those who attempt to describe the atrocities that they have witnessed also risk their own credibility. To speak publicly about one's knowledge of atrocities is to invite the stigma that attaches to victims. (1–2)

The trauma of incest and patricide combined with natal alienation have given Daphne a distorted sense of herself, requiring her to create a different self as a means of self-protection. Being light-skinned also set Daphne apart from other Blacks and perhaps gave her a color complex. Like Clare Kendry in Nella Larsen's *Passing*, Daphne Monet has tried to be both Black and white in America where strict racial bifurcation is habitually required. Interestingly, Mouse provides a racial analysis to Rawlins on Daphne's and his desires:

> She wanna be white. All them years people be tellin' her how she light-skinned and beautiful but all the time she knows that she can't have what white people have. So she pretend and then she lose it all. She can love a white man but all he can love is the white girl he thinks she is....That's just like you Easy. You learn stuff and you be thinkin' like white men be thinkin.' You be thinkin' that what's right fo them is right fo' you. She look like she white and you think like you white. But brother you don't know that you both poor niggers. And a nigger ain't never gonna be happy 'less he accept what he is.' (252–53)

Here Mouse makes the point that Daphne/Ruby will forever be a divided individual; the only thing worse than lying to other individuals is lying to yourself. Because of internalized white supremacy, many Black people have developed a perspective that light-skinned individuals are more attractive than dark-skinned individuals; light-skinned individuals develop a false sense of superiority and dark-skinned individuals develop a false sense of inferiority. Daphne's body thus becomes a site for considering how the intersectionality of gender, class, and race ideologies are constituted and denied; accordingly her body functions as a marker of sexual and racial transgression. For her to develop a long-term relationship would signal the inescapable class implications of crossing the racial boundary. As argued by one scholar,

> the phenomenon of passing for white is a kind of Faustian paradigm that represents a profound paradox which both challenges the doctrine of white supremacy (the essentialism of whiteness) and requires a denial of one's blackness at the same time that it reaffirms the existing racial hierarchy of white power and white privilege. Personhood is whiteness, and whiteness means possibility and privilege. (Thompson *The Tragic Black Buck*, 8)

For Daphne/Ruby to deny her race means that at times she had to deny any family connection to Frank Green and any other Black family members. This psychological denial causes enduring mental anguish, and Daphne loses everything that she attains by passing for white. As Nathan Irvin Huggins postulates there are psychological penalties involved in passing:

> Since being white made all the difference in American life, who would not be
> white if he [or she] could? But such reasoning exacted a psychic penalty. The man
> [or woman] who worked as white but kept alive relations with Black family and
> friends knew the immediate fear of detection. On the other hand, he [or she]
> who tried to play it safe by moving to another place and "disappearing" into the
> white world doubtless nurtured guilt because of deception and the abandonment
> of race and family. And the fact, that Afro-Americans did "pass" only served to
> deepen white anxieties about racial identification. (245–46)

It is interesting to note that both Daphne and her half-brother are involved
in criminality; Frank, "the Knifeman" was involved in highjacking liquor
trucks and cigarette shipments from California to Nevada, and Daphne was
involved in racial misrepresentation which lead to the violent deaths of four
individuals.[25] Daphne's criminality is also associated with the thirty thousand
dollars she took from Todd Carter; it is this money that directly leads to the
death of Coretta James, Howard Green, Richard McGee, and Matthew
Teran. Also, DeWitt Albright and Joppy are killed by the money-hungry
Mouse who kills as easily as lifting a fork to eat. During the times she was
with Easy, Daphne was passing as a white woman and enjoyed the notion
that this Black man thought that he was having passionate sexual relations
with a white woman. This helps us understand why Rawlins was confused
after having relations with Daphne; she was attempting to behave like she
thought a white woman would behave with a Black man. Her sexual behavior
could be characterized as bizarre and suggests how she has developed some
essentialism around race and sexuality. Daphne expressing racial
essentialism believes that Black females act a certain way and white females
act in a certain manner. Mouse's criticism of Rawlins learning things and
"thinkin' like white mens be thinking" also suggests some racial essentialism
on his part. Mouse relates that certain "nigger jobs" such as gardening and
cleaning that Easy had done in the past made him Black, and now owning a
home and "fuckin some white man's girl" have made Rawlins white. This is
racial essentialism, the absurd notion that one's race dictates one's career
or sexual preferences; this perspective comes out of a system of white
supremacy and Jim Crow segregation. Rawlins' desire to own his home is
tied to a legacy of the exploitation of sharecropping, and his desire for
white women is based on the racial taboo of miscegenation. Like the
progressive Blacks in Wallstreet, Oklahoma, and Rosewood, Florida, who
owned homes and businesses before they were attacked by white
supremacists, Rawlins understands that hard work and home ownership are
critical elements in one's success regardless of one's race. Moreover, it must
be stressed that as a veteran of World War II, Rawlins' worldview has been
forever changed. As Gail Buckley makes clear:

In 1945, Black veterans once again came home to a country where they could be lynched for wearing a uniform. America was the same, but veterans, again, were different. In 1918, Black vets had looked to Communism for ways to change their country. In 1945, they looked to democracy, coming home to use the Declaration of Independence, the Bill of Rights, and the Constitution to nourish the frail shoots of civil rights and to make sure that Black soldiers would never again fight and die for a country that did not treat them like Americans. (333–34)

Buckley's analysis underscores a fundamental aspect of Rawlins' often challenging encounters with all of the white males in the novel and his view of Daphne Monet. The one subject where Mouse's criticism of Rawlins might be valid is Easy believing that he could have a long-term relationship with Daphne. Earlier, Rawlins was concerned about being stopped by the police while Daphne was with him; perhaps Daphne has a better understanding of their racial dynamics and knows that their relationship would not work. It would be over twenty-five years before, in the *Loving versus Virginia* case of 1967, anti-miscegenation laws were deemed unconstitutional.[26] One night of feral and painful sexual relations with Daphne somehow convinced Rawlins that miscegenation between a Black man and a white woman would not be an enduring problem. Although there were no legal restrictions concerning Black people's ownership of land and property, there were widespread laws concerning miscegenation.

The final resolution of this misadventure for Easy Rawlins involves meeting Todd Carter and dealing with the white authorities. Fundamentally, Carter views Rawlins as a failure because his fiancée and his thirty thousand dollars are gone. However, Rawlins convinces him that at least Daphne Monet has her freedom as opposed to being dead. Rawlins tells Carter "I saved her life, man. I let her get away with your money and her skin. Any one of the men involved with this would have seen her dead" (256). Carter despondently learns that although Daphne loves him she would never have any peace with him; at the same time that he is telling Carter this, Rawlins is thinking "about making love to her when she was still a white woman" (255). Acknowledging his preference for the white Daphne as opposed to the light-skinned Black Ruby reinforces and reinscribes the intraracial conflict that comes out of interracial conflict. Placing this issue of color within a historical context Russell, Wilson, and Hall note:

Before the Civil War, passing was understandable, as it enabled Blacks to escape slavery and brutal racism. Today, passing is viewed with distain by other Blacks, and while some African American pass "part-time" for economic reasons, by far the majority of those who could pass don't—and would never dream of doing so. Blacks who do decide to pass for White pay a heavy price for their betrayal. They must renounce their heritage, terminate all contact with darker-skinned relatives, and constantly monitor their speech patterns and social behavior. Many even forgo having children for fear a baby's color will blow their cover. (*Color Complex*, 73)

Daphne Monet encapsulates yet challenges this description. While she uses a fake French accent and changes her names, she did have a close relationship with her half-brother Frank; here again Mosley suggests incestuous desire. Her duality is mirrored by Easy's desire for this "white woman." Growing up under segregation, Rawlins obviously learned that white females were taboo, but now, after fighting in the Second World War where he had relations with white women, he feels he has a right to have white women and prefers Daphne's whiteness. One of the central issues to be resolved is the enduring protection of Daphne, especially since they found DeWitt Albright dead in his car north of Santa Barbara. With Albright dead, both Daphne and Easy have an added sense of freedom because Albright would have come after them with murderous intent. Although Carter and his white lawyer accompany Rawlins to meet with the assistant to the chief of police and the deputy mayor, Rawlins has a more difficult time equivocating to them, especially with Miller and Mason in the room. The central deception here is to frame the story in a way that involves the men and eschewing any mention of Daphne, Black men, and white men killing and dying over money. With the wealthy Carter and his lawyer, Jerome Duffy, as powerful foils, the questioning of Rawlins is long and extensive; Miller and Mason are skeptical and with Miller later threatening to arrest Rawlins every other day for jaywalking, spitting, and creating a general nuisance, Rawlins reluctantly suggests that they could "try Junior Fornay against that print" (260). Like the killing of Joppy, Junior must be sacrificed for Easy's freedom; Easy's American Dream becomes stained with blood, but this is reflective of America being founded on the bloody and whipped and scarred bodies of enslaved Africans. Since the days of slavery, white male power has been a fundamental aspect of American life. Mosley's point here is that these white police officers have a tremendous amount of power and can operate with impunity. Knowing that these white police only care about the deaths of whites (in this case white males), Rawlins' freedom from white legal authority requires him to give up another Black man who was violently impulsive and careless in killing a white man. The lesson here is that when a white man dies and there is evidence that a Black male is involved, some Black male must pay a profound price, his freedom or even his life. Coretta James' horrific death and the equally gruesome death of Howard Green are only incidental to the deaths of white males, Richard McGee and Matthew Teran, especially since a Black man, Joppy, was responsible for bludgeoning Coretta and Howard. Having slept with the seductive Coretta while his friend Dupree was asleep in the next room reveals the immoral side of Easy Rawlins' character, suggesting that he will act impulsively sexually. However,

Rawlins' feelings of shame and guilt might explain his relative indifference to Mouse killing Joppy.

Even in the characterizations of death and murder, white supremacy reigns. White individuals are shot or stabbed, and Black individuals are bludgeoned into unrecognizable pulps of flesh. One cannot help but make the connection between Joppy's traumatic life as a boxer ("the punishments he had taken in the ring") and the brutal killings. Daphne's murder of the pedophile, Matthew Teran also falls into this category of a psychological response to trauma; Daphne nonchalantly states:

> I pulled the trigger, he died. But he killed himself really. I went to him, to ask him to leave me alone. I offered him all my money but he just laughed. He just laughed. He had his hands in that little boy's drawers and he laughed...I don't know if it was a laugh or a sound of disgust. And so I killed him. (250)

Here Daphne's willingness to use all of her money to protect herself reflects the significance of her racial secret and her willingness to protect her life within the white world from the scrutiny and revelation of her blackness. Racial passing, which reflects a death of the individual, leads to the death of others to protect the self. This desperateness to protect Daphne's racial secret is evident when Rawlins and Mouse question Frank Green about her whereabouts. Easy states: "I could see that Daphne meant enough to him that he was ready to die to keep her safe" (197). Here "safe" means keeping Daphne's secret of racial passing despite the accumulation of dead bodies tied to her clandestine masquerade. Even in death Jim Crow segregation still makes its repulsive presence; outside the South, the state of California passed more Jim Crow laws (seventeen) than any other state in the country. Jim Crow legislation which created systematic discrimination in housing, employment, and education ensured that the races would remain separate. Several states prohibited hearses from carrying both races, and cemeteries were required to maintain separate graveyards; this is particularly paradoxical as it relates to Black and white soldiers.

Easy Rawlins' discussion with his friend and father figure, Odell Jones, at the conclusion of the novel reflects his guilty in having to give up Junior Fornay to the police; Easy has approximately ten thousand dollars (this blood money is analogous to the money he obtained when Mouse killed his stepfather) buried in his backyard, a rental property, and an innovative yet precarious profession, working for himself as a private detective. It was the his making the connection of Junior Fornay's Zapatas cigarette to the murder of Richard McGee and his overall tenacity—along with the deadly assistance of Mouse (his alter ego)—that established Easy Rawlins' future as a detective. As in any warfare there is success and there is loss, and Junior had to be sacrificed for Easy's liberating future. For Rawlins his problems with white males such as Benny Giacomo, DeWitt Albright, Todd Carter, and the white police officers have led to his socioeconomic independence. However, with a number of contradictions in Easy Rawlins' character and conduct, Odell Jones represent the ongoing guidance that Easy will need if he is to be a successful sleuth, especially within this culture of violence. Tensions between whites and African Americans too often come down to this national narrative in which African Americans have faced centuries of racialized violence and racial hegemony designed to exclude them from all vestiges of socioeconomic subjectivity associated with the American Dream poignantly symbolized by Jay Gatsby (Thompson, *Eating the Black Body,* 19). Unlike Gatsby, Easy has attained his idea of the American Dream, a dream that gives him power and subjectivity. Thus he learns some poignant lessons about the infrastructure of white male domination inside and outside the legal arena and the dynamics of racial representations, and more importantly he learns some powerful lessons about himself and what he is willing to do to maintain his piece of the American Dream.

Notes

1   Walter Mosley' Easy Rawlins books are set in various decades of Rawlins' life and infused with Black life and historical context. *The Red Death* puts Rawlins in the 1950s in the context of the FBI's conflict with the communists; the setting for *A Yellow Dog* is the 1960s and the relentless violence due to the rapid increase in drug traffic.

2   Spike Lee has announced plans to make a movie about the struggle against Nazi occupiers in Italy during World War II that he hopes will highlight the contribution of African American soldiers who fought and died to liberate Europe. The film will spotlight the courage of Black soldiers who, despite suffering discrimination back home, made a contribution that has so far gone largely unnoticed in other Hollywood movies. Lee said. "We have Black people who are fighting for democracy who at the same time are classified as second-class citizens. That is why I'd like to do a film to show how these brave Black men, despite all the hardship they were going through, still pushed that aside and fought for the greater good." Based on the novel *Miracle at St. Anna* by James McBride, the movie will tell the story of four Black American soldiers, all members of the Army's all-Black 92nd "Buffalo Soldier" Division, who are trapped behind enemy lines in an Italian village in Tuscany in 1944.

3   The American hard-boiled detective novel finds its origins in the 1920s and is analogous to the British counterpart in organization, but extremely different in content. Generally, the hard-boiled novel begins with the introduction of the detective, propels him into conflict in pursuit of some mystery which turns into a crime, trails him through a labyrinth-like investigation, and ends with the mystery being solved. Simply put, confusion turns into clarity after some twists and turns.

4   It is interesting to note that on the back cover of the novel the name is Daphne Money. Phonetically, her name suggests money and the desire for money encapsulates the entire novel.

5   Black soldiers returning from World War II were subjected to physical violence and some Black soldiers were lynched in their uniforms.

6   Walter Mosley, *Devil in a Blue Dress* (New York: Washington Square Press, 1990) 168.
All further references to this text will be given parenthetically.

7   In Eric Foner's *Nothing but Freedom: Emancipation and Its Legacy* (Baton Rouge:
Louisiana University Press, 1983), Foner argues the significance of Blacks obtaining
land in the Sea Islands under the auspices of the Freedman's Bureau and the army:
"Throughout the South, possession of the land was the focal point of conflict in
early reconstruction, but few regions witnessed as sustained a struggle as the South
Carolina and Georgia low country. Here, where blacks had long enjoyed a unique
degree of autonomy, black troops were spreading the gospel of land ownership. Federal
authorities had sold land to Sea Island blacks during the war, and the Freedmen's
Bureau seemed committed to further redistribution of the land. By the end of 1865,
President Andrew Johnson, reversing the Bureau's initial policy, had pardoned the
great majority of large planters and authorized the return of their lands. The actual
process of restoration was a prolonged and bitter one, often requiring the intervention
of Union soldiers. Throughout the low country, virtually the entire white population
had fled, and blacks, who had cultivated the soil in 1865, had no intention of giving
up their crops or abandoning their claim to the land" (82).

8   Like the Slave Codes, the Black Codes were designed to keep Black people under
control and in an inferior socioeconomic position. With brutal violence by poor white
patrollers, Blacks had little choice in how they would live and work. For example,
certain laws prevented Blacks from owning or renting property, and vagrancy laws
were strictly enforced even to the point where a Black individual who refused to sign
a work contract with a white employer would be considered a vagrant. Mississippi
codes allowed white employers to hunt down Black workers—just like the fugitive
slave laws. And in South Carolina, vagrants could be sentenced to years of hard labor.
Under these restrictions, white employers could whip their Black workers and in some
cases they were raped, mutilated, and murdered. In other situations the white police
and government officials directed mobs to attack and destroy Black schools, homes,
businesses, and churches; hundreds of Black people were killed and many wounded. As
Truman Nelson points out in the Introduction to W. E. B. Du Bois' *The Gift of Black
Folk: The Negro in the Making of America* (New York: Washington Square Press, 1970)
"The answer of the defeated and vindictive white South was to pass their infamous
'Black Codes,' local laws which compelled every black person who wanted to practice
a trade to be licensed by a white judge. Every black who wanted a weapon to defend
himself, every black who tried to study and learn without a hoe in his hand had to
apply to a white judge for permission. Thus the black man, striving to be free, had to
stand hat in hand before men whose fondest wish was to prove that freeing the slave
was the greatest disaster of all time and whose judicial life was dedicated to insuring the
failure of black freedom either by active force or passive noncompliance with federal
law. The black man stood 'doomed in his own person and his posterity to live without
knowledge and without capacity to make anything his own and to toil that another
may reap the fruit.'" (xvi).

9   See *Slavery by Another Name: The Re-Enslavement of Black Americans from the Civil
War to World War II*

10 As James W. Loewen explains in *Sundown Towns: A Hidden Dimension of American
Racism* (New York: The New Press, 2005): "A sundown is any organized jurisdiction
that for decades kept African Americans or other groups from living in it and was thus
'all white' on purpose.... Other towns passed ordinances barring African Americans

after dark or prohibited them from owning or renting property; still others established such policies by informal means, harassing and even killing those who violated the rule. Some sundown towns similarly kept out Jews, Chinese, Mexicans, Native Americans, or other groups" (4).

11 See Ralph Ginzburg's *100 Years of Lynching* (Baltimore: Black Classics Press, 1988).

12 For a discussion on race and racial passing in *The Great Gatsby,* see Carlyle Van Thompson's *The Tragic Black Buck: Racial Masquerading in the American Literary Imagination* (New York: Peter Lang Publishing, 2004).

13 In John Berger's *Ways of Seeing* (New York: Penguin Books, 1977) Berger makes a fundamental argument when he states: "Seeing comes before words....But there is also another sense in which seeing comes before words. It is seeing which establishes our place in the surrounding world; we explain that world with words, but words can never undo the fact that we are surrounded by it. The relation between what we see and what we know is never settled" (7).

14 It should be noted that Irene Redfield occasionally passes for white, but is married to a Black man, whereas Clare Kendry is married to a racist white man named Jack Bellew who calls her "Nig."

15 The importance of Black males fighting in World War I and World War II cannot be overemphasized. Those who did return were forever changed; many were unwilling to live under segregation, and this resulted in a plethora of race riots, especially the Red Summer of 1919. This was signified on in Toni Morrison's *Sula,* where she desired Black soldiers in "shit colored uniforms." Here Morrison is relating both how Black veterans were treated and the fact that some Black soldiers were lynched in their uniforms and that they would defecate and urinate on themselves as a result of the lynching.

16 Both of these race riots originated with racial conflicts over white women. In Rosewood, a white woman made a false allegation that a Black man beat her and that resulted in the prosperous Black town of Rosewood being destroyed. In Wallstreet, there was a minor incident between a white female and a Black male, and this led to the wealthy Black town being destroyed with hundreds of people killed and many Black businesses destroyed.

17 As related by Kareem Abdul-Jabbar and Alan Steinberg in *Black Profiles in Courage: A Legacy of African-American Achievement* (New York: HarperCollins, 2000), "Before Emmett and several cousins boarded the Illinois Central, Mamie Till drilled her son on how to act down South: Say 'Yes, sir' and 'No sir.' Never look a white person straight in the eyes. Mind the COLORED ONLY and WHITE ONLY signs. And especially: 'If you have to get on your knees and bow when a white person goes past, do it willingly' " (223). A black individual on their knees is also a theme that Walter Mosley uses with regard to racial relations.

18 It is generally in high school and college that the racial prohibitions breakdown, and Blacks and white explore the sexual taboos that they have been socialized to accept. The case at Duke University involving white male lacrosse players and a Black female exotic dancer who allegedly accused them of raping her represents a graphic example of white males' desire to sexually consume the Black female body.

19 Here John Berger makes a relationship about how men treat women based on their gaze: "Men survey women before treating them. Consequently how a woman appears to a man can determine how she will be treated. To acquire some control over this process, women must contain it and interiorize it. That part of a woman's self which

is the surveyor treats the part which is the surveyed so as to demonstrate to others how her whole self would like to be treated. And this exemplary treatment of herself by herself constitutes her presence. Every woman's presence regulates what is and is not 'permissible' within her presence. Every one of her actions—whatever its direct purposes or motivation—is also read as an indication of how she would like to be treated" (46–47).

20   All of these actions require bending over. More importantly, the issue of fellatio is not a farfetched issue if we consider Toni Morrison's novel *Beloved*, in which white slave masters forced Black male slaves on the coffle to give them fellatio if they wanted to eat.

21   In Johnson's novel the protagonist sums up a white man's success in one word, money.

22   Historically, Easy Rawlins' hallucination suggests the heroism of Dorie Miller, a hero of Pearl Harbor and the first Black winner of the Navy Cross and the first American hero of World War II. As Gail Buckley relates in *American Patriots: The Story of Blacks in the Military from the Revolution to Desert Storm* (New York: Random House, 2001): "The first American hero of World War II was Black. On December 7, 1941, at Pearl Harbor, Dorie Miller was a mess man on the burning deck of the *U.S.S. Arizona*. Miller, the shy twenty-two year old son of a Texas sharecropper, carried the ship's mortally wounded captain to safety, then manned an antiaircraft gun to bring down what witnesses said were four Japanese planes (officials listed two). Miller had never been taught to fire the antiaircraft gun; it was against Navy regulations for Blacks to do so. Only when the ammunition was exhausted and the *Arizona* was sinking beneath him did he abandon ship. It took three months for his heroism to be officially recognized....In the aftermath of Miller's heroics, Navy regulations were changed to require that all hands, including mess men and stewards, receive antiaircraft training" (275).

23   In Frederick Douglass's *Narrative* there is a similar scene where the young Douglass watches from a closet as his Aunt Hester is whipped by Douglass's white master and father.

24   The tragic mulatto is a stereotypical fictional character that appeared in American literature during the 19th and 20th centuries. The "tragic mulatto" is an archetypical mixed race person, who is assumed to be despondent or even self-destructive because he/she fails to completely fit in the "white world" or the "black world." As such, the "tragic mulatto" is depicted as the victim of the society he/she lives in, a society divided by race. Because of society's reluctance to acknowledge ambiguity in racial classifications, this character is particularly vulnerable.

25   In some states it was a crime to misrepresent one's racial identity and it some cases Black men were lynched for passing as white.

26   As pointed out by Gloria J. Browne-Marshall in *Race, Law, and American Society: 1607 to Present* (New York: Routledge, 2007): "Richard Loving, a White man, and his wife Mildred, a Black woman, were arrested for violating Virginia's anti-miscegenation law. The couple was married in Washington, D.C., in 1958 and returned to Virginia. Soon, three White police officers entered their bedroom and arrested them for violating Virginia's Racial Integrity Act of 1924. Neither knew that Virginia had anti-misce-genation laws dating back to 1619. The Lovings pled guilty to violating the statute and were convicted for leaving the state in order to marry. Under the law, 'if a white person and colored person shall go out of the State, for the purpose of being married

and with the intention of returning , and be married out of it, and afterwards return to and reside in it, cohabiting as man and wife, they shall be punished.' The punishment was confinement in the penitentiary for not less than one and no more than five years" (109–10). The Lovings appealed to the United States Supreme Court, and the Court determined that anti-miscegenation laws were designed to support a system of white supremacy and States were prohibited from infringing upon the freedom to marry a person of another race.

5. From a Hog to a Black Man: Black Male Subjectivity and Ritualistic Lynching in Ernest J. Gaines' A Lesson Before Dying

Many questions were troubling the explorer, but at the sight of the prisoner he asked only: "Does he know his sentence?" "No," said the officer, eager to go on with exposition, but the explorer interrupted him. "He doesn't know the sentence that has been passed on him?" "No," said the officer again, pausing a moment as if to let the explorer elaborate his question, and then said: "There would be no point in telling him. He'll learn it on his body."

—*Franz Kafka*[1]

How does any Black man construct his subjectivity in America's institutionalized white supremacist culture during a time and place in which Black lives seemingly count for nothing? How does an educated Black man who struggles to construct his subjectivity help another scarcely literate Black man face an unjustifiable execution with dignity when a white supremacist society attempts to prevent all Black men from standing tall? How does this educated Black man help transform this unenlightened, psychologically unenlightened and barely literate Black man whom many whites believe represents a "hog" into a hero for an entire Black community? When a white man dies by the hands of a Black man in America's Jim Crow South, the expeditious death of that Black man, regardless of his actual culpability, is as certain as the change of the seasons. Too often, during segregation, the death of this Black man—and by extension the whole Black community— would be in the form of an extra-legal ritualistic lynching-burning.

In Ernest J. Gaines' powerful novel *A Lesson Before Dying* (1993), the retributive nature of America's white supremacist culture is powerfully on display as Jefferson, a twenty-one-year-old slightly retarded Black man, is arrested and convicted for a murder he did not commit. He waits for his electric chair execution after a white man, Alcee Grope, has been violently murdered during a robbery and shoot-out at a Cajun liquor store. Confused and in shock, Jefferson waits in the store and when two white men find him; he is blamed for armed robbery and murder. As the only survivor of this shoot-out in which three men (one white and two Blacks) are killed, Jefferson, as an unwitting witness to this tragedy, faces the death penalty. Because of his innocence and ignorance, Jefferson's execution via the electric chair symbolizes a ritualistic lynch-burning.[2] However, Gaines' eloquence and moral resonance illustrate the truly redemptive power of the human spirit by juxtaposing Grant Wiggins, a rather cynical Black elementary school teacher who has taught at the local school for six years, with the barely literate Jefferson (his only name); this relationship is orchestrated by Grant's Tante Lou and Jefferson's beleaguered godmother, Miss Emma Glenn (Nanna), who desires that her godson walk to his death with dignity and pride. Although he has the solace and encouragement of his light-skinned lover, Vivian Baptiste (also an elementary school teacher), Grant Wiggins faces an extremely difficult teaching challenge. By examining the relationship between these two very different Black men in a white patriarchal and racist society designed to keep all Black men, regardless of education, from achieving subjectivity, Gaines illustrates the fundamental humanity of all people in the face of overwhelming and oppressive conditions. Here, I will explore how many Black men become ritualistically lynched in accord with the enduringly blood-letting rituals evident in America's white supremacist culture, but despite this abhorrent human tragedy, a redemptive and hopeful spirit emerges gradually breaks down the barriers of interracial and intraracial hegemony as Jefferson loses an ingrained sense of racial inferiority. More specifically, I will examine how Jefferson, who is labeled an "old hog" and who temporarily accepts this self-deprecating definition,[3] is transformed into a dignified Black man and a Christ figure whose journey to subjectivity challenges the mythology of white supremacist culture.[4] In the context of Jefferson's transformation, we also see the transformation of Grant Wiggins and how shame and self-esteem are critical factors in the subjectivity of these Black men. Equally important Gaines underscores how these Black men have been marked by the trauma of abuse, abandonment, and natal alienation. As bell hooks argues, psychological factors are at the root of our history under racism and white supremacy:

> We discover the psychohistory of African Americans it becomes apparent that the foundation of the shaky self-esteem that assaults our sensibilities is rooted in the experience of traumatic violence. Whether it is the emotional violence caused by the pain of abandonment or the violence that is a consequence of domination (whether racism sexism, or class elitism), it is the normalization of violence in our lives as black people that creates the foundation for ongoing trauma reenactment. (*Rock My Soul*, 21)

Notwithstanding these conditions, Jefferson's majestic metamorphosis leads to Grant Wiggins's metamorphosis and the potentiality of diminished interracial and intraracial antagonism in this Cajun community.

Ernest J. Gaines places his novel in a small Cajun town in Louisiana during the 1940s—the heart of the Jim Crow period, when the lynchings of Black men were diminishing but political and socioeconomic restrictions on Blacks were extremely oppressive. Beyond these restrictions the psychological effects of white supremacy were pervasive. During 1936–1970, the number of Blacks lynched across America was annually fewer than ten.[5] However, lynching gave way to oppressive legal sanctions. The Civil Rights Act of 1875 had been declared unconstitutional, and the Supreme Court legally instituted segregation through its decision in *Plessy v. Ferguson* in 1896. This segregation is evident in the jail in which Jefferson is incarcerated: there is a separate cell block for Black inmates and separate restroom facilities for Black visitors to the jail. In *Plessy v. Ferguson* the Court upheld the principle of "separate but equal" facilities for Blacks and whites. This system is called "de jure" segregation; the laws that accomplished de jure segregation in the South are known as Jim Crow laws, named after a pre-Civil War minstrel show character. It would not be until 1954 with the Supreme Court decision in *Brown v. Board of Education* in Topeka, Kansas, that public school segregation would be declared unconstitutional. However, outlawing segregation did little to change the culture of racial oppression, especially in Louisiana.[6] The historical context for Gaines' narrative centers on an execution in 1947. Gaines discloses: "[T]his young man had been sentenced to the electric chair twice—I think it was 46 or 47. Because the chair had failed to work properly the first time....What I did learn from that incident was that the state had had a portable electric chair that they would run wires through the window for the night before."[7] Beyond the tangible violence of lynching, legal measures were taken to keep Black people in a dependent state and exclude them from enjoying the fruits of a nation built on the unpaid labor of enslaved Blacks. During this time, America' white supremacist society, supported by the violence of the Ku Klux Klan and many other white supremacist groups, attempted to keep most Blacks oppressed by substandard socioeconomic conditions and by making black skin a badge of degradation and dehumanization. Along with the quasi-slave system of sharecropping, local ordinances in the North and South restricted Blacks from earning competitive incomes, and without sufficient income, few were able to secure decent food, education, health care, and housing. Under Jim Crow segregation, Black people are metaphorically killed before they die; the daily humiliation they experience represents ritualistic lynching. As Orlando Patterson asserts in his seminal work *Slavery and Social Death: A Comparative Study* (1982): "The nation as a whole, and Afro-Americans in particular, are still paying the ethnocidal price of slavery and the neo-dulotic Jim Crow system" (166).

In America's patriarchal society, Black men are especially affected by the physical, psychological, and economic violence of white supremacy because they often feel powerless when they cannot safeguard and provide for themselves and their families. As a system Jim Crow segregation touched every aspect of Black life, producing an environment of hopelessness. Lawrence M. Friedman sums up the Jim Crow period:

> Segregation was, however, only one leg of the southern system. Labor arrangements made up the other leg. Here law and custom joined together to keep blacks, in essence, tied to the soil. To put it bluntly, the southern labor system was a form of serfdom. There were, of course national laws against peonage, and slavery had been officially abolished by the Thirteenth Amendment to the Constitution. Getting rid of slavery was, to be sure, a great social advance, and it meant a great deal to southern blacks—that is undeniable. When slavery ended, the mass of blacks could legally marry, own property, and to a limited degree, run their lives. But their rights and powers continued to be severely circumscribed. For one thing, most blacks were desperately poor. They were farm workers—sharecroppers or contract laborers. Practically speaking, they were tied to the soil. An elaborate structure of laws, designed to preserve intact "the southern way of life," buttressed the labor system. The point of these laws was to keep blacks 'in their place.' (56)

Like the brutal lynching-burnings where Black men were disembodied, castrated, and consumed (burned alive), the daily socioeconomic oppression that Black men experience becomes a communal rape by whites, especially whites who project their sexual desires and apprehensions onto the bodies of Black men. Like a horde of pigs at slaughter, the bodies of Black males become sites for fearful and lustful white men to release their castrating depravity. As argued in *Eating the Black Body: Miscegenation as Sexual Consumption in African American Literature* (2006):

> ...it is critically important to note that the lynching of African American people, as a sexualized ritual of racial hatred represents the unconscious guilt feelings on the part of the race-haters. They displace this animosity towards those who are different and less able to defend themselves; moreover, these white Americans displace their sexual desires and sexual frustrations on to their African American victims whom they consume. (23–24)

Like Richard Wright, Ernest J. Gaines uses the theme of consumption quite deftly in *A Lesson Before Dying* to convey how this racist society consumes Black labor and consumes those Black individuals like Jefferson who violates the rules of segregation

Gaines' sustained structure in the novel is that of paradox, and it begins in the first sentence. "I was not there, yet I was there. No I did not go to the trial, I did not hear the verdict, because I knew all the time what it would be. Still, I was there. I was there as much as anyone else was there,"[8] announces our reluctant narrator, Grant Wiggins. While not physically in the courtroom,

Grant understands the psychological effect of Jefferson being on trial for the murder of a white man. As a Black man in the South, Grant understands and empathizes with Jefferson's tragic plight. Further, Grant believes he understands the effect this would have on Jefferson's godmother, Miss Emma Glenn, Tante Lou, and the Black community of Bayonne. As Grants relates: "A white man had been killed during a robbery, and though two of the robbers had been killed on the spot, one had been captured, and he too would have to die" (4). Under Jim Crow segregation, the racial mathematics is simple: a white man killed plus a Black man's involvement equals the death of that Black man. Even in relating the story of how Alcee Grope, Bear, and Brother were involved in the shootout the narrative is tragically laden with paradox:

> Soon there was shooting from another direction. When it was quiet again, Bear Grope, and Brother were all down on the floor, and only Jefferson was standing....The old man was still alive. He had seen him. He would tell on him. Now he started babbling. "It wasn't me. It wasn't me, Mr. Grope. It was Brother and Bear. Brother shot you. It wasn't me. They made me come with them. You got to tell the law that, Mr. Grope. You hear me, Mr. Grope?" But he was talking to a dead man. (5–6)

Jefferson is illiterate, but he clearly understands the legal importance of this situation and the need for this dying white man, Mr. Grope, to speak for him and speak the truth. Indeed, Jefferson understands that a white man's word is analogous to the law. When white men speak, the law responds in legal or extra-legal terms.[9] Indeed, white males are the primary benefactors of legal statutes, especially during segregation. Based on previous violent incidents involving the murder of a white individual, Jefferson is fortunate to have a trial; immediate lynching would generally be the response to a white man being robbed and killed by Black males. Unfortunately, Jefferson was speaking to a dead man in Mr. Grope, and of course Jefferson is also dead at this point, dead man talking. Under a legal system of white supremacy, Black men are presumed to be guilty as in the internationally notorious case of the Scottsboro Boys in 1932 (*Powell vs. Alabama*). It is not difficult to assume that Gaines also had this case in mind in the construction of this novel. Here the issues were miscegenation and rape after some white boys charged nine Black boys with gang-raping two white girls, Ruby Bates and Victoria Price. As Gloria Browne-Marshall documents, this case amounted to a legal lynching:

> The Scottsboro Boys were indicted on the very day they were arraigned. The defendants entered pleas of not guilty. They did not have counsel representing them at the arraignment. The trail judge appointed all the members of the bar to represent the defendants at the arraignment. The defendants were tried in three groups. As each of the three cases was called for trial, each defendant was arraigned and, having the indictment read to him, entered a plea of not guilty.

Each of the three trials was completed within a single day. Under the Alabama statue, punishment for rape was decided by the jury and within its discretion may be from ten years' imprisonment to death. The juries found defendants guilty and imposed the death penalty upon all of them. The trial court overruled motions for new trials and sentenced the defendants in accordance with the verdicts. The judgments were affirmed by the state supreme court. (212)

With an appeal to the Supreme Court and other legal challenges along with Ruby Bates recanting her story, it would be fifteen long years before members of the Scottsboro Boys regained their freedom. This trial exposed the justice system as blatantly unfair to Black people from arraignment to jury selection. The concept that these Black men were innocent before proven guilty or that they should be treated fairly simply did not exist.

Early in *A Lesson Before Dying* a jury of twelve white males will decide the ultimate fate of Jefferson who is charged with a white man's violent murder and the robbery of a liquor store. According to the ethics of Jim Crow society, a Black man who could murder a white man could also rape and murder a white woman, and white society must be protected from this societal threat. Paradoxically, Jefferson's white defense lawyer draws on the philosophy of Thomas Jefferson to defend his young Black client from almost certain death by the white body politic. Despite his majestically worded document explicating freedom, justice, and equality, Jefferson's political philosophy advocating white supremacy stands as America's linchpin of racial hegemony. Pondering the place of Blacks in America, Thomas Jefferson believed they should be returned to Africa. In *Notes on the State of Virginia* (1793), Jefferson, a wealthy white landowner, who owned over two hundred Black slaves, has a "suspicion" that Black people are inherently physically and intellectually inferior to white people:

> I advance it therefore as a suspicion only, that the Blacks, whether originally a distinct race, or made distinct by time and circumstances, are inferior to the whites in the endowments both of body and mind. It is not against experience to suppose that different species of the same genus, or varieties of the same species, may possess different qualifications. Will not a lover of natural history then, one who views the gradations in all the races of animals with the eye of philosophy, excuse an effort to keep those in the department of man as distinct as nature has formed them? This unfortunate difference of colour, and perhaps of faculty, is a powerful obstacle to the emancipation of these people. (143)

Prefiguring the survival of the fittest theory and the eugenics movement in the 1920s, Jefferson's discourse of biological essentialism rationalized the continued enslavement of African people and laid the philosophical foundation for Black people to always be considered intellectually inferior and aesthetically repulsive. Using the strategy of reverse psychology, the white lawyer defiantly claims that Jefferson is intellectually incapable of murder and robbery and that the two Black men, Brother and Bear,[10] who were killed were solely responsible for the death of Alcee Grope. The defense lawyer argues that the money that Jefferson took from the cash register was an act of "hunger and plain stupidity" (7). Gaines' description of the aftermath of the shootout aptly conveys Jefferson's hunger and ignorance.

> He [Jefferson] looked from one dead body to the other. He didn't know whether he should call someone on the telephone or run. He had never dialed a telephone in his life, but he had seen other people use them. He didn't know what to do. He was standing by the liquor shelf, and suddenly he realized he needed a drink and needed it badly. He snatched a bottle off the shelf, wrung off the cap, and turned up the bottle, all in one continuous motion. The whiskey burned him like fire—his chest, his belly, even his nostrils...Now he began to realize where he was. Now he began to realize fully what had happened. Now he knew he had to get out of there. He turned. He saw the money in the cash register, under the little wire clamps. He knew taking money was wrong. His nanna had told him never to steal. He didn't want to steal. But he didn't have a solitary dime in his pocket. And nobody was around, so who could say he stole it? Surely not one of the dead men. (6)

Obviously, it never occurs to Jefferson that white people outside heard the shots and would come to investigate. So Jefferson is found by two white men with "the money stuffed inside his jacket pocket, the half bottle of whiskey clutched in his hand" (6). A further irony is that Jefferson (without a "solitary dime in his pocket") was on his way to the White Rabbit Bar and Lounge when he encountered Brother and Bear. Reinforcing and reinscribing Thomas Jefferson's philosophy of white supremacy, the white lawyer, in a dehumanizing effort to save the Black Jefferson from a legalized lynch-burning in the electric chair, importunes the twelve "honorable" white men on the jury:

> '*Look at the shape of this skull, this face is flat as the palm of my hand—look deeply into these eyes.* Do you see a modicum of intelligence? Do you see anyone here who could plan a murder, a robbery, can plan—can plan—can plan anything? A cornered animal to strike quickly out of fear, a trait inherited from his ancestors in the deepest jungle of Blackest Africa—yes, yes, that he can do—but to plan? To plan, gentlemen of the jury? No gentlemen this skull here holds no plans. What you see here is a thing that acts on command. A thing to hold the handle of a plow, a thing to load your bales of cotton, a thing to dig your ditches, to chop your wood, to pull your corn....What justice would there be to take this life? Justice gentlemen? Why, I would just as soon put a hog in the electric chair as this.' (7–8 emphasis added)

This passage is intriguing in a number of aspects concerning Black male subjectivity. First, the white court-appointed defense attorney signifies on creationists Louis Agassiz and Samuel George Morton and evolutionists Paul Broca and Francis Galton who exploit the data of brain size to make their invalid and invidious distinctions among different racial groups. Essentially the morphological argument is that Black people have smaller brains and posterior prominences when compared to whites. During the 1920s, eugenicists like Henry H. Goddard would extend the range of social phenomena caused by differences in innate intelligence until it encompassed almost everything that concerns human behavior. As a proponent of scientific racism, Goddard states: "The people who are doing the drudgery are as a rule in their proper places" (Gould, 161). Of course, this suggests the Hamitic myth that Black people as slaves are forever to be the carriers of water and hewers of wood, and any attempt by Blacks to transcend this position is against natural law. The reference to the "deepest jungles of Blackest Africa," beyond being blatantly racist, conjures up images from Joseph Conrad's *Heart of Darkness* (1920), in which an entire continent becomes defined by violence, disease, death, and chaos. *Heart of Darkness* suggests that this is the natural result when racist white men are allowed to operate outside a socioeconomic system with safeguards and stability: power, especially power over other human beings, inevitably corrupts. At the same time, this begs the question of whether it is possible to call an individual insane or wrong when he is part of a system that is so thoroughly corrupted and corrupting. *Heart of Darkness,* thus, at its most abstract level, is a narrative about the difficulty of understanding the world beyond the self, about the ability of one man to judge another. One quote from this novel suggests a connection to *A Lesson Before Dying:* "The conquest of the earth, which mostly means the taking it away from those who have a different complexion or *slightly flatter noses than ourselves,* is not a pretty thing when you look into it too much" (4, emphasis added). Obviously the analogy between imperialism and Jim Crow segregation comes to mind as Jefferson is a creation of this oppressive system and his freedom is being taken away.

According to the white lawyer, Jefferson's lack of intelligence and inability to plan a murder and a robbery have their origins in biology and not in the socioeconomic conditions in a Jim Crow society with its philosophy of interposition and nullification. Even still, the tragic results of segregation's waste land such as mendicancy, analphabetism, and crime are used as the justification for the continuance of bigotry. Like a mule, Jefferson becomes a "thing" to fulfill the wishes of white men on the jury who now sit in judgment. For these white males, Jefferson may be viewed as some wild hog, who must be killed and who must be a lesson to other Black males. By focusing on Jefferson's Black body, the white defense attorney reinforces and reinscribes the aesthetics of white supremacy. As Cornel West argues in *Race Matters* (1993):

> White supremacist ideology is based first and foremost on the degradation of black bodies in order to control them. One of the best ways to instill fear in people

is to terrorize them. Yet this fear is best sustained by convincing them that their bodies are ugly, their intellect is inherently underdeveloped, their culture is less civilized, and their future warrants less concern that that of other peoples. Two hundred and forty-four years of slavery and nearly a century of institutionalized terrorism in the forms of segregation, lynchings, and second-class citizenship in America were aimed at precisely this devaluation of black people. (85)

Quite simply, West's analysis confirms that the white defense attorney's characterizations go to the heart of white supremacist culture; Jefferson is not only dangerous and illiterate, but he is characterized as physically repulsive. It could be argued that in the minds of the all-white jury and all white supremacists that the two most heinous crimes a Black man could commit are the killing of a white man and the rape of a white woman, and any Black man who would attempt or commit one could easily commit the other. It is in this context that Jefferson's trial and execution can be characterized as a legal lynching, an act that helps to solidify the racial subordination of African Americans while reinforcing the culture of Jim Crow segregation. Timothy V. Kaufman-Osborn makes the connection between the extra-legal and legal operations of justice: "Whereas lynching visibly marked the bodies of its victims as black and so reconsolidated the color line that was indispensable to the reproduction of racial subordination, key elements of the contemporary practice of capital punishment veil that line and so render its contribution to racial subordination more difficult to apprehend and so to contest" (23). Jefferson and his black body become part of America's history with Black people being the most visible objects of racist white people's public consumption of blackness. Despite his reverse psychology, the white defense attorney's dehumanizing rhetoric paradoxically seals Jefferson's tragic fate by marking his body for ritualistic consumption. At the very core of white supremacy is the reduction of Black people to bodies or commodities of complex histories. As a representation of the white community and Jim Crow segregation, the all-white male jury's culpability is displaced as black criminality and violence legitimize Jefferson's execution.

Lastly, the defense lawyer connecting Black men to bestiality makes the grossly offensive analogy of Jefferson and a hog. Coincidentally, one of the main economic resources in the town is "a slaughter house mostly for hogs" (25), and like a beast in the marketplace, Jefferson faces slaughter. By using the word "hog" the white lawyer encapsulates the horror of Black people's enslavement; and Jefferson's godmother "heard nothing said in the courtroom. Not by the prosecutor; not by the defense attorney... (Oh yes, she heard one word—one word for sure: 'hog')" (4). As a "hog," the young Black Jefferson becomes another thing for racist male whites to slaughter, to consume, and to debauch. Also, the genetic connotation is equally disturbing, if Jefferson is a hog, then Miss Emma Glenn is a sow. A deep sense of shame becomes established here, despite the white lawyer's attempts to plead for mercy. Like naked Blacks on the auction blocks, Jefferson and his godmother become vulnerable to shame. As articulated by Gershen Kaufman and Lev Raphael in *Coming out of Shame*, the transgenerational transgression of trauma is rooted in shame:

> Shame is a deeply disturbing human emotion that becomes triggered anew throughout the life cycle, from birth to death. Shame is by no means confined to just one time of life. During each successive, unfolding phase of development from childhood and adolescence and old age, there are distinctive sources of shame. It is ever-present in our lives, however masked it may be. This perplexing emotion is also passed from generation to the next; the transfer is mediated directly by critical scenes of shame which become internalized through imagery but which then are reactive and reenacted with others. (quoted in *Rock My Soul*, 37)

As she grew up during the period of Jim Crow segregation, there is little doubt that Emma Glenn has experienced many incidents that have brought her deep-seated feelings of masked and unmasked shame; hearing Jefferson labeled a "hog" represents a continuation of this unmasked shame.

Equally significant, Gaines directly signifies on Claude McKay's powerful poem of resistance to racist violence during the "Red Summer," a period of race riots in major cities such as New York, Chicago and Washington, DC. In its entirety "If We Must Die" (1919) reads:

> If we must die, let it not be like hogs
> Hunted and penned in an inglorious spot,
> While round us bark the mad and hungry dogs,
> Making their mock at our accursed lot.
> If we must die, O let us nobly die,
> So that our precious blood may not be shed
> In vain; then even the monsters we defy,
> Shall be constrained to honor us though dead!
> O kinsmen! we must meet the common foe!
> Though far outnumbered let us show brave,
> And for their thousand blows deal one deathblow!
> What though before us lies the open grave?
> Like men we'll face the murderous, cowardly pack,
> Pressed to the wall, dying, but fighting back![11]

McKay's poem articulates Miss Emma's unrelenting desire for her godson to die like a man with respect and dignity because at this point Jefferson is emptied of his agency and can only be read as the material signifier of the marginalized position accorded him in southern racial discourse. By naming the young Black protagonist, Jefferson, Gaines symbolizes the mythological and morphological Black male image in the white mind of wealthy white supremacists as Thomas Jefferson, a rather paradoxical spokesman for the

American Enlightenment. The Black Jefferson (known by one name) suggests the practice of the slave being named for the master and the Hegelian dialectic of the slave and master.

Pained by the white lawyer's analogy of a young Black man as swine and the genetic connotation, Jefferson's godmother, Miss Emma Glenn, and Tante Lou harangue Grant Wiggins in their attempt to have Jefferson die with dignity, but at every turn, an embittered Grant becomes emasculated, humiliated, and symbolically castrated (ritualistically lynched) by white men in power. The legacy for the Black man's emasculation resides in the enslavement of Black people. By using the name Grant, Gaines conjures up the historical and libratory significance of Ulysses S. Grant, who with his unrelenting assault led the Northern troops during the bloody Civil War, leading to the legal emancipation of Black people. (Paradoxically, history reveals that Ulysses S. Grant was not shy in admitting that, especially in his early military career; he was often frightened and would rather have been somewhere else when the bullets were flying.) Ulysses S. Grant also attempted to eradicate the Ku Klux Klan. The Klan was founded in 1865 by veterans of the Confederate Army to restore white supremacy in the aftermath of the Civil War. The Klan resisted Reconstruction by intimidating northern whites and free Blacks. The KKK quickly adopted violent methods; the increasing murders finally resulted in a backlash among Southern elites, who viewed the Klan's excesses as an excuse for federal troops to continue occupation. The organization declined from 1868 to 1870 and was destroyed for a time by President Ulysses S. Grant's prosecution and enforcement under the Civil Rights Act of 1871. One of the chief reasons for this act's passage was to protect southern blacks from the Ku Klux Klan by providing a civil remedy for abuses then being committed in the South. The statute has been subject to only minor changes since then but has been the subject of voluminous interpretation by courts. Grant' Wiggins' humiliation in his journey to liberate Jefferson from an undignified death begins when he has to escort Miss Emma and his Aunt Lou "up the quarter" to the home of the brother-in-law of the white sheriff, Henri Pichot. Miss Emma's request for Jefferson's life before death is concise and straightforward: "I don't want them to kill no hog," she said. "I want a man to go to that chair, on his own two feet" (13). Miss Emma is truly heroic in her desire to save Jefferson from a humiliating and shameful death and by extension prevent her own humiliation and shame. Emmett Till's death in Money, Mississippi, recalls another Black woman's heroism in having the casket open during his funeral in Chicago despite the horrific smell. Mamie Till-Mobley recalls:

> It was the most terrible odor. We began to smell it about two blocks from the funeral home as we drove toward it. *At first, I thought about the stockyard, where they slaughtered hogs and cattle.* There was always a lingering odor from the

stockyards that you could pick up even fifteen blocks away. This was much worse.
This was overpowering. And the closer we got, the worse it got. It was the smell
of death and it was everywhere. It seemed to cut a pathway right to the top of
my skull. I will never forget that smell. It was Emmett. (*Death of Innocence*, 132;
emphasis added)

Considering the analogy of Jefferson and a hog, Miss Emma's reference to
"his own two feet" eschews the implicit redundancy. Grant's trenchant and
sarcastic response to this request reveals his sense of emasculation; he tells
Miss Emma, "...I teach what the white folks around here tell me to teach—
reading, writing, and 'rithmetic. They never told me how to keep a Black boy
out of a liquor store" (13). Grant's slave-like response underscores his feelings
of emasculation even in the classroom. Grants' response also underscores
how some Blacks knowingly or unknowingly reinforce racism and white
supremacy but justify their behavior by articulating this is what they must do
to keep their position. Upon reaching Pichot's "antebellum house," like a
slave, Grant, with the two old Black women, has to go to the side gate and
through the backdoor of this former white slave master's house. The irony
here is that Tante Lou never wanted Grant to go through the backdoor once
he left the Quarter[12] for the university ten years ago. Grant recalls his Aunt
Lou proudly telling him: "Me and Emma can make out all right without you
coming through that back door ever again" (19). Grant encounters a double-
edged shame and humiliation because these Black women make him revisit
his powerlessness, and he becomes silently enraged as Miss Emma importunes Henri Pichot to ask the sheriff, Sam Guidry, for permission to allow
Grant to visit her godson, Jefferson who is "...locked up in that cage like an
animal" (182). Grant remembers that Miss Emma's connection to the Pichot
plantation goes back to the days of slavery: "She had cooked for the old
Pichots, the parents of Henri Pichot. She had cooked for Henri and his
brother and sister, as well as for his nieces and nephews....She cooked, she
ran the house; my aunt washed and ironed; and I ran through the yard to get
things they needed to cook or cook with" (18). Drawing on this past service,
Miss Emma requests that Grant be allowed to visit Jefferson; she tells Henri
Pichot, *"I didn't raise no hog and I don't want no hog to go set in that chair.* I want a
man to go set in that chair, Mr. Henri" (emphasis added 20). Miss Emma's
statement conveys the central narrative desire which brings conflict to the
older Black women and Grant along with conflict between Grant and Jefferson
and Grant and Sheriff Guidry. Here, Grant is only tolerated by Henri because
of his relationship to Miss Emma and Grant is repeatedly questioned about
putting Miss Emma up to this. As a schoolteacher, Grant realizes that he is "too
educated for Henri Pichot; he had no use for me at all anymore" (20). Clearly,
in a Jim Crow society, an educated Black man who does not know his place is
an abomination for most white males like Henri Pichot, especially because

most of the Black labor is needed for framing and harvesting sugarcane. Indeed, the reduced school year is based on Black children supporting their families in the fields. Hence the education of Black children is antithetical to white power, white wealth, and white leisure.

Grant's humiliation by racist white males begins when he is summoned to the Pichot household by an old Black man, Farrell Jarreau, "a messenger to run errands" for Henri Pichot. Before this, Grant Wiggins's conversation with his light-skinned girlfriend, Vivian Baptiste, at the Rainbow Club reveals his frustrations about being put in a situation in which he has little control and little power, a situation where his charge is to transform a "hog" into a Black man with a presence commanding respect from the white males who will execute him. An aggravated Grant asks the married but separated Vivian, "Do I know what a man is? Do I know how a man is supposed to die? I'm still trying to find out how a man should live. Am I supposed to tell someone how to die who has never lived?" And then he arrogantly asks, "Why not let the hog die without knowing anything?" (31). Reinforcing the novel's structure of paradox, Grant confesses that his own masculinity is an issue in this racist society; Jefferson's condition is even worse because he "has never lived" and soon will be executed. Regardless of one's status, these questions reveal the spirit-crushing nature of life in a Jim Crow society for Black men. Grant and Vivian are schoolteachers, but Grant, who teaches in a plantation church, seems especially affected by the inherent narrow-mindedness of whites. With the school being a church and being on the former Pichot plantation, we sense the control that Henri Pichot has over Grant and other Black workers. A frustrated Grant expresses his desire to go someplace where he feels that he is living, but like many Blacks who sacrifice themselves and have to bear the burdens for other Black people, Vivian conscientiously reminds him of their societal commitment, a commitment to teach impoverished Black children like Jefferson.

Understanding the larger issue of sacrifice and commitment, Vivian persuades Grant to visit Jefferson if he obtains permission; Grant is allowed to ask to make the visits only after waiting nearly two and a half hours standing in Pichot's kitchen, while the white males eat, drink, and socialize. Grant's sense of self-respect and dignity will not allow him to sit in the kitchen or accept any food from the Black cook, Inez. Inez informs Grant that "Mr. Louis in there trying to get a bet" (43). Here powerful white males are betting whether Grant can get Jefferson 'ready to die' (43). Like wealthy white males at a horse race or a cockfight, these white males reduce Jefferson to an animal, betting "a whole case of whiskey" (43) on whether he will die as a man or like the dumb hog that they think he represents. While waiting to see Sam Guidry and Henri Pichot, Grant considers the reality of Jim Crow etiquette: "Whether I should act like the teacher that I was, or like the nigger that I was supposed to be....To show too much intelligence would have been an insult to them. To show a lack of intelligence would have been a greater insult to me" (41). Once he is allowed into the dining room, Grant is viewed as a "smart nigger" when he chooses not to respond to a question that would force him to side either with Sheriff Sam Guidry or with Guidry's wife. Grant's response: "I make it a habit never to get into family business" (49). Ironically, Grant is here on "family business" because Jefferson belongs to everyone in the Black community, especially Tante Lou and Miss Emma. Since Grant lives with his Tante Lou, her "family business" becomes his business as well. At this point, Grant lacks the awareness to see any connection to his teaching and helping Jefferson die with dignity. His rage in being forced into this obsequious position blinds him. Although Grant is allowed to visit Jefferson, Guidry expresses his desire to "...see a contented hog go to that chair than an aggravated hog" (49) and with echoes of the white defense attorney's discourse and eugenics movement he proclaims "There ain't a thing you can put in that skull that ain't there already" (50). Interestingly, there is also a nameless white male repeatedly identified as the "fat man" who "grunted" and "snorted" during Sheriff Guidry's arrogantly hostile interrogation of Grant. Considering the references by Sheriff Guidry to Jefferson as a "hog," Gaines signifies that this derogatory term may be a psychological projection. It becomes clear to Grant that the decision to allow him to visit Jefferson has already been made, and this session is designed strictly to humiliate him. Along with Sheriff Guidry's overt racism, Grant receives specific instructions regarding bringing things to the jail and then he is dismissed. Guidry's instructions are full of contempt: "Don't bring anything up there you don't want taken away from you—knife, razor blade, anything made of glass. Not that I expect him to do anything—but you can never be sure" (50). It is not enough to insult Grant with his blatant racism but to suggest that the college-educated, Grant would bring these sharp items to the jail is absolutely preposterous. Grant is viewed as a "smart" nigger who is perhaps "just a little too smart" for his own good. Sam Guidry's contemptible and bitter sarcasm for Grant is evident when he tells him: "But I wouldn't plan on a diploma" (50). Once these four satiated whites leave the kitchen, a deeply shamed and humiliated Grant Wiggins leaves through the backdoor of Pichot's kitchen, remembering how Tante Lou and Miss. Emma stood there the night before begging Henri Pichot to talk to his brother-in-law, Sheriff Guidry.

Grant's frustration and humiliation extend to his position as a schoolteacher (of first to sixth grade), Black students from six years old to thirteen and fourteen. The physical conditions of the classroom in the church–school are disheartening and the resources are severely inadequate. Grant's students use the benches upon which their parents and grandparents sit during church meetings as desks and the "students either got down on their knees and used the benches as desks to write upon, or used the backs of their books upon their laps to write out their assignments" (34). Teaching only takes place during the five and a half months from late October to the middle of April, when the children are not needed in the cane fields. Grant's frustration of being thrust into this role of savior and the humiliation he has to endure are evident in the classroom. Grant informs his students of Jefferson's distressing fate and the assignment he is being coerced to perform:

> 'Do you know what his nannan wants me to do before they kill him? The public defender called him a hog, and she wants me to make him a man. Within the next few weeks, maybe a month, whatever the law allows—make him a man. Exactly what I'm trying to do here with you now to make you responsible young men and young ladies. But you prefer to play with bugs. You refuse to study your arithmetic, and you prefer writing slanted sentences instead of straight ones. Does that make any sense? Well does it?' (39)

Grant's arduous task is to attempt to help these Black students avoid the tangled of web of oppression spun by white people's pernicious hatred and the ensuing injustice that his former student, Jefferson, has encountered. Here the psychological weight of attempting to help Jefferson affects Grant's teaching. When a student is caught figuring a simple multiplication problem on his fingers, Grant "slashed him hard across the butt with the Westcott ruler…brought the Westcott down into his palm" (35–6). While Grant's specific frustration with regard to helping Jefferson, his behavior reflects the violence in Black schools after emancipation. Discussing the violence in black schools, in *Been in the Storm So Long* (1979), Leon F. Litwack explains:

> Whether deservedly or not, black teachers were reputed to be the harshest disciplinarians, and some of them refused to be defensive about it. After all, a black teacher in New Orleans noted many of his pupils had been plantation slaves and consequently knew no motive for obedience other than fear of punishment. 'Coax 'em and they'll laugh at you; you've got to knock 'em about, or they won't think you've got any power over 'em.' Nor were black parents necessarily averse to seeing their children punished, if necessary to instill proper learning habits, but they made it clear that they would tolerate a whipping only if meted out by "a Yankee teacher" and not a native white. (482)

Clearly the transgenerational transgression of trauma associated with physical violence in reflected in Grant's teaching and in the treatment of Jefferson. Separated from the other Black prisoners, because he is waiting for death, Jefferson can leave his six-foot by ten-foot cell once a week and spend an hour in the dayroom. The sparseness of the cell—one bunk, equipped with a mattress and a wool blanket, a toilet, a washbowl with only a single bulb hanging from the center of the ceiling and a small, high barred window—reinforces the depressing confinement. Once a week he obtains a shower (127). (Interestingly, Gaines mentions Angola Prison, which would have been where Jefferson would have served a life sentence if the all-white jury had spared his life.[13]) Like a tormented slave pinned in a cage, Jefferson's spirit up until this point seems to be broken by the incommodious space and humiliating conditions.

When the white superintendent of schools, Dr. Joseph Morgan visits Wiggins' classroom (with echoes of the days of slavery, Grant obtains the news from Farrell Jarreau who finds out from Henri Pichot), Grant's humiliation escalates, echoing similar treatment at Henri Pichot's house. He repeatedly calls Grant, "Higgins." Also, like naked enslaved African on the auction block whose orifices were penetrated, probed, and played with by lustful white males, this white man, "a short, fat man with a large red face and a double chin" (52) inspects the teeth of Grant's Black students, having "the poor children spreading out their lips as far as they could while he peered into their mouth" (52). Grant recalls: "At the university I had read about slave masters who had done the same when buying new slaves, and I had read of cattlemen doing it when purchasing horses and cattle" (56). Of course, Gaines' point here is to link the dehumanization of Jefferson and the less grotesque dehumanization of these children. When Grant notifies the superintendent that he needs more books, chalk, pencils, paper and a better heater, the dismissing response is, "We're all in the same shape, Higgins" (57). This white man's tone and attitude suggest that he views Grant as an uppity or "smart nigger" who does not know his place. He asks him, "Are you questioning me, Higgins?" Thoroughly exasperated, the superintendent's visit concludes with him telling Grant, "More drill on the flag" and "More emphasis on hygiene" (57). Grant again challenges him on the issue of hygiene concerning toothbrushes, and the white man's response glaringly reveals the disturbing image of Blacks in the mind of many whites. Once outside the classroom, the superintendent points out the hundreds of pecan trees in the yard; he tells Grant: "Get them off their lazy butts, they can make enough for a dozen toothbrushes in one evening" (58). Like the abject humiliation and disrespect that Grant encounters in Henri Pichot's kitchen, we view his emasculation in this plantation school as this superintendent–teacher relationship represents the Hegelian master–slave dialectic. The added insult here is that Grant Wiggins is disrespected in his own classroom in front of his own students and at time when he is under pressure to transform Jefferson into a man. However, Gaines uses the motif of the white man as pig again as it relates to Dr. Morgan whose "large stomach nearly touched the edge of the table" (54). When Dr. Morgan gets out of his car he "grunted and looked around the yard," when he sits down at the desk he "grunted, which meant thanks" and "grunted" when asking the children questions. Like the "fat man" in Pichot's dining room, Dr. Morgan is portrayed as a hog engaged in excessive consumption. As in lynching where the Black victims were dehumanized by being torture, mutilated, and killed, the dehumanization of the participants is also evident. To be involved in the heinous ritual of a lynching results in the loss of one's humanity; these individuals are forever changed because both witnesses and the victim are traumatized. By extension the entire system of Jim Crow dehumanizes all people with counterfeit notions of racial superiority or racial inferiority. Clearly, the confrontation between Dr. Morgan and Grant Wiggins suggests the *Brown vs. Board of Education* decision of 1954 which legally sounded the death knell for the philosophy of "separate but equal" for the different races; thus making the *Plessy v. Ferguson* decision of 1986 unconstitutional.[14] Despite this decision, the law only applied to public education, and it had little effect on the culture of racism and white supremacy. As John P. Muffler points out: "States, local districts and now even the federal government have used a variety of means to circumvent the spirit and intent of both *Brown I* and Civil Rights Acts" (35). Equally important, Black children in predominantly white schools faced some of the most vicious psychological aspects of white supremacy and racism. Drawing on her own childhood, bell hooks deftly argues that desegregation produced trauma for many Black children:

> The self-esteem that had been fostered in a social and political atmosphere of racial uplift was assaulted in the world of racial integration. Black folks living in segregation worlds who had spent only a measure of their lives thinking about white folks were more and more becoming obsessed with race. Naturally, the more contact we had with white folks the more intensely we experienced racist assaults. Even the well-meaning and kind white teachers often believed racist stereotypes. We were never away from the surveillance of white supremacy in the world of racial integration. And it was this constant reality that began to undermine the foundation of self-esteem in the lives of black folks. (*Rock My Soul*, 13)

Institutionalized racism at Jefferson's trial becomes mirrored in the area of education by Dr. Morgan's sustained focus on nutrition and hygiene, as Grant relates:

> Finally, when he felt that he had inspected enough mouths and hands, he gave the school a ten-minute lecture on nutrition. Beans were good, he said. Not only just good, but very, very good. Bean, beans, beans—he must have said beans a hundred times. Then he said fish and greens were good. And exercise was good. In other words, hard work was good for the young body. Picking cotton, gathering potatoes, pulling onions, working in the garden—all of that was good exercise for a growing boy or girl. (56)

Under white supremacy the education of Black children is designed to support the socio-economic structure of racism. Like the process of fattening frogs for snakes, Black children are to be miseducated to serve the economic needs of the dominant white society. Here with Dr. Morgan's focus on "picking cotton" and other manual labor, Black children are reminded that their present is connected to their ancestors' enslavement. As Leon F. Litwack argues in *Trouble in Mind: Black Southerners in the Age of Jim Crow*:

> The history to which black children were exposed in the classroom and the primers made a virtual gospel of the superiority of Anglo-Saxon institutions and ways of thinking and acting. They imbibed the same lessons taught in the white schools, essentially a sanitized history of Anglo-Saxons and northern Europeans: Pilgrims, Puritans, and Founding Fathers. It was not their history, nor had it much relevance to their lives or to the lives of their parents and neighbors. What little they learned of their own history consisted often of disparaging caricatures of black people as the least civilized of the races—irresponsible, thoughtless, foolish, childlike people, satisfied with their lowly place in American life, incapable of self-control and self-direction. The history of black people was a history of submission gladly endured and of services faithfully rendered. Transported from the darkness of heathen Africa to the civilized and Christian New World, grateful slaves found contentment and happiness. Illustration of blacks, if they appeared at all, depicted well-fed, carefree laborers frolicking in the fields: amiable, deferential Uncle Toms greeting their patronizing and loving masters, hat in hand, evincing a demeanor of contentment, docility, and faithfulness. The occasional malcontent, like a Nat Turner, was said only to have launched a "horrible massacre" that killed many innocent white people. The treatment of emancipation depicted blacks passively waiting for Massa' Lincoln to strike off their shackles. And Reconstruction saw the enthronement of black ignorance and inexperience, with the Ku Klux Klan in some accounts redeeming Anglo-Saxon civilization from alien rule. (71)

With Grant telling Miss Emma and Tante Lou that "I teach what the white people folks around here tell me to teach" (13), we understand how he has become socialized to support a system of institutionalized white supremacy. Like a good and subservient house slave, Grant does what he is told but being forced into helping Jefferson, Grant has to learn some new sociological lessons. Lastly, Gaines contextualizes Grant's humiliation by his visit to Henri Pichot's house and the visit by Dr. Joseph Morgan; in both incidents Grants is demeaned, however, white males are characterized as gluttonous livestock.

The sociological content for Grant Wiggins's constant humiliation and his desire to escape Jim Crowism reside in his relationship with another teacher—his mentor, Matthew Antoine. Antoine, Grant's former teacher, was a big Creole mulatto from Poulaya who "hated himself for the mixture of his blood and the cowardice of his being and he hated us [Black students] for daily reminding him of it...He could teach any of us only one thing and that one thing was flight" (62–63). Forced to retire because of ill health, Matthew's self-hatred and pain are so pervasive that he is constantly cold. Frantz Fanon reminds us that many of the psychological problems of the oppressed result from their slavish socioeconomic conditions and an epiderminization of inferiority. Fanon argues: "White men consider themselves superior to Black men. There is another fact: Black men want to prove to white men, at all costs, the richness of their thought, the equal value of their intellect."[15] Matthew reflects this racial paradigm. As a student in the same plantation school, Grant provokes more hatred from his mulatto teacher because he wanted to learn and because he challenges him when the other Black students do not. Matthew despises him because Grant wanted to teach and his gruesome advice to Grant reflects a vicious cycle of frustration produced by slavery's dehumanizing legacy: "When you see that those five and a half months you spend in that church each year are just a waste of time, you will. You will. You'll see that it'll take more than five and a half months to wipe away—peel—scrape away the blanket of ignorance that has been plastered and replastered over brains in the past three hundred years" (64). Likewise, Matthew, feeding his cancer of internalized white supremacy, reveals how interracial conflict breeds intraracial conflict because he defiantly tells Grant, "I am superior to any man Blacker than me" and he hates the dark-skinned, Grant "Because that superior sonofabitch out there said I am you" (65). As Kathy Russell, Midge Wilson, and Ronald Hall argue in *The Color Complex: The Politics of Skin Color Among African Americans* (2000):

> Several interrelated factors explain the 'light on top' phenomenon in Black America leadership. In a society that is politically and economically controlled by Whites, those members of minorities with the lightest skin and the most Caucasian-looking features have been allowed the greatest freedom. The unique privileges granted to mulattoes under slavery enabled them to advance further, educationally and occupationally, than Blacks who were dark skinned. The result was a leadership pool of light-skinned Blacks with both money and education. Within that pool, it was often those Blacks light enough to pass who became the Black community's most vocal and active leaders. (34–35)

Matthew's discourse of internalized white supremacy reveals the hypo descent theory that "one drop of Black blood" makes an individual Black; this theory marginalizes all Black people regardless of complexion. As Orlando Patterson points out, this theory fundamental to white supremacy is historical:

> This unusual mode of racial classification has a vicious ideological history rooted in the notion of racial purity and in the racist horror of miscegenation. Traditionally, it was used as a major ideological bulwark of legalized segregation, and was at the heart of the 'white' supremacist opposition to any form of integration. There is no gainsaying the fact that this conception of 'race' historically rationalized the most pernicious legal, social, and political injustices against Afro-Americans. (69)

Matthew's discourse reveals that the color hegemony supports the Jim Crow segregation that marginalizes him and his teaching. Before his death at the age of forty-three, Matthew advises Grant that, " 'You have to go away to know about life. There's no life here. There's nothing but ignorance here. You want to know about life? Well it's too late. Forget it. Just go on and be the nigger you were born to be, but forget about life ... Just do the best you can. But it won't matter' " (65–66). For Matthew Antoine, segregation breeds a profound sense of self-hatred despite his statements of innate superiority.

Intraracial prejudice as represented by Matthew Antoine is also evident in Grant's physical altercation with two mulatto bricklayers at the Rainbow Club. Miscegenation between white males and Black females during the period of enslavement produced light-skinned Black individuals who could either pass for white or claim color superiority. Some of these light-skinned Black individuals received preferential treatment by their white masters, and this among other factors created the intraracial conflict that developed during and after the brutal period of enslavement. While at the Club, these "two brick-colored bricklayers" make contemptible statements about Jefferson; Grant relates the legacy of their intraracial bigotry:

> Since emancipation, almost a hundred years ago, they would do any kind of work they could find to keep from working side by side in the field with the niggers. They controlled most of the bricklaying business in this part of the state. Even took that kind of work from the white boys, because they would do it so much cheaper than the white boys would. Anything not to work alongside the niggers. With school it was the same. Many of them would drop out of school, would get a trade—bricklayer or carpenter—rather than sit in class side by side with the niggers. Their sisters went to high school and college, but they would not. Rather take a trade than to sit next to the niggers. And these two who were talking now were of that way of thinking. Dumb as hell, but prejudiced as hell. They had no other place to go to do their drinking—they would not dare go to any of the white clubs—so they would come here and bring their prejudiced attitude with them. (198)

Incensed by their remarks that Jefferson should "have burned" months ago, Grant gets into a fight with them until the owner, Thelma Claiborne, breaks up the fight. Gaines point here and later with Paul Bonin is that racial conflict is complex between and within racial groups. With Grant willing to fight for Jefferson, it is clear that he may no longer view him as a hog and his understanding of his communal responsibility is increasing despite the bigotry he encounters. This physical confrontation represents Grant's frustration, a frustration he acknowledges has affected his sexual relationship: "Things have not been going too well for Vivian and me in bed, and I knew it was because of Jefferson, me worrying about him" (196). Vivian, who comes to aid Grant after the fight, has not adopted the bigotry that these mulatto individuals have internalized, and it is this characteristic that leads Miss Emma and Tante Lou to view her as a "lady of quality." It is difficult to imagine Grant going through this humiliating and emasculating process without the love and support of Vivian Baptiste.

Grant's initial visit with Miss Emma to the incarcerated Jefferson continues the teacher's humiliation and emasculation by white male authority figures. The Bayonne red-bricked courthouse with "a statue of a Confederate soldier" and "national, state, and Confederate flags" (68–69) becomes the place where Grant undertakes an process that gradually disrobes him of the subjectivity and self-esteem he has attained through his education at the university and being the only Black male school teacher in Bayonne. After the young white deputy goes through the basket of food and the handbag of clothes, Grant must empty his pockets and then be patted down to make sure he took everything out of his pockets; Grant relates that the chief white deputy, with a taxonomic gaze, who looks at him with contempt "didn't look decent at all" (70). Like Easy Rawlins going to meet DeWitt Albright, Grant Wiggins is treated like a "common criminal." Like the bathrooms in the courthouse and like all public parts of the town, the jail cells are segregated. "The white prisoners were also on this floor, but in a separate section" and Grant "counted eight cells for Black prisoners, with two bunks to each cell" (71). Here, Grant and Miss Emma encounter a rather taciturn Jefferson who does not acknowledge their presence and while lying on his bunk, mainly looks at the gray concrete ceiling. Like an animal in a enclosure, Jefferson has a desolate jail cell, roughly six by ten with only a "metal bunk covered by a thin mattress and a woolen army blanket; a toilet without a toilet seat or toilet paper; a washbowl, brownish from residue and grime, a small metal shelf upon which was a pan, a tin cup, and a tablespoon" (71). Being fixated only on his impending death, Jefferson's laconic statements center on his execution and he asks, Grant, if he's the one who will " 'jerk that switch.' " Jefferson's instinctive trepidation and anger are matched by Grant's own antagonism and frustration. Moreover, Grant senses that Jefferson mocks him with his questions of his former teacher playing a role in his execution, but, during slavery, white masters with their divide and conquer strategy, would routinely have slaves whip, torture, and discipline rebellious slaves. The perverse logic of racism is to achieve genocide. In Jefferson's cell, Miss Emma's fried chicken, bread, sweet potatoes, and tea cakes go uneaten; shortly, they leave, and she tells the white deputy to give any food that Jefferson does not eat to the "rest of them [Black] children" in the jail. Jefferson's unwillingness to eat Miss Emma's food represents his anger and denial of reality, the initial stages of psychological trauma. Like the fetal position that he assumes on the cot, Jefferson becomes childlike in his behavior. In a real sense, most racist whites view all Black people as children who can be treated as inferiors without reprisal, and Grant's humiliating visitations to Henri Pichot's kitchen and the Bayonne courthouse in support of Miss Emma and Jefferson take their toll on him; at some point, he defiantly tells Tante Lou:

> 'The humiliation I had to go through, going into that man's kitchen. The hours I had to wait while they ate and drank and socialized before they would even see me. Now going to that jail. To watch them put their dirty hands on that food. To search my body each time as if I'm some kind of common criminal. Maybe today they'll want to look into my mouth, or my nostrils, or make me strip. Anything to humiliate me. All the things you wanted me to escape by going to school. Years ago, Professor Antoine told me that if I stayed here, they were going to break me down to the nigger I was born to be. But he didn't tell me that my aunt would help them do it.' (79)

Here again Gaines makes the paradoxical point of a college-educated Black man being reduced to a slave-like individual in order to help an uneducated individual, foreshadowing a role reversal. In Grant's mind, he views his aunt as a co-conspirator in his emasculation, not realizing than his gender and status make him the best person to help Jefferson; of course, Grant's former teacher, Matthew Antoine taught him enough to allow him to be in a position to help Jefferson. Hence Grant's pain-filled proclamation represents the fundamental paradox in the novel. This paradox is compounded when one of the white deputies, Paul Bonin, shows Grant that he has a sincere concern for Jefferson; Paul hates having to search Grant when he visits and lets Grant know that he is just following the policy of the jail. Paul represents an exception to the other racist white men, especially those who are betting on how Jefferson will die. Jefferson's salvation will come through Grant's temporary emasculation. Although his Aunt Lou understands this fundamental paradox, Grant will gradually learn a lesson before Jefferson dies. In the face of ubiquitous racism, certain Black individuals such as Jackie Robinson and Joe Louis understood the value in acquiescing to tyrannical white authorities and individuals for the greater good of the Black community. Furthering the historical context to his novel, Gaines draws on the subjectivity of sports figures like Jackie Robinson and Joe Louis to signify on the relationship between Grant Wiggins and Jefferson. Jackie Robinson playing baseball for the Brooklyn Dodgers and Joe Louis fighting in the boxing ring, faced tremendous obstacles during a time when racial violence in the form of lynchings and race riots was widespread in major American cities. These heroic Black men represented redemptive forces for Black people all across America. Like the Black slaves who created folklore such as the Brer Rabbit and Brer Bear stories to dispel their just vehemence and frustrations with their white masters; these Black sports figures become larger than life heroes who fight the socioeconomic, political, and legal battles of all beleaguered Black people. While at the Rainbow Club, Grant encounters two old Black men proudly discussing the achievements of Jackie Robinson: "They could recall everything Jackie had done in the past two years. They remembered when he got his first hit, and who it was against. They remembered the first time he stole two bases in one game and the first time he stole home" (87). One of the men goes beyond just remembering and proudly acts out Jackie hitting the baseball and stealing the base as the other man validates his extemporaneous performance. And a seventeen-year-old Grant remembers the jubilation and the pride he saw "in those faces" when the Brown Bomber, Joe Louis, defeated Max Schmeling. Black heroes like Jackie Robinson and Joe Louis have a profound effect on Black communities, so profound that God becomes displaced as Grant recalls the story of a young boy in Florida crying as he is dragged to and strapped into the electric chair: "Please, Joe Louis, help me. Please help me. Help me...Mr. Joe Louis, help me. Mr. Joe Louis, help me" (91). Grant wonders if the young Jefferson in that "cold, depressing cell uptown" will "call on Jackie Robinson as the other one had called on Joe Louis" (91). The heroic actions of these Black men dramatically dispel the notion of white supremacy. Grant Wiggins will have to step up to the plate or go into the boxing ring in a similar fashion as Jackie Robinson and Joe Louis in his relationship with Jefferson to confront the prevailing philosophies of white supremacy.

Initially, the possibility of Jefferson calling on Jackie Robinson, Joe Louis, God, or anyone else is quite remote because when Grant visits him again without Miss Emma but with a bag of her food, Jefferson's behavior suggests that he has internalized the white supremacist ideology of his white defense lawyer. Jefferson, enraged and separated from his own sense of self-respect and dignity, believes he is an "old hog." When Grant asks, Jefferson if he is hungry, Jefferson, with an attitude of self-contempt asks, for corn because "That's what hogs eat" he says, turning his head now to look at Grant. Jefferson continues, "I'm a old hog they fattening to kill" (83). More disturbing, Jefferson prostrates himself on the cold floor and "put his head inside the bag and started eating without using his hands. He even sounded like a hog" (83). Gaines provides a profound characterization of Jefferson's deep-seated shame, a shame so profound that feels compelled to take on the role of a swine to hurt others. Here, like a slave who accepts his inferior status, Jefferson has seemingly accepted Thomas Jefferson view of Black people as beasts of burden. Grant begins to understand Jefferson's painful, cynical grin and his refrain of "That's how a old hog eat" as he attempts to make Grant feel guilty for being there. Gaines' point here is that both Black men are trapped: Jefferson is physically and psychologically trapped in jail and Grant is psychologically and physically trapped by his job and having been forced by Tante Lou to visit Jefferson. Unlike Jefferson, who mainly has the love and support of Miss Emma, Grant has the love and support of Vivian Baptiste. At this point, both Jefferson and Grant are depressed and in conflict with themselves and each other. Discussing how Black people have been transformed into aberrations of their true selves in *12 Million Black Voices*, Richard Wright can only say: "We Black men and women in America today, as we look back upon scenes of rapine, sacrifice, and death, seem to be a devilish aberration, descendants of an interval of nightmare in history, fledglings of a period of amnesia on the part of men who once dreamed a great dream and forgot" (27). This great American Dream has eluded both Grant and Jefferson as they wage a psychological warfare with each other in order to conceal their trauma. However, like a professor who challenges his fearful student who uses psychological projection as a defense mechanism to hide his or her intellectual inadequacies, Grant begins to confront Jefferson and asks him if he wants him to stay away and let the "white man" win the battle over his subjectivity. Perhaps Grant is thinking of the future of his most challenging student, Louis Washington, when he looks into Jefferson's anguished face and reflects on Vivian telling him to go to the jail "For us, Grant" (32). With no blackboard, chalk, or concrete lesson plan, Grant confronts Jefferson with his most formidable pedagogical task: transforming an old hog into a proud young Black man facing death by electrocution.

The novel confirms Grant's arduous task when Miss Emma goes to the jail cell with the Black preacher, Reverend Mose Ambrose. Jefferson again asks for corn and claims to be a hog. Screaming "You ain't no hog, you hear me? You ain't no hog" (122), Miss Emma slaps Jefferson, falls upon him, and cries. In a perverse manner Jefferson accepts the demeaning characterization because it allows him to be angry as a temporary way of dealing with the pain. Like the racist signifier "buck," the epithet "hog" conveys the Black man as some grotesque animal, incapable of reasoning and thought. As Leonard Cassuto explicates in *The Inhuman Race: The Racial Grotesque in American Literature and Culture* (1997): "The grotesque is a threat to the system of knowledge by virtue of its liminal position within that system. This liminality demands resolution; for a human being caught between the categories of human and thing, the pressure will be exerted toward a return to the human category, for that is the only choice that offers the possibility of resolution" (XVII). Back in the Quarter, saying that someone must do something for her before she dies, Miss Emma importunes Grant to go back to the jail and save her dehumanized and demoralized godson from a humiliating death. Still psychologically torn and wanting to flee, Grant responds to his aunt with rage: "What for, Tante Lou? He treated me the same way he treated her [Miss Emma]. He wants me to feel guilt, just as he wants her to feel guilt. Well. I'm not feeling guilty. Tante Lou. I didn't put him there. I do everything I know how to keep people like him from going there. He's not going to make me feel guilty" (123). Like a massive boulder in the road, Tante Lou's response is unwavering: "You going back....You ain't going to run from this, Grant" (123). Grant's tone reflects a sense of self-righteous-ness, especially since he says he only teaches what the white folks tell him to teach, and his repeated references to guilt suggest that he may feel guilty about how he teaches the Black children at his school. On the other hand, Tante Lou's response suggests that Grant Wiggins has "run away" before or that she has experienced other Black men running from their responsibili-ties. There is even the possibility that Tante Lou will not allow Grant to do what Grant's father did, run away from his responsibilities. Gaines' narrative silence on the subject of Jefferson's father and Grant's father suggests the issue of natal alienation and the ensuing trauma of young Black men not knowing and having the guidance of their fathers. Thus the teacher–student relationship between Grant and Jefferson morphs into a father–son relation-ship.

Grant's next visit results in more conversation with Jefferson, but the increasingly surly and distraught prisoner bitterly accuses his former teacher of vexing him. Not knowing that Vivian Baptiste ardently supports Grant Wiggins, Jefferson, revealing his intraracial color complex, disrespects the couple by telling Grant that his light-skinned girlfriend is an "old yellow woman" and further that "Her old pussy ain't no good" (129, 130). Suspending the desire to whack Jefferson with his fist, Grant tells him that his "lady," keeps him coming to "this damn hole" (130). However, the psychologically beneficial aspect of Jefferson's mean-spirited verbal attacks is that he articulates his indignation as opposed to denial and silent seeth-ing. Equally important, Jefferson's verbal attack conveys his lack of sexual experience and the reality that he will never have any sexual experience with a Black woman like Vivian or have any children. Indeed, there is no narrative evidence to suggest that Jefferson ever had a girlfriend or any sexual encounter. Out of frustration, Jefferson attacks Grant via Vivian's sexuality. The issue of the womb is also suggested here because Jefferson was in a fetal position during the first visit and now he makes a crude attack on Vivian's genitalia. There is no reference to Jefferson's mother in the novel, and Vivian might represent a surrogate mother figure who makes Grant go to the jail. As Vivian is light-skinned, there is the added possibility that Jefferson resents Grant because of her skin color. His anger causes him to associate Vivian with a more privileged class. As bell hooks argues in *Rock My Soul: Black People and Self-Esteem,* this association is rooted in slavery:

> Long after slavery ended, a more privileged class of black folks who were fairer skinned participated in creating and sustaining hierarchical and social arrange-ments where they lorded it over their darker counterparts. Since they often lacked concrete material privilege, skin color itself became the mark of status. Like the racist white master and mistress, a fair-skinned black person could deploy sham-ing on the basis of color to ridicule and treat contempt darker folk. Naturally,

individual dark-skinned black folks rebelled against this internalization of racist thinking, but their rebellion did not win the day. (39)

Still, Jefferson's anger aimed at Grant and indirectly targeting Vivian humanizes him. In essence, Jefferson begins to break through the psychological trauma created by white supremacy. As Judith Lewis Herman articulates in *Trauma and Recovery*:

> The knowledge of horrible events periodically intrudes into public awareness but is rarely retained for long. Denial, repression, and disassociation operate on a social as well as an individual level. The study of psychological trauma has an "underground" history. Like traumatized people, we have been cut off from the knowledge of our past. Like traumatized people, we need to understand the past in order to reclaim the present and the future. Therefore, an understanding of psychological trauma begins with rediscovering history. (2)

Gaines' characterizations of Jefferson reveal that he has gone through the psychological stages of trauma outlined by Herman and that Grant, as a result of being forced into this situation, undergoes a similar process of denial, repression, and disassociation.

Grant draws on the history on Black people being continually traumatized by white people and their resistance in order to transform Jefferson from "an old hog" to a Black man. The transformation slowly approaches its apex when the sheriff allows Jefferson to meet his visitors in the dayroom. Grant narrates that a psychologically beaten Jefferson enters the dayroom "shackled, walking with short steps, his head bowed and his shoulders stooped...his shoulders hanging low and closer together than they should be" (137). Gaines uses a number of paradoxical analogies to comment on Jefferson's low-spirited subjectivity. First, the food presented to Jefferson reflects an antilogy; there are pork chops. Pork, especially the internal organs of hogs (chitterlings), a rather staple food during slavery and in the present Black community, is being given to a Black man who views himself as a hog. Making the Jeffersonian analogy between "youmans" and himself, he says, "Hog don't give nothing. Hogs don't leave nothing...This hog know. Fattening, up for Christmas. Kill him at Christmastime" (139, 140). Second, with this occurring before the Christmas season, Jefferson inquires about Christ's birth and death. Constructing an analogy between Christ and Jefferson, Gaines juxtaposes a crucifixion with a lynching with Jefferson as the sacrificial hog going to the slaughter. Like Richard Wright's surreal poem "Between the World and Me" that describes a horrific lynch-burning, religious signification and personification make the connection between Jesus Christ and thousands of Black men being mutilated and brutally lynched. In the poem where the narrator metamorphoses into the tortured Black male victim, Wright writes, "There was a charred stump of a sapling pointing a blunt finger accusingly at the sky."[16] Using personification and religious signification, Wright illustrates Christ on the cross who asks God why he was forsaken. With the tar and feathered lynched-burned Black man unable to articulate the horror of his barbarian murder, the sapling that he is bound to symbolically asks God, why did He forsake this man as "through the morning air the sun poured yellow surprise into the eye sockets of a stony skull" (437). Unlike this nameless Black man, Jefferson does have his godmother, Miss Emma, who supplicates God, "What I done done? What I done my Master to deserve this?" (122) Consequently, Gaines's narrative structure and signification straightforwardly convey that Jefferson, an innocent victim, symbolizes a modern-day Christ figure bound not to a cross but soon to be bound to an electric chair.

Like the symbolism of Jefferson as a hog, Gaines' use of Jefferson as a Christ figure is significant. In other texts by Gaines such as "The Sky Is Gray" the role of religion is paradoxical; in this short story a Black preacher is characterized as a supporter of Black people's oppression when in a white dentist's office he tells Black people that they should not question God or the reality of their lives under Jim Crow. A young Black man challenges the preacher: "You believe in God because a man told you to believe in God....A white man told you to believe in God. And why? To keep you ignorant so he can keep his feet on your neck" (96). In a non-Christian manner the preacher slaps the young man who turns the other cheek. We witness a similar confrontation between Grant and Reverend Ambrose, but Jefferson as a Chris-figure configures the synthesis of these two Black men and represents a new form of religion. As argued by Lee Papa: "Instead, Gaines is indicating that the appearance of a new Christ means the dawn of a new religion on the terms of the black characters, not a revisiting of the repressive system of Christianity that has been forced on them....For Ernest J. Gaines' characters, the greatest leaps forward are instigated by the inward search for the old—self and culture and community—which can create the new" (192). Like the young Black man in "The Sky Is Gray" Jefferson represents a new hope in religion and racial relationships.

Unlike Miss Emma who questions her fate and the burden placed on her, Grant speculates on the socioeconomic factors that have led to Jefferson's tragic fate. He asks, "When will a man not have to struggle to have money to get what he needs....When will a man be able to live without having to kill another man?" (174). By understanding his own subjectivity, Grant communicates to Vivian the paradox that all Black men like Jefferson and himself face living in the South:

> We Black men have failed to protect our women since the time of slavery. We stay
> here in the South and are broken, or we run away and leave them alone to look
> after the children and themselves. So each time a male child is born, they hope

he will be the one to change this vicious circle—which he never does. Because even though he wants to change it, and maybe even tries to change it, it is too heavy a burden because of all the others who have run away and left their burden behind. So he, too must run away if he is to hold on to his sanity and have a life of his own....They [the women and girls] look at their fathers, their grandfathers, their uncles, their brothers—all broken. They see me—and I, who grew up on that same plantation, can teach reading, writing, and arithmetic. I can give them something that neither a husband, a father, nor a grandfather ever did, so they want to hold on as long as they can. Not realizing that their holding on will break me too. That in order for me to be what they think I am, what they want me to be, I must run as the others have done in the past. (167)

Grant who has learned to "wear the mask" believes that it will be Jefferson who will take this burden of Black masculinity. However, the concept of Black masculinity is extremely problematic within a white supremacist culture that by definition must keep all Black males in a subordinate position. Grant is viewed as a "smart nigger" who is emasculated at the jail, at his own school, and at Pichot's house. Grant has the respect of the Black community because of his middle-class status, but that same status brings him the contempt of most whites. Discussing the Black middle class, W. E. B. Du Bois' *Philadelphia Negro* published in 1899 paints a disturbing picture that is relevant to this discussion of Grant Wiggins: "They are not the leaders or the ideal-makers of their own group in thought, work, and morals. They teach to the masses, to a very small extent, mingle with them but little, do not largely hire their labor...the first impulse of the best, the wisest and the richest is to segregate themselves from the masses." Grant's attempt to segregate himself from his blackness is challenged by all three Black women: Miss Emma, Tante Lou, and Vivian. As Patricia Williams points out in *The Rooster's Egg: On the Persistence of Prejudice* (1995), the Black middle class has been traditionally the favored "sons and daughters" who are full of wrath and have isolated themselves: "So upstanding they're enraged. So exceptional they're desperately lonely. So virtuous they're bitter with the sacrifice, never enjoying, the always being on display. So frozen in the viewfinders of racial anxiety they're don't move much. Can't afford a single wrong step" (63). With only his lover, Vivian, as his confidant, Grant has marginalized himself, especially from other Black males. Ironically, it is not the educated and "talented tenth" (Grant) who can escape the blatant discrimination of the South but the barely literate Jefferson who cannot run away, who will be the Savior, the one to break the vicious circle by representing the Black race, especially Black manhood, with dignity and pride.

Grant's visit to Jefferson after the date for the execution has been set marks the turning point in Jefferson's journey to manhood. For the first time, Grant and Jefferson have a substantive and sustained conversation. And this visit represents the first time that Jefferson does not refer to himself as "an old hog." In fact, when Jefferson, as a soon-to-be-executed body, understands that he will have a whole day that is his to enjoy, he desires for his "last supper" a whole gallon of vanilla ice cream, and he plans to eat it not in the way an old hog would eat it out of a trough but with a pot spoon. Here, repetition is a form of change as Jefferson repeatedly says that he will use a pot spoon to eat the ice cream. "But now I'm go'n get me a whole gallon. That's what I want—a whole gallon. Eat it with a pot spoon...I want a gallon. Eat it with a pot spoon. Every bit of it—with a pot spoon" (170). Although Jefferson affirms his humanity by his desire to eat a "whole gallon" of "vanilla ice cream," there is something rather juvenile and crude here in his statement, and the consumption of whiteness is paradoxical to his own consumption that awaits him. Beyond this acknowledgment of his humanity, Jefferson now obtains an "inner calmness" as Grant relates the news from the Quarter. Jefferson reflects about his friend, Gable, who has a baby with Stella. "He was remembering the day he was supposed to go into the swamps with Gable but instead had ended up with Brother and Bear at the liquor store" (171). This reflection is important in two ways. First, it conveys that the enduring cycle of life in the Quarter continues even in the face of impending death, and second, it takes Jefferson back to the scene of murder and robbery as he contemplates the catastrophic consequences of going with Brother and Bear, a tragic choice with tragic consequences. Jefferson continues to regain his subjectivity and humanity by agreeing to let Grant bring him a little radio. When Grant buys the radio, he encounters the deeply pervasive bigotry of a white female salesperson, who attempts to convince him to buy the store model instead of a packaged radio. Just before Grant pays for the radio,

> another white woman came into the store. The clerk set the radio beside the cash register and went to see what the white woman wanted. The other woman was not buying anything; she only wanted to talk. So they stood there about ten minutes before the clerk came back to wait on me. After ringing up the bill, she asked me if I needed a bag. But she asked it in a way that I knew she didn't want to give me one. (176)

As Gaines points out in "Writing a Lesson Before Dying," the radio and the notebook are significant in advancing the narrative. Gaines states: "The idea of the radio was not planned, but it turned out to be a most important turn in the story. From that moment on, there was some communication, although limited, between the two of them. Still Jefferson refuses to open up completely to Grant, to his grandmother, Miss Emma, or the minister of the church. So we know little of what he is thinking about or what he thinks about life" (60). The radio thus symbolizes some relief from the overarching tragedy of the impending execution. With the Confederate soldier and the Confederate flag outside the courthouse as symbols of Southern segregation and constant reminders to

Grant Wiggins of the legal and extra-legal injustices to Blacks, bigoted white people like this white female salesperson treat Black people with contempt regardless of their socioeconomic status. During this lesser form of social malfeasance, Grant becomes invisible not because of some ectoplasm experiment, but because this white woman refuses to see him as another human being with obligations and desires. This pervasive climate of hate and bigotry prevents Black people from fully participating in this society.

Grant Wiggins's humiliation when buying the radio causes him an internecine conflict with his elders, but Grant completely understands the role of the little radio with regard to Jefferson's growing subjectivity; he sarcastically warns his Aunt Lou and the preacher, "The only thing that keeps him from thinking he is not a hog is that radio. Take that radio away, and let's see what you can do for the soul of a hog" (183). Then he points out the remarkable significance of his last visit: "It was the first time he didn't call himself a hog" (183). His next meeting with Jefferson is even more remarkable than the last. Grant brings large pecans and roasted peanuts from his students, a half dozen apples, some candy, and two or three comic books. More importantly, Jefferson agrees to always meet Miss Emma, Tante Lou, and Reverend Ambrose in the jail's dayroom and accepts Grant's offer of a little notebook and a pencil in order to record his thoughts. Before Grant leaves, Jefferson says, "Tell—tell the children thank you for the pe-pecans" (186). This expression of gratitude conveys a monumental change in Jefferson's subjectivity, and Grant exclaims, "I caught myself grinning like a fool. I wanted to throw my arms around him and hug him. I wanted to hug the first person I came to. I felt like someone who had just found religion. I felt like crying with joy. I really did" (186). As the "old hog" disappears and with Jefferson's time on earth deliberately marching towards death, reciprocity of Black male subjectivity occurs bringing Grant a profound sense of joy and Jefferson acceptance not only of the food but the affection associated with it.

Gaines' use of food as a metaphor for love, affection, and sometimes humiliation plays a powerful role in the novel relative to Black male subjectivity. Having Jefferson being defined as a "hog" by the white defense attorney connects to one of the major economic industries (a slaughterhouse for hogs) in Bayonne and to the regular consumption of pork by Black people in the Quarter. One day, Grant's "breakfast was two fried eggs, grits, a piece of salt pork, and a biscuit" (35); Miss Emma brings "fried chicken, bread, baked sweet potatoes, tea cakes" (70) to Jefferson. On two occasions Jefferson mockingly asks for corn: "Corn for a hog" (122) he says. Jefferson's paradoxical request represents the traumatic effect of the white defense attorney's label of bestiality and his attempt to hurt others by accepting the grotesque signifier. While Grant waits in the kitchen to speak to Sheriff Guidry: "Inez dished up the food. She had cooked a pot roast with potatoes and carrots, onions, bell pepper and corn bread" (45). This food and the aromas add to Grant's humiliation as the meal is delivered to the group of white men who know he is in the kitchen waiting. Also, when Jefferson is allowed to come into the day room shackled and chained: "Miss Emma dished up the food. Mustard greens with pieces of pork fat mixed in it. There was stewed beef meat, rice, and biscuits" (137). Here Jefferson refuses to eat and the hurt on Miss Emma's face is profound. Like most Black women, Miss Emma's most powerful way to show her love and concern for Jefferson is represented in the meals she prepares for him. Jefferson's initial rejection hurts her soul. A few days later, Grant asks Jefferson to eat the food he brought. "There was store brought bread, fried pork chops, and baked sweet potatoes" (138), and again a grunting Jefferson is stubborn and claims his status as a hog. On another occasion Grant asked "the children at the school to bring large pecans and roasted peanuts" (183). On still another occasion when Grant, Rev. Ambrose, Miss Emma, and Tante Lou go to the jail, "Miss Emma put rice in each pan, then poured gumbo over the rice until the pan was nearly full. Besides shrimp, she had put smoked sausage and chicken in the gumbo, and she seasoned it well with green onions, file, and black pepper" (189); again Jefferson refuses to eat until Grant has a long conversation with him about the myth of white supremacy and the difference between what some people think Jefferson is and what he can be. This is a profound moment bringing Jefferson and Grant to tears; later they eat Miss Emma's gumbo. All of these uses of food reinforce the relationships between the individuals, especially with regard to Black male subjectivity. Miss Emma expresses her enduring love and affection for her godson, Jefferson by preparing him food. As note earlier, food becomes part of the process of humiliation when Grant goes to speak to Sheriff Guidry and Grant echoes Jefferson's behavior in the jail when he refuses to eat when he is annoyed with Tante Lou. When Jefferson refuses to eat it hurts those who love him (especially, Miss Emma) and when he does eat, it reverses the self-loathing he feels. On the other hand, when Grant is alone with Vivian they share a meal: "She dished up beans over the rice and placed a pork chop on each plate" (207–208). Gaines also uses food to connect Jefferson's anger to Grant's anger because when Grant is upset with Tante Lou he refuses to eat. The exchange between Tante Lou and Grant reveals his understanding of the deep hurt he causes:

> When I stopped in front of Miss Emma's house, my aunt got out of the car with her. 'Im going to Bayonne,' I told my aunt. She had not shut the door yet. 'I'll be home to cook in a little while,' she said. 'I'll eat in town,' I told her. Tante Lou held the door while she stood there looking at me. Nothing could have hurt her more when I said I was not going to eat her food. I was supposed to eat soon after she had cooked, and if I was not at home I was supposed to eat as soon as I came in. She looked at me without saying anything else, then she closed the door quietly and followed Miss Emma into the yard. (24)

This incident with Grant and Tante Lou occurs immediately after Grant is forced to drive his elders to Henri Pichot's house where Miss Emma pleads for Grant to be allowed to visit Jefferson. This confrontation marks the beginning of Grant's encounters with the white legal authorities, especially Sheriff Guidry. Lastly, we get Sheriff Guidry's meal hours before the execution: "His breakfast was two homemade biscuit sandwiches. The biscuits had been split open; one contained a pork sausage patty and the other figs. Lillian, their colored maid, had preserved figs the past summer" (238). The author's constant references to hog and pork keep our focus on Jefferson and the fact that he will be metaphorically consumed as well as the possibility of his transformation from a hog to a man. Moreover, with regard to the Black community food represents a psychological bond and an expression of love and concern for those who presently have little else to give. Even in the face of death, food represents life and Miss Emma's desire for Jefferson to live and die like a man.

Along with the food, Gaines also uses the metaphor of black birds and a blue bird to connect to the theme of Black male subjectivity and the desire for freedom. Here these dark birds represent flight for Grant and freedom for Jefferson; both of these aspects will be realized metaphorically and psychologically. Grant notices "a swarm of black birds flew across the road and alighted in a pecan tree in one of the backyards to the left" (107). While in his jail cell, "Jefferson sat on the bunk, slumped forward a little, his big hands clasped together down between his legs. He was looking through the barred window toward the sycamore tree, where several black birds were perched on a limb" (127–128). The swarm of black birds in both of these passages infers some collective sense of identity in the sense that Jefferson is not alone in this tragedy. In a journal entry, Jefferson writes: "the bird in the tre soun like a blu bird" (234). During the last moments in his jail cell, "A bird sang in the sycamore tree outside the window....The bird continued its chirping in the tree outside the window" (244). At this point, the black birds become a singular blue bird, a representation of the transformation and future ascension of Jefferson. Gaines' final image of flight is not a bird, but a butterfly; assuming that the Jefferson has been executed, Grant notices "a butterfly, a yellow butterfly with dark specks like ink dots on its wings" (252). These birds represent flight for both Grant and Jefferson; while the Black men have not left the Quarter of Bayonne, they have moved psychologically. Through their often confrontational interactions that lead to transformations, Jefferson and Grant broke out of their psychological cocoons and learned to fly.

In his next to last visit, Grant gives Jefferson his most important lesson, a lesson concerning the mythology of white supremacy advocated by Thomas Jefferson and Jefferson Davis, who took the oath of office as Confederate president in 1861. Since the days of Black people's enslavement until this

Jim Crow period and beyond, Black men were especially made to feel powerless by a brutal system of segregation. During slavery, whipping, branding, and forced breeding were common, and during the Jim Crow period, murders, lynchings, and castrations were common—all designed to instill fear and frustration in any Black man who dared to challenge a white male dominated society with its laws and sanctions of white privilege. As George Lipsitz explains, the construction of whiteness is about materiality: *The Possessive Investment in Whiteness: How White People Profit from Identity Politics* (1998):

> Whiteness has a cash value it accounts for advantages that come to individuals through profits made from housing secured in discriminatory markets, through the unequal education allocated to children of different races, through insider networks that channel employment opportunities to the relatives and friends of those who have profited most from present and past racial discrimination, and especially through intergenerational transfers of inherited wealth that pass on the spoils of discrimination to succeeding generations. I argue that white Americans are encouraged to invest in whiteness, to remain true to an identity that provides them with resources, power, and opportunity. (vii)

The religious rationalization for this was that Black people were the descendants of Ham who looked upon his father's (Noah's) nakedness and therefore were cursed to be the drawers of water and the hewers of wood. Along with this racist and reactionary religious discourse, there was the biological essentialism of white supremacists like Thomas Jefferson who is alleged to have had an intimate relationship with his Black slave, Sally Hemings. With Jefferson's head and heart in conflict, he represents the fundamental paradox of the white founders of this country, soon to be wealthy white slaveholders seeking freedom for themselves. However, there were Black men seeking freedom for themselves and for other Black people, individuals like Frederick Douglass, Nat Turner, Denmark Vesey, Gabriel Proser, and David Walker. These are perhaps some of the heroic Black men that Grant has in mind when he teaches Jefferson a lesson on the nature of heroism and the history of a people perched on the fragile branch between action and fear in the pursuit of complete justice and equality. Grant tells Jefferson: "A hero is some-one who does something for other people. He does something that other men don't and can't do. He is different from other men. He is above other men. No matter who those men are, the hero, no matter who he is, is above them" (191). Courageously, Grant tells Jefferson that he is not a hero because he does not like and even hates teaching, only doing it because it is "the only thing that an educated Black man can do in the South today." (191) Grant wants to run, to live for himself and for Vivian and for nobody else. Acknowledging that he is not a hero, Grant tells Jefferson that he wants him to be a hero. "You could give something to her [his nannan], to me, to those children in the Quarter. You could give them something that I never could. They expect it from me, but not from you. The white people out there are saying that you don't have it–that you're a hog, not a man. But I know they are wrong. You have the potentials. We all have, no matter who we are" (191). Here, we have the quintessential paradox of the novel, the possibility of an uneducated, barely literate and deprived young Black man, named Jefferson challenging the racial dogma and mythology of Thomas Jefferson. Grant requests the Black Jefferson to challenge the epistemology and the philosophy of the white racist Jefferson represented by Sheriff Guidry, and Dr. Morgan and the narrow-minded preference by pigmentocracy prejudice of Matthew Antoine.

Gaines' narrative structure suggests a double entendre when Grant speaks to Jefferson about the philosophy of white supremacy:

> Do you know what a myth is, Jefferson...White people believe that they're better than anyone else on earth—and that is a myth. The last thing they ever want is to see a Black man stand, and think, and show that common humanity that is in us all. It would destroy their myth. They would no longer have justification for having made us slaves and keeping us in the condition we are in. As long as none of us stand they're safe. They're safe with me. They're safe with Reverend Ambrose. I don't want them to feel safe with you anymore. (192)

Although Thomas Jefferson speculated of Black people's innate inferiority, many whites took this speculation as actuality and rationalized their oppression and marginalization of Blacks. Also, in this dialectical analysis, challenging racial hegemony, the Black Jefferson moves to the apex of the triangle with the more accomplished Grant and the Reverend Ambrose assuming a separate point at the base of this triangulation. And the separation between Grant Wiggins and Reverend Ambrose is profound because the non-believer, Grant, is viewed by Ambrose as a lost soul, especially when Grant refuses to discuss God with Jefferson. In perhaps one of the most heated exchanges in the novel, Reverend Ambrose tells Grant: "No, you not educated, boy....You far from being educated. You learned your reading, writing, and rithmetic, but you don't know nothing. You don't even know yourself....When you act educated, I'll cal you Grant. I'll even call you Mr. Grant, when you act like a man" (215–216). For Reverend Ambrose Black male subjectivity is defined by belief in God; for Grant his subjectivity is defined by his education, his teaching, and his relationship with Vivian Baptiste. While the relationship between Reverend Ambrose and Grant can be characterized as a confrontational father and son relationship, the relationship between Grant and Jefferson is that of a teacher and a student with a paradox. Reversing the traditional teacher and student relationship, Grant tells Jefferson,

> I need you more than you could ever need me. I need to know what to do with my life. I want to run away, but go where and do what? I'm needed here and I know it, but I feel that all I'm doing here is choking myself. I need someone

to tell me what to do. I need you to tell me, to show me. I'm no hero; I can just give something small. That's all I have to offer. It is the only way that we can chip away at that [Jeffersonian] myth. You—you can be bigger than anyone you have ever met...You have the chance of being bigger than anyone who has ever lived on that plantation or come from this little town. You can do it if you try. (193)

Like those self-sacrificing Blacks who laid down their lives so that all Black people could stand with dignity and pride, Grant offers Jefferson the opportunity to use this tragedy as a moral lesson for Blacks up in the Quarter struggling against white supremacy and racist whites who view him as only "an old hog" going to the slaughter. Furthermore, Grant offers Jefferson an enabling form of consciousness that may contribute to the reconstruction of the psychological, social, and cultural relationships between Blacks and whites. Hence Gaines establishes the role reversal that has been foreshadowed, Jefferson can become the teacher and Grant becomes the student.

Grant achieves an emotional breakthrough because Jefferson begins to cry, and using the analogy of a rough piece of scrap wood being transformed into something new and pretty, Grant urges Jefferson to become a new Black man: "I am still that piece of drifting wood, and those out there are no better. But you can be better. Because we need you to be and want you to be. Me, your godmother, the children, and all the rest of them in the quarter" (193). Grant's lesson and explanation here are that Jefferson's life is connected to the Black community, and he has the ability to make a tremendous impact based on how he embraces this tragedy. Grant also cries at this point "not from reaching any conclusion by reasoning," but because despite his self-deprecation, he is "still part of the whole" (194). Gaines' suggestion here is that by breaking down the intraracial class and color hegemony evident with Matthew Antoine and the two mulatto bricklayers, Black people can facilitate the breakdown of interracial conflict.

The concluding visit by Grant reveals that his jailhouse lessons are having a transformative effect on Jefferson's psyche and subjectivity. Grant discovers that Jefferson has been writing. Like the ex-slave Frederick Douglass who wrote himself into existence in three autobiographical slave narratives, Jefferson writes himself into subjectivity. Jefferson writes:

> *I dreampt it last night. They was taking me somewhere. I wasn't crying. I wasn't begging. I was just going, going with them. Then I woke up. I couldn't go back to sleep. I didn't want to go back to sleep. I didn't want to dream no more....If I ain't nothing but a hog, how come they just don't knock me in the head like a hog? Stab me like a hog?...Man walk on two foots; hogs on four hoofs.* (author's emphasis 220)

Although the trials that many Black children faced during Jim Crow often went beyond anything their parents imagined, Miss Emma's desire for someone to do something for her before she dies becomes realized in

Jefferson's dream as he walks to his death with dignity. In his dream, Jefferson becomes a "dead man" walking to his execution with a nobility of manner. Implicitly, Jefferson rejects the racist analogy of Black men as animals or beasts used by his white defense attorney and that he in his truly torturous moments of self-contempt and self-deprecation had internalized. Through his rudimentary diary, Jefferson, in his attempt to write himself into existence, becomes a man who takes psychological risks, what Toni Morrison calls a "free man":

> This is a man who is stretching, you know he's going all the way within his own mind and within whatever his outline might be. Now that's the tremendous possibility of masculinity among Black men. And you see it a lot....They may end up in sort of twentieth-century, contemporary terms being also unemployed. They may be in prison. They may be doing all sorts of things. But they are adventuresome in that regard.[17]

Thinking on the self-abnegating and adventuresome life of Jesus, Jefferson desires to bear his cross without "mumbling a word." However, he does question Grant about his proposal to bear the cross for the entire Black community up in the Quarter, a question that reveals his slave-like abandonment and natal alienation. "Me Mr. Wiggins. Me. Me to take the cross. Your cross, nannan's cross, my cross. Me, Mr. Wiggins....Who ever car'd my cross, Mr. Wiggins? My mama? My daddy? They dropped me when I wasn't nothing. Still don't know where they at this minute....You too, Mr. Wiggins. You never thought I was nothing else. I didn't neither" (224). These questions and acknowledgments reflect Jefferson's advanced Lacanian moment, the moment when the child understands his unique identity as an element unconnected to his or her parents. Jefferson also painfully affirms the brutal physical and psychological nature of a white supremacist society, where he is cursed, beaten, and worked for "nothing" and he is expected to grin to get by. No longer with his head down in his chest, Jefferson tells the head-bowed Grant "You can look at me Mr. Wiggins; I don't mind" (224). Upon looking up, Grant views Jefferson standing "big and tall and not stooped as he had been in chains" (225). Roles of teacher and student are reversed, as Grant feels compassion for his former student's tragic predicament and possible remorse for his earlier condemnations of Jefferson. Now, Jefferson becomes the teacher, and Grant becomes the student, claiming "You're more a man, than I am Jefferson." Grant is healed not by the escape that he desires but by engagement with Jefferson. Lastly, like a liberated man sitting in his home with a friend, Jefferson asks Grant if he would like to eat one of the sweet potatoes that he brought to the jail.

In the section named "Jefferson's Diary," Gaines signifies on Thomas Jefferson's memoirs, *Notes on the State of Virginia*, by having Jefferson explicate his Notes on the State of Louisiana. In a crude grammatical form with no capital letters, no punctuation, and misspellings, his writing reflects this young Black man's journey to attain his voice and subjectivity. Like a slave narrative, Jefferson's writing is an African American narrative of embodied agency. There are a number of entries that reflect how Grant has helped Jefferson to be transformed from an "old hog" to a Black man. In a number of telling journal entries, Jefferson relates his slave-like status that echoes Thomas Jefferson's Hamitic view of Black people's intrinsic inferiority: "it look like the lord just work for the wite folks cause ever sens I wasn nothin but a litle boy I been on my on haulin water to the fiel on that ol water cart...i kno I care for nanan but I dont kno if love is care cau se cuttin wood and haulin water and things like that I dont know if thats love or jus work...i ant done this much thinkin and this much writin in all my life befor" (227–229). Ironically, the sheriff in his attempt to humiliate him, makes sure that Grant does not bring any "hairpins, no pocket knives, no razor blades, no ice picks" to the jail (70), but Jefferson relates that when the sheriff, Henri Pichot, and Mr. Morgan visit Jefferson to see how he is doing, Pichot gives him a "brand new pencil" and his pocket knife so that Jefferson can sharpen his pencil. More importantly, Jefferson's autobiographical diary reveals that like drunken white slave masters gambling over their Black slave property, Pichot and Morgan have a wager going concerning as to how Jefferson will face this undeserved execution: "picho say you want double that bet you want add that troter an mr mogan say it still aint fidy yet" (229). Even at this moment, white males view Jefferson as a hog and dehumanize him by betting on whether he will go squealing like a pig and begging or will he be standing tall with dignity. Despite the seeming kindness of Pichot, Jefferson is not bamboozled and knows which white men are decent: "paul trying to be hod when he aint like he dont want get too close to me no mo an all the time he is the only one rond yer kno how to talk like a youman to people I kno you paul an I kno ole clark an I kno you too shef guiry and you mr picho an mr morgan an all the rest of yall I jus never say non of this before but I know yall ever las one of yall" (230). Not knowing or caring who will see his diary, Jefferson realizes that he has "no rights which a white man was bound to respect" challenges these racist white men and their dehumanizing juridical system. Yet there is some strong evidence that Sheriff Guidry has through his actions come to respect Jefferson as a human being and not a hog. Jefferson writes:

> shef guiry come by after i et an ax me hom im doin an i say im doin all right an he ax me he say i aint never pik up yo tablet an look in it an he ax me what all i been ritin an i tol him jus things an he say aint he done tret me rite an i tol him yesir an he say aint his deptis done tret me fair an i told him yesir an he say aint he done let peple vist me anytime an i say yesir an he say didn't he let the chiren an all the peple from the quarter com an vist me jus two days ago an i say yesir an he say n in yo tablet i tret you good all the time you been yer an he say he had to

go hom cause he hadn et his super yet but for me to call a depty if i need somthin
an he ax if i wan the lite to stay on all nite in case i want rite som mo an i tol him
yesir an he say all rite i coud have all the lite i want (233)

For Sheriff Guidry to request that Jefferson document his treatment while
in the jail is significant, a shift in the racial power dynamics. Implicitly,
Sheriff Guidry does not at this point view Jefferson as a hog but views him as
an individual capable of reasoning and thought. Also, Sheriff Guidry seems
to realize the historical significance of this moment and desires to be
included in Jefferson's diary in a favorable manner. Lastly, the light in
Jefferson's jail cell metaphorically suggests a form of enlightenment for
both Jefferson and Sheriff Guidry as they engage in a man-to-man dialogue.
Like John Newton's lyrics in *Amazing Grace,* Jefferson's journal entries are
informal and crude, but they represent a testimony to his transformation.

The last section of Jefferson's diary relates the emotional impact of
Black people from the Quarter visiting him and the profound gratitude he
has for Grant Wiggins. Jefferson returns to his cell and cries after Grant's
students visit him. Jefferson acknowledges the emotional significance of
Grant bringing his students to the jail:

lord have mercy sweet jesus mr wigin where all them people come from when
you ax me if some chiren can com op here an speak to me i didn't kno you was
meaning all them chiren in yo clas an jus sitin ther on the flo all quite in they
clean close lookin at me an i could see som was scard o me but mos was brave an
spoke an my little cosin estel even com up an kiss me on the jaw an i coudn hol
it back no mo (230)

Jefferson cries because nothing like this has ever happened to him; a whole
Black community comes out to express its love and concern for one of its
own. By Grant bringing his students to the jail to visit Jefferson, we see the
synthesis between the formal and informal instruction; these students learn
a powerful lesson that they could never experience in a classroom, a lesson
about redemption for a teacher and his student. More importantly in terms
of narrative structure, Miss Emma's desire is dramatically fulfilled when
Jefferson sees his Nannan, and he says "I tol her I love her an I tol her I was
strong an she jus look lor and tied an pull me to her an kiss me an it was the
firs time she never done that an it felt good an I let her hol me long is she
want cause you say it was good for he an I tol her I was strong an she didn
need to come back no more cause I was strong" ((231). Miss Emma leaves
the jail for the last time knowing that her prayer for Jefferson has been
answered. Like the slave narrative of Frederick Douglass, who wrote himself
into existence, a newly invented Jefferson becomes the man that Miss Emma
wanted him to be. Jefferson also writes himself into existence in a manner
that the whole of Bayonne will remember, especially Grant's students.

Certain sections of Gaines' earlier reference to the Reverend Ambrose's termination song, "Amazing Grace" (106) capture Jefferson's and Grant Wiggins' transformations; "Amazing Grace, how sweet the sound/ That saved a wretch like me/ I once was blind, but now am found/ Was blind, but now I see." With Jefferson being abandoned by his parents and being cursed, beaten, and worked for nothing, his transcendence to his current subjectivity ("when I was a litle boy I was a waterboy an rode the cart but now I got to be a man an set in a cher") reflects John Newton's lyrics "Through many dangers. toils and snares/ we have already come/ T'was Grace [Grant] that brought us [Jefferson] safe thus far." After apologizing to Grant for his contemptuous words to his girlfriend, Vivian, who visits him at the jail, Jefferson's last words in his introspective diary are: "good by mr wigin tell them im strong tell them im a man good by mr wigin im gon ax paul if he can bring you this" (234). With only Tante Lou mentioned as a family connection in the novel, Grant might have issues of natal alienation that have affected his worldview. In one of the many moments when Tante Lou is frustrated and annoyed at Grant, she declares to him: "I raised you better" (182). Reverend Ambrose confirms the sacrifices that Tante Lou has made for Grant; he tells Grant:

> That's how you got through that university—cheating herself here, cheating herself there, but always telling you she's all right. I've seen the blisters from the hoe and the cane knife. At that church, crying on her knees. You ever looked at those scabs on her knees boy? Course you never. 'Cause she never wanted you to see it. And that's the difference between me and you, boy; that make me the educated one and you the gump. I know my people. I know what they gone through. I know they cheated themselves, lied to themselves—hoping that one they all love and trust can come back and help relieve the pain. (218)

Here Grant as the teacher receives a personal history lesson on the nature of sacrifice for the larger good; Tante Lou has made a bloody sacrifice for Grant to go to the university and but it has taken Grant some time to see the larger communal good in helping Jefferson. With the obvious disrespect of them calling Grant a "boy" several times, the author reflects on the paradox of white men calling Black men "boys." Yet being forced into this role, the process has fed Grant's soul despite the conflicts it has brought him with Tante Lou and Vivian. Paradoxically, Jefferson's final meal cooked by his nannan, "som okra an rice an som pork chop an a conbread an som claba...an I et it ever bit an it was the bes meal I kno my nanan ever cook" (232) illustrates that a newly resolute and self-assured Black man consumes pork and he is not an "old hog" consuming another hog. Here Gaines makes powerful use of the metaphor of food being connected to Black male subjectivity; the pork is here to be consumed but the hog is gone. Jefferson has finally made peace with himself and his tragic destiny. His last words to the benevolent deputy sheriff, Paul Bonin, are "Tell Nannan I walked" (254). Jefferson's simple statement is profound because he "walked" with dignity and pride, smashing to pieces the racist mythology posed by Thomas Jefferson and those white males in Bayonne who viewed him as a "dumb hog" or as one white woman explains to her son, as an "old bad nigger" that had to be put away (242). While Jefferson lived as a poor, illiterate individual, he dies with the respect of most of the Black community and a few respectable and fair-minded whites such as Paul Bonin.

When the young white deputy sheriff comes to the Quarter for the first time to bring Jefferson's diary to Grant, Gaines suggests the possibility of some redemptive healing between Blacks and whites. Like the biblical Paul who brings God's new message to the Corinthians, Paul brings good news of Jefferson's subjectivity. True to his words in his diary, Jefferson "was the strongest man there" (253) as Paul confirms Grant's resolute faith in Jefferson's manhood. "I saw the transformation, Grant Wiggins... I saw the transformation, I'm a witness to that" (254) Paul testifies. In variance to most white males, Paul uses Grant's full name as a sign of respect, asks if they can be friends, and asks Grant to tell his students that Jefferson "was the bravest man in that room today. I'm a witness, Grant Wiggins. Tell them so" (256). Gaines places emphasis on Paul's role as a mediator when we consider that when Vivian and Grant contemplate her being pregnant, the name "Paul" (used by the New Testament's Saul of Tarsus who drops his Old Testament name, which symbolizes his rejection of Judaism) is suggested if the child is a boy. However, Grant, considering an escape from the Quarter, tells Vivian, "I don't know if I want Paul to grow up here" (109). Contemplating the name Paul for their son suggests the possibility of better racial relations between Blacks and whites and within each racial group, racial transformation. Jefferson's tragic lesson in his death has been a life-transforming lesson for Grant and the entire Black community in the efficacy of redemptive suffering. Jefferson's diary thus represents a speak-erly text that Grant will use in teaching his Black students. Perhaps no longer will Grant just teach what "the white folks tell him to teach," but he may be more innovative in his pedagogy. This possibility is evident in his statements and self-questioning about God and the America's legal system:

> Don't tell me to believe. Don't tell me to believe in the same God or laws that men believe in who commit these murders. Don't tell me to believe that God can bless this country and that men are judged by their peers. Who among his peers judged him? Was I there? Was the minister there? Was Harry Williams there? Was Farrell Jarreau? Was my aunt? Was Vivian? No, his peers did not judge him—and I will not believe. (251)

Here Grant questions both God and man's legal dictates; the trial judge and Reverend Ambrose, the authorities on legal and spiritual laws, are challenged. For Grant neither God nor America's legal system is viewed as just in their treatment of Black people. Further, Grant contradicts his earlier statement that he "was there" in the courtroom; he realizes that he was not "there," and even the Black people who were physically present in the courtroom were not there because they could not participate in providing judgment on their peer, Jefferson. Believing for Grant is based on some practice and evidence of some equality and justice. This will change Grant's teaching. As Grant profoundly states: "Nothing will ever be the same after today" (248). Jefferson's diary combined with Grant's and Paul's testimonies will create a profound lesson on redemption in the face of a tragedy. Both Grant and Jefferson find redemption and meaning in the struggle to pursue meaningful subjectivity. Jefferson exceeds the dedicated lack of knowledge and dehumanizing limitations of Jim Crow cultural hegemony. By reconstructing Jefferson's masculinity, Grant reconstructs his own subjectivity as a teacher; equally significant, white supremacy becomes deconstructed. Redemption can only occur after a fall; Grant falls somewhat and Jefferson's manhood is restored. Grant converts Jefferson, and Jefferson converts Grant, and the possibility exists that other conscientious non-racist whites like Paul will be converted. Gaines's characterization of Paul suggests that racist white people become enslaved when they engage in the oppression of Black people. With the white deputy coming to the Black community for the first time and extending his gratitude and friendship to Grant for his role in transforming an "old hog" into a dignified Black man, there is the significant possibility that despite this white supremacist culture, Grant Wiggins and Vivian Baptiste will stay in the Quarter and continue to be inspirational agents for transformation, especially for young Black males like Jefferson, a resurrection and a manifestation of infinitely redemptive hope. Jefferson's truly redemptive death symbolizes a rejuvenation of optimism against the perversity of racial injustice; this ritualistic lynching becomes a climatic resurrection of both Grant Wiggins' and Jefferson's subjectivity. Jefferson meets death with dignity and Grant lives a life with purpose and meaning. Lastly, when Grant goes back into the classroom and releases the racial hurt with tears, this symbolizes the collective release of the Black community from the long tyranny of white supremacy and Jim Crow segregation. Grant and Paul represent new social relationships and new attitudes towards race and social interaction and the possibility that the legal system will be transformed to treat Black people with humanity and respect. Consequently both Grant Wiggins and Jefferson become metaphorical and real martyrs for the Black community of Bayonne with the possibility that the South can be transformed into a place no longer strangled by race.

This brings us to the subject of writing as a redemptive process and an act of discovery. As previously stated, a comparison can be made between

Frederick Douglass and Jefferson; for Black people the enslavement period and the period of Jim Crow segregation were both filled with trauma, dehumanization, and relentless physical violence. Like Douglass, Jefferson's writing represents bringing himself into existence, a self-discovery. In his final days, Jefferson in his own limited manner comes to understand Jim Crow society and his precarious place in a world where opportunities are severely restricted. However, despite the overwhelming restrictions of psychological and physical violence, Black authors like Phillis Wheatley, David Walker, Harriet E. Wilson, Harriet Jacobs, and Frederick Douglass discovered themselves and permanently written themselves into existence. On writing as a process of discovery, Ernest J. Gaines explicates:

> Writing for me is discovery. If I knew everything when I began a novel, I'm afraid it would be boring to write. I do not know everything that's going to happen in the book. I don't want to know everything. I want to discover, as you, the reader, wants to discover, what it's all about....I try to create characters with character to help develop my own character, and maybe the character of the reader who might read me. (*Mozart and Leadbelly*, 62)

Gaines' metacognitive explication allows us to conclude that Grant Wiggins' and Jefferson's initially painful interaction lead them through the thorny and meandering path to self-discovery and redemption. These Black men discover themselves, and their self-discoveries transform the entire community of Bayonne. The prevailing theme is that Black bodies regardless of religion, class status, or education become living testimonies to Black people's suffering and trauma under white supremacy, but redemption is always possible. Redemption is significant not only for the injured and traumatized psyches of African American people who come under the bone-crushing weight of racism but for those bodies that are not Black.

Notes

1   Franz Kafka, "In the Penal Colony," *The Complete Stories,* ed. Nathan N. Glazer (New York: Schocken, 1971), 144–145.
2   By 1950 the electric chair was in operation in Louisiana.
3   Gaines uses the word "hog" 52 times in the novel.
4   In *Conversations with Ernest Gaines,* edited by John Lowe (Jackson: University of Mississippi Press, 1995), Gaines discusses Black male subjectivity: "You must understand that in this country the Black man has been pushed into the position where he is not supposed to be a man. This is one of the things that the white man has tried to deny the Black ever since he brought him here in chains....My heroes just try to be men; but because the white man has tried everything from the time of slavery to deny the Black man this chance, his attempts to be a man will lead toward danger....So whenever my men decide that they will be men regardless of how anyone feels, they know that they will eventually die. But it's impossible for them to turn around. This

is the sense of Greek tragedy that keeps coming back in my writing, that men are destined to do things and they cannot do anything but that one thing. Whatever that one thing is, it is to be done as well as the man can do it" (30).

5   Richard Maxwell Brown, *Strain of Violence: Historical Studies of American Violence and Vigilantism* (New York: Oxford University Press, 1975) 325.

6   As Neil R. McMillen relates in *The Citizen's Council: Organized Resistance to the Second Reconstruction 1954–64* (Chicago: University of Illinois Press, 1994), Louisiana was extremely defiant to the Supreme Court's decision: "Almost alone among southern states, its legislature was in session on 'Black Monday,' and it wasted little time in responding to the threat posed by the *Brown* doctrine to the state's system of segregated schools. On May 20, lawmakers introduced in the lower house a resolution censuring the nation's highest tribunal for its 'unwarranted and unprecedented abuse of power.' Passing that body with only three dissenting votes, the measure carried every vote but one in the Senate. On this note of recalcitrance, the legislature proceeded to build a legal barricade against desegregation in the public schools which by 1964 included more than 131 acts and resolutions—more than twice the number enacted by any other state" (59).

7   John Lowe, ed. *Conversations with Ernest Gaines* (Jackson: University of Mississippi Press, 1995) 307.

8   Ernest J. Gaines, *A Lesson Before Dying* (New York: Vintage Books, 1993) 3. All further references to this text will be given parenthetically.

9   Undoubtedly, the most horrific extra-legal lynching in America's history was the 1918 murder of Mary Turner. In May of 1918, Hampton Smith, a thirty-one-year-old white plantation owner in Brooks County, Georgia, was shot and killed by Sidney Johnson, one of his Black workers. During a physical altercation, Smith was shot and killed by Johnson. Mob violence ensued with the deaths of thirteen individuals including Mary Turner. Protesting her husband's death during the mob violence, twenty-year-old Mary Turner, eight months pregnant at the time, publicly objected. Mary Turner was taken to the Folsom Bridge; her ankles were tied and she was hung upside down from a tree. Gasoline was poured on her body and all of her clothes were burned off. One sadistic white male then cut her stomach open, and her unborn baby dropped to the ground and was stomped and crushed. Mary's body was then riddled with bullets; the makeshift grave was marked with a whiskey bottle and a cigar stuffed in the neck of the bottle.

10   Like the name Brer Rabbit a synthesis of Brother and Bear gives us Brer Bear. Hence, Gaines draws on Black folklore where enslaved Blacks constructed tales to rationalize their relationship with white slave masters.

11   Claude McKay, "If We Must Die," *Norton Anthology of African American Literature* Edited by Henry Louis Gates Jr. and Nellie Y. McKay (New York: W. W. Norton & Company, 1997), 984.

12   The "Quarter" refers to the land around River Lake Plantation—near New Roads, Poite Coupee Parish, Louisiana which is the land around the Pichot plantation, near Bayonne.

13   Angola (also known as "The Farm") is the Louisiana State Penitentiary and is estimated to be one of the largest prisons in the U.S. with 5,000 inmates and 1,800 staff members. Located on an 18,000-acre plantation in unincorporated West Feliciana Parish close to the Mississippi border, it is surrounded on three sides by the Mississippi River, making flooding a constant menace. The transformation of Angola Plantation to Angola Prison reinforces the ongoing criminalization and exploitation of Black people

and white America's need for cheap labor. In the prison, inmates work from sunup to sundown for little or no wages. Louisiana State Penitentiary has a large population of aging men serving long sentences with little hope of reprieve. Eighty-five percent of the 5108 inmates currently incarcerated at Angola are expected to die there.

14 As cited in John P. Muffler's "Education and the Separate but Equal Doctrine" in *Black Scholar* (May/June 1986): "Segregation of white and black children in public schools has a detrimental effect upon the black children. The impact is greater when it has the sanction of the law; for the policy of separating the races usually is interpreted as denoting the inferiority of the Negro group. A sense of inferiority affects the motivation of the children to learn. Segregation with the sanction of the law, therefore has a tendency to retard education and the mental development of Negro children and to deprive them of some of the benefits they would receive in a racially integrated school system" (37).

15 Frantz Fanon, *Black Skin, White Masks* (New York: Grove Press, 1967), 10.

16 Richard Wright, "Between the World and Me" *Black Voices* (New York: Paul R. Reynolds Inc., 1968), 437. All further references will be given parenthetically.

17 bell hooks, *Black Looks: Race and Representation* (Boston: South End Press, 1992), 96.

Conclusion

> Black Americans throughout their history have always been challenged by the harsh and often brutal reality of institutional racism. As a system of unequal power, political racism led to the disenfranchisement of African Americans after the Reconstruction's brief experiment in democracy.
>
> —*Manning Marable* (quoted in *And don't call me a racist*)

The African American male experience has been and still represents a constant struggle against enduring forces from the period of Black people's enslavement to the present. Like a virulent disease America's white supremacist culture constantly mutates, and its insidious effect on the Back body politic remains a conestant. The transgenerational transgression of trauma caused by forced migration, enslavement, natal alienation, lynchings, segregation, warfare, interracial conflict, intraracial conflict, race riots, unemployment, underemployment, inferior housing, miseducation, environmental pollution, police brutality, racial profiling, redlining, subprime loans and the ever-increasing incarceration has taken a deadly toll on Black people, especially males. Unfortunately, there is little evidence to suggest that white supremacy, white privilege and the socioeconomic policies that maintain them will be eviscerated any time soon or ever. With these four African American novels in mind, a critical examination of America's white supremacist culture reveals the too often precarious situation of many Black males have in relation to the legal authorities and the enduring challenges to these authorities. Despite the exceptional success of some sports figures, entertainers, and politicians, the masses of Black males are in extremely desperate socioeconomic conditions as represented by prison rates, graduation rates, unemployment rates, and family structure. Not surprisingly, the Black male body is constantly racialized, that is marked for difference and for consumption.[1]

With the films *Training Day* and *American Gangster* in mind director Bill Duke's film *Deep Cover* (1992) illustrates the ultimate cinematic representation of the Black male outlaw, a Black police officer who goes undercover to arrest criminals involved in selling large amounts of drugs such as cocaine and heroin. In the clandestine process, this Black undercover officer significantly blurs the line between a cop and a criminal. Here Laurence Fishburne plays the role of Russell Stevens Jr., who at the age of ten years old (Cory Curtis) watches his drug-addicted father, Russell Stevens Sr., (Glynn Turman) being shot and killed in Cleveland, Ohio on a snowy evening after robbing a liquor store. After snorting some coke, his father's last and prophetic words to his beloved son are: "Don't you never do this shit, you hear me? Don't you never be like me, all right? Don't do it." The constant self-negation provides the catalysis for a son's journey into manhood. Although the father's further response addresses his son's vague desire for Christmas, Stevens' father tells him: "Boy you better know what you want...Else, how do you expect to get what you want if you don't know what you want?" Knowing and self-knowledge become critical to the film's narrative structure. Stevens' seductively poetic voice-over narrates the sequence of tragic and traumatic events and provides an explanation: "So gather round while I run down and unravel my pedigree. My father was a junkie...My father, when I saw him die like that, saw him find his grave in the snow, I had only one thought. It wasn't gonna happen to me." Like the complex protagonist, Oknokwo in Chinua Achebe's *Things Fall Apart* (1959) who believes that his father, Unoka is weak and lazy, Stevens' affirmation to be his own uncorrupted man reveals the ongoing transgenerational transgression of trauma despite one's will to surmount the tragic past.[2] Becoming the very antithesis of drug-addicted criminal with a gun robbing a store with his young son in the automobile, Stevens, some twenty years later becomes a police officer in Cincinnati. This desire sets the stage for Stevens' encounter with a Drug Enforcement Agency supervisor named Gerald Carver (Charles Martin Smith), a diminutive white father figure who becomes Stevens' handler between two different worlds. The film's poignant racial tensions become established in Carver's gloomy nondescript office where he conducts interviews with potential Black male undercover officers. His encounter with Stevens occurs after a sequence of meeting with three uniformed Black police officers who are asked the same controversial and racially explosive question: "Do you know the difference between a Black man and a nigger?" Shifting uncomfortably in his chair with an equally uncomfortable smile, the first Black officer answers "no" to the provocative question; on the other hand, the second officer named Winston jumps up and grabs the Machiavellian Carver out of his chair and rages "who the fuck do you think you're talking to?" Interestingly, Carver's arrogant response to the first smiling officer is: "Most niggers don't." Carver's obsequious response to Winston is to thank him for coming to the interview. Stevens, the third officer, with a stoic expression calmly and deliberately responds "the nigger is the one that would even answer that question." Leaning forward and smiling at Stevens' intelligent and swift-thinking response, Carver believes that he has the right man for his undercover operation. Stevens' response personifies the middle road of a Du Boisian double consciousness where the first two Black police officers represent acceptance and rejection of white supremacy and its ideology of racial essentialism. Within the context of slavery, Stevens' response positions him in the middle of the proverbial house nigger and field nigger paradigm, a nigger in limbo and the quintessential status of one unsure about his identity.

In the ensuing conversation between Stevens and Carver that we see the film's dominant themes of the blurred line of demarcation between a cop and a criminal and the problematic racial essentialism of Black males as inherently criminal. Informing Stevens that the job entails an undercover officer buying and selling drugs in an attempt to target the high-level drug dealers for arrest and prosecution, Stevens' response is that he would be a "snitch." Here Carver does a psychological profile on Stevens that sanguinely suggests that he is exactly the right person for the operation because he has a criminal profile and demeanor despite the fact that he is a police officer. If Stevens accepts the assignment, he will be on loan to the DEA and a "scumbag" on the right side of the law. With his father's death a fundamental part of his psyche, Stevens' response reinforces his purity of staying away from drugs and declares that "I've never even had a drink. I never have, and I never will." Clearly understanding the source of his virtuous statement and proclaiming that "I'm God. I know everything," Carver asks if his abstinence has anything to do with his father being killed robbing a liquor store? Like a "natural born" killer Carver informs Stevens that he is a "natural-born" criminal because he scores "almost exactly like a criminal." More specifically, Carver, while reading and referencing the specifics of his Metro Police Personnel File, tells him that he resents authority, he has a rigid moral code but has no underlying system of values, and that he has an insufficiently developed sense of self. Beyond these disturbing characteristics, Carver says: "Look at all this rage, look at all the repressed violence" and informs Stevens that if he goes undercover all of his "faults will become virtues." The confidential personnel file also reveals that Russell Stevens Jr. is also known as John Q. Hull (an obvious phonetic signifier for John Q. Law and the antithesis of John Q. Public); the Du Boisian double consciousness is again established as his dual identity succinctly foreshadows Hull (the name Carver uses for his undercover officer) being a police officer acting like a drug-selling criminal. Providing a context to the racial aspects of the film, Mark Berrettini in "Transgression, Racialized Policing and the Limits of Identity: *Deep Cover*," argues:

While he [Stevens] confronts racism within the police institution from the film's outset, the shift in Stevens' professional life is represented as problematic since it seems to depend upon his skin color, cultural heritage, and negative associations with blackness rather upon his skills as a police officer. The film simultaneously represents this racism within the police and societal prejudices against African American men both as a boon to his undercover policing but as damaging to his personal life. (148)

Having tragically established the death of Stevens' father, there are a number of father figures that provide him with guidance; Carver's fatherly and emphatic advice to his new mentee is "don't blow your cover." Carver's mandate does not address the other two possibilities of going undercover: getting flipped (crossing the line to becoming a criminal) and getting deeper (making your way into the dark world of crime and breaking up the drug ring). While the third criterion is implicit in going undercover, the tension in the film is Hull walking the line between committing felonies that could land him in jail for a considerable amount of time and stopping the criminal enterprise of drug dealing. Thus playing intensely on racial tensions just as he did in *A Rage in Harlem,* Duke shows Russell being manipulated by the arrogant and self-righteous Carver, an individual who despite his diminutive stature symbolizes the larger white supremacist and capitalistic society. Briefed two weeks later in Los Angeles by Carver about the two high-level targets for his undercover work, Felix Barbosa (Gregory Sierra) and Anton Gallegos, Hull as an white male authorized and sanctioned Black outlaw is beset by two other father figures who represent the legal and extra-legal aspects of society. Like Antonio Harris in *Training Day* with his three white male handlers, John Q. Hull has three father figures (two white individuals and one Black individual), Carver, David Jason (Jeff Goldblum), a corrupt, white Jewish lawyer who works for the Latin American drug cartel, and an African American detective named Charles Martin Smith Taft (Clarence Williams III) who keeps a protective eye on Hull, not knowing that he is an undercover police officer.

John Hull's relationship with David Jason reinforces the depths of criminality that Hull must engage in to masquerade as a criminal and as a junior outlaw, moving him closer to the nefarious behavior of his dead father. Seamlessly embracing the street culture, Hull becomes a street-level drug dealer who attracts the attention of one of Jason's dealers, Eddie (Roger Guenveur Smith). Eddie's betrayal of Hull when he is arrested brings Hull closer to Barbosa when Jason becomes his lawyer and has his drug case dismissed. Having kept the confidence of his suppliers, Hull gains the admiration of Jason and Barbosa. Before Jason as the charismatic lawyer comes to Hull's defense, detective Charles plays the role of the Christian and benevolent father seeking to give guidance to his wayward son. Charles attempts to establish a relationship with Hull by showing him pictures of his two daughters while making the point that he would do whatever is necessary to stop drug dealing. Charles states that Hull's drug dealing is analogous to putting a gun to the heads of his "African American beautiful babies" and despite the fatherly concern for Hull, he warns him that he will be all over him "like stink on doo doo," a crude reference to the process of intravenous drug use "shooting shit." Despite his bravado, Charles senses that Hull is not what he appears to be. Ironically in the court room where Jason represents Hull, Carver sits behind Hull and Charles sits in the corner; the three father figures are all concerned about Hull, but with very different agendas, motivations, and interests. Both Jason and Carver seek to use Hull for various clandestine purposes and Charles seeks to protect him from a life of criminal activity.

Later, as a police officer undercover, Hull witnesses the brutal killing of Eddie by Barbosa as he beats him to death with a pool stick; unable to "blow his cover," Hull like the James Weldon Johnson's Ex-Colored Man passing for white at the scene of the lynch-burning must look on in horror as another Black man is beaten to death. Eddie's death leads to Hull's advancement as he is introduced to Jason and Barbosa's money-laundering partner, Betty McCutheon (Victoria Dillard), an African American art dealer who specializes in "ethnic" art while working for the drug cartel. Like Jason's immediate reaction to Hull, Betty states that she does not trust him, but her fears are slowly diminished as Hull continues to play the nefarious role of the drug-dealing criminal "selling drugs to kids and pregnant women." The significance of Betty's statement is that it foreshadows the fact that almost no one can be trusted in this realm of cat and mouse duplicity. Lamenting in the voiceover that he "hates what he is doing," Hull also proudly acknowledges that he is good at it and that "being a cop was never this easy." Juxtaposed with Hull's desire to be an effective drug dealer is Jason's sexual predilection for blackness articulated by his taxonomic gazes at Betty. When he comes out of an attractive Black woman's apartment, he asks Hull: "How come I like balling Black chicks so much?" Director Duke establishes an analogy between Gerald Carver and David Jason, two white males on different sides of the law using Black bodies for their own self-righteous means. Hull's satirical response to Jason's unashamed racism places emphasis on the Hegelian master and slave dialectic as he states: "Maybe you feel like fucking a slave." This candid response becomes more complex when we consider how the manipulative lawyer, DeWitt Albright in *Devil in a Blue Dress* exploits Easy Rawlins, Jason exploits Hull and Betty and has little remorse for the brutal death of Eddie; echoing the horror-filled days of slavery, Black bodies are to be used, consumed, and discarded. Furthering the concept of consumption and disposability of Black bodies, Betty refers to John Hull as the "new Eddie" and that "The other one wore out." David Jason relates that Eddie was "The factory recall" and Hull represents "the advanced model." Not surprisingly, Jason's language conveys his white supremacist views when he compares Hull to a "beautiful panther," a "jungle storm," and a "dangerous, magnificent beast [who has] the gift of fury." David Jason's racist and hyperbolic description of the Black male body occurs after Hull murders a rival African American drug dealer named Ivy (James T. Morris). Having watched Eddie being killed, the death of Ivy by Hull solidifies his descent to lowest depths of criminality as he becomes like his manipulative white father figures, Jason and Carver.

Similar to most narratives of father and son conflict, the symbolic or literal death of the father must occur if the son is to achieve his subjectivity; this occurs three-fold in *Deep Cover*. In one of the final scenes with Carver, Hull informs his superior officer that he has an upcoming meeting with Gallegos, the second highest member of the cartel. Carver responds that Hull's clandestine operation is over because true to his psychological profile he violated a direct order. This conflict escalates as Carver pulls his gun and threatens to arrest Hull. The father and son paradigm is reversed as Hull grabs his guns and throws him on the hood of the car. High-level prevarications are revealed as Carver tells Hull that Gallegos is no longer a target because Gallegos's uncle, Guzman (Rene Assa) who is also entangled in the drug cartel, is now a political ally of the United States government. Realizing the depth and breadth of the deception Hull acknowledges the paradox of his identity; Hull in response to another job in Washington, tells Carver: "I can get more money and clout on the street than [I can] following your ass to Washington ... This whole fucking time I'm pretending to be a drug dealer. I ain't nothing but a drug dealer pretending to be a cop. I ain't gonna pretend no more. I quit." Hull's rejection of his police persona and his acceptance of his drug dealer persona provide a synthesis between his identity as a police officer and his identity as a criminal as earlier articulated by Carver. The second and third father and son conflict involves Hull and Jason as they attempt to sell synthetic drugs to Guzman when Charles Taft attempts to arrest everyone at this midnight meeting on the docks. Here Charles pleads with Hull and Jason to turn themselves in after Guzman uses his diplomatic status to flee the scene, but Charles is shot and killed by Jason. Hull's emotional response to his "father's" death leads him to identify himself as a police officer and as the altercation between Hull and Jason escalates, Hull shoots and kills his criminal father, Jason.

With these two father figures dead, Hull must make a final break with Gerald Carver, by testifying in a hearing about the successful nature of the deep cover operation. With eleven million dollars of stolen drug money along with Betty and the young son, James (Joseph Ferro) of a deceased drug addict named Belinda Chacon (Kamala Lopez), the film ends with Hull attempting to begin a new life outside of law enforcement and criminal activity. When Carver demands to know where the money is, Hull responds by self-righteously asking Carver the same test question that began this clandestine operation, and then answers the question himself: "the nigger is the one who would even think about telling [where the money is]" and then hits Carver in the stomach, a symbolic castration of the father. Like the redemptive shooting and killing of racist Jason, this is a reversal of the father and son paradigm as Hull attains full subjectivity in relation to the three father figures. John Hull's reconfiguration of the Black family provides us with some sense of redemption for his legally sanctioned criminal activities that have resulted in the brutal killings of three Black men and countless individuals addicted to the drugs he sold, especially pregnant women and children. Like Easy Rawlins in *Devil in a Blue Dress* and Grant Wiggins in *A Lesson Before Dying*, John Hull discovers that for Black men the quest for the American Dream is always a difficult process because of the persistence and permanence of racism in the society, too often leaving Black men with a finite number of long-term options for subjectivity outside of the pernicious parameters of criminality. Because we had little to go on in terms of Hull before he went undercover except for the desire not to be like his father, the film concludes with the issue of who will he be outside of these white male dominated identities. What we see in *Deep Cover* as well as in the four novels discussed in this book in many different forms is the clearly justified Angry Black Man syndrome articulated as Black Rage, a phenomenon that James Baldwin described as to be Black and conscious in America is to be in a constant state of rage or as comedian Richard Pyor stated: "I got a right to be hostile, my people are being persecuted!" What we are left with is the treatment of Black criminality as an investigation of Black identity politics within the context of a white male dominated and racist society. As John Jackson Jr. argues in *Racial Paranoia: The Unintended Consequences of Political Correctness* (2008): "Racism is still 'an American dilemma,' but it is a dilemma that has been transformed by the structural changes remapping our country's social hierarchies: the move from chattel slavery to sharecropping and agriculture to urbanization, the migrations from South to North, and the radical renunciations of blatantly racist social policies" (191). Fueled by racism and classism, established boundaries and identities become blurred; however, for Black men, especially Black police officers the dynamics of race too often place them in the role of the outsider, the outlaw. White supremacy continues to mutate and this transmutation is most evident in the too often racist social policies in education, employment, housing, and law enforcement where Black males are too often under the gun.

Again, why is another group of Black parents having to fear for their Black male children? Again, why are these angry Black people waving their clenched fists in the air, seeking some justice from a failed legal system? Again, why are these police officers standing in front of another police precinct (this one in Queens County in New York City) with faces fixed like polished stone? The gruesome death of Sean Bell and the wounding of his two friends, Joseph Guzman and Trent Benefield, in front of Club Kalua nightclub in Jamaica, New York, on November 25, 2006 and the despicable racist remarks of Michael Richards at the Laugh Factory in West Hollywood on November 19, 2006 offer excellent opportunities to examine the ongoing racial dynamics. The majority of white people in America have a Ku Klux Klan mentality when it comes to education, employment, and housing with their trepidations of miscegenation as the bedrock for their decisions. Sadly far too many Black people have internalized the fundamental tenets of America's white supremacist culture. Like many young Black men, Sean Bell was a casualty of a castrating and emasculating white supremacist educational system that left him with few opportunities for socioeconomic advancement. Numerous menial jobs did not allow Sean to provide for his girlfriend, Nicole Ashley Paultre, and two young children, four-year-old Jada Bell and six-month-old Jordyn Bell. Paradoxically, before he was killed Sean articulated the desire to join the electrical union, another bastion of white supremacy and white male privilege. Like the New York City Police Department and the New York City Fire Department, the construction industry represents one of the most racist and white male dominated sectors of New York City. In America, many Black men like Sean Bell die before they are killed. The dropout rate for Black and Latino students in New York City high schools is an alarming 50%, and it coincides with the 50% plus unemployment rate of Black males. One grim statistic should stay with us: Only 51% of all Black students and 52% of all Hispanic students graduate high school, and only 20% of all Black and 16% of all Hispanic students leave high school college ready. More likely than not Black and Latino academic institutions get the bulk of the 31% of Blacks and 36% of Hispanics that need remediation. Many Black and Latino students work, live, eat, and sleep the philosophical, epistemological, and cosmological realities of white supremacy, and they need pedagogical approaches to address these realities. Like many of my Black male students who are outraged at yet another police killing of an innocent and unarmed Black man, it would be very painless for to articulate an anti-police perspective similar to that of the old school rappers like NWA, Ice T, Ice Cube, Paris, Public Enemy, Dead Prez, and of course Tupac Shakur. Michael Richards despicable statement to a Black man that: "Fifty years ago we'd have you upside down with a fucking fork up your ass," represents a public articulation of the silent racism that many Black people face. Richards's use of "we'd" is especially revealing as he aligns himself with the Ku Klux Klan and other white supremacist groups involved in the over 3,000 lynchings of Black people and countless acts of terrorism in this country from the end of the nineteenth century to 1968; these lynchings were festive occasions on which white families with picnic baskets would watch the torture, mutilation, and sadistic killing of Black people, especially Black men. The word "nigger" rolled off Richards's tongue as smoothly as soy butter on hot blueberry muffins. The educational genocide only foreshadows the slow death by incarceration and the more expedient death by police deadly force. Medgar Evers took the radical road and challenged the system of white supremacy despite the lethal consequences. Since are all going to die anyway, the real question is how we will live and what we will stand for in this genocidal white supremacist culture designed to murder Black people especially Black males with or without deadly force. Forty-one shots last time, fifty shots this time, how many shots next time?

Police thought a gun was present in the Sean Bell case and lied about a fourth Black male being present. Using the media, the police attempt to transform lies into facts. Head of the Organized Crime Control Bureau Chief Anthony J. Izzo headed the undercover unit that killed Sean Bell and wounded his two friends. President of the Detective Union Poladino claimed that the shooting is justified. Police defend white supremacy and capitalism in the same manner that the soldiers are killing and raping innocents in Iraq. Simply put, military terrorism is similar to police terrorism. The New York City Police Department's Office of Public Relations presents information that tends to criminalize those Black innocent victims. Some 137 persons have been killed by the New York City Police Department since the Amadou Diallo murder and the murder of Sean Bell. So Blacks repeatedly ask, "How do white police respond when Black men are involved?" This question became real in the "friendly fire" shooting and killing of New York City Police Officer Omar Edwards who was killed in May 2009 while chasing a man who had broken into his car. A white officer shot Edwards three times, the final shot in the back. As Edwards lay handcuffed on the ground, cops cut off his shirt to reveal a Police Academy T-shirt and found a NYPD shield in his pants pocket. Officer Edwards is survived by his wife Danielle and eighteen-month-old Xavier and seven-month-old Keanua. "My son is dead, my son is dead," Edwards's heartbroken mother, Natalia Harding told a friend while she held her son's babies. "They killed my son." Police Commissioner Raymond Kelly spent fifteen minutes with the family and never had any further contact with them, and Mayor Michael Bloomberg made some perfunctory comments about improving police procedures. Regardless of the verbiage that surrounds Edwards' killing a fundamental issue remains about white police officers in their encounters with Black males, especially in Black communities. Most white male police officers do not live in the communities where they work and often view these communities as unpredictable war zones. Consequently, many African Americans do not trust white police officers and are extremely apprehensive about any confrontation or interaction. A Black man running with a gun in a Black community is viewed first and perhaps only as a criminal; the possibility of him being a police officer was not a consideration. Although many whites may fervently believe that race is not a factor in this shooting, the other incidents of police shootings of police in New York City all involve white officers shooting Black officers and not the reverse.

Despite the white supremacist Republicans with their legacy of Willie Hortonistic tactics and dirty tricks of demonization by association, America as represented by Blacks, whites, Asians, and Latinos, and Native Americans elected Barack Obama as the forty-fourth president of the United States of America. Considering the fact that African Americans while enslaved by whites laid the steps to the Capitol building and had a hand in building the White House in Washington, D.C., this election of the first African American man is beyond historical in its national and international importance.

New studies on the plight of Black men in America reveal a dire situation in terms of employment and education. Huge pools of poorly educated Black men are becoming even more disconnected from the mainstream society. As Erik Eckholm relates in "Plight Deepens for Black Men, Studies Warn": "Especially in the country's inner cities, the studies show, finishing high school is the exception, legal work is scarcer than ever and prison is almost routine, with incarceration rates climbing for blacks as urban crimes rates have declined" (18).

During the second week of July 2009, two incidents involving Black men and the legal authorities captured the national and international spotlight. In the first incident, federal agents came to the Virginia home of Michael Vick, the former quarterback with the Atlanta Falcons, to remove an electronic monitoring device from his ankle. This brought an end to a significant part of Vick's conviction and sentence of twenty-three months in prison for federal criminal charges of running a dog-fighting operation. Vick was not eligible to restart his football career until he was reinstated by NFL Commissioner Roger Goodell. Tragically for him and his family, Vick was out of football for two years—he was suspended even before he went to prison—and his options may be limited. He is twenty-nine, still young enough for many productive seasons, but he was becoming a less accurate thrower as his career went on, and few teams may be willing to take him on as a starting quarterback. The outrage over this dog fighting caused many to wonder if Vick could redeem himself.

Many white Americans reacted to the cruelty to animals by Vick and his friends in a louder and more tumultuous manner than we see with the systematic cruelty to Black people in terms of education, health care, employment, and police brutality. Rich white individuals sent planes to evacuate animals from Katrina, and the care and feeding of animals in America represents a billion-dollar industry. Perhaps the larger issue here is that Michael Vick believed that his status as a NFL quarterback and his tremendous wealth would somehow allow him to act in a cruel manner to animals. Some white NFL players have been convicted of manslaughter and have done less prison time than Vick. On July 27, 2009, Commissioner Goodell reinstated Michael Vick, allowing any NFL team to sign him up. Goodell stated: "I never thought about this in the context of the commercial success of the NFL, the intent here was to do the right thing in a young man's life....I believe he is sincere in his remorse; he recognizes what he was engaging in was horrific and cruel....He didn't focus significantly on the loss of career and the loss of money." It is hard to believe that money and career are not issues because there are numerous other Black men without the monetary resources and athletic skills of Vick who are not allowed to pursue redemption. Not surprisingly, on August 13th 2009, after Vick filed for bankruptcy, the Philadelphia Eagles signed Vick to a two-year renewable six million dollar contract.

In the second incident the mix of the perception of racism and questionable police behavior in one Northeastern college town created a national and international fervor that would involve the president of the United States. On July 16th 2009, Henry Louis Gates Jr., the noted African American scholar, Director of the W. E. B. Du Bois Institute for Research in African and African American Studies and a University Professor at Harvard University in Cambridge, Massachusetts, was arrested for disorderly conduct at his home by a white police officer, Sergeant James Crowley. Gates was returning home from filming a documentary in China and could not open the front door of his residence; he and the cab driver attempted to force the door open when a white woman, Lucia Whalen reported "seeing two large men, one looked kind of Hispanic, but I'm not really sure, and the other one entered, and I didn't see what he looked like at all." Furthermore, Lucia Whalen's lawyer categorically denies that his client had any conversation with Sergeant Crowley and notes that she "never said to any police or to anybody anything about 'two black men.'" However, Crowley suspected that two Black men were burglars. Once he was able to enter the house through the rear door, Gates was confronted by the police and the conflict began. Like two freight trains approaching each other on the same track, this confrontation was messy, involving less obvious racial dynamics and more proper police procedure, power, privilege, property, and pride. With no physical witnesses (Crowley's radio allowed the confrontation to be recorded), the narratives of Gates and Crowley could not be more dissimilar, with much more professionally at stake for Gates. Gates viewed Crowley as a "rogue" who racially profiled him, initially not believing that he was a professor at Harvard and the sole resident of the house. On the other hand, Crowley documents in his police report that Gates was "loud and tumultuous" and so angry, verbally combative, and out of control that he initially prevented a proper investigation. As Crowley was summoned to the house, it is difficult to assume racially profiling is an element here, especially if the allegation is true that Gates refused to provide proper identification when the confrontation ensued. Ironically, Sergeant Crowley is an instructor at the police academy who teaches police cadets about racial profiling. On the other hand, Henry "Skip" Gates's academic and professional work centers on transcending race, not reinforcing racial stereotypes, and avoiding racial essentialism. It appears that Sergeant Crowley's expertise and Professor Gates' professionalism did not survive this out-of-the-classroom examination. Perhaps both individuals will have to rethink the very things that define their expertise before they return to their respective classrooms because this is clearly a teaching moment, especially since both relate very different versions of the encounter. According to Charles J. Olgetree (a close friend of Barack Obama, a Harvard professor, and the lawyer representing Gates), Gates claimed that he showed photo identification, but Crowley did not believe Professor Gates lived at that house. Frustrated, Professor Gates requested Sgt. Crowley's name and badge number, which he refused to give. The police version was that Gates refused to show identification and accused Crowley of racism by yelling: "Why because I'm a black man in America?" The report stated that Gates followed the officer outside, yelled at him and was arrested for disorderly conduct. Gates and Crowley are also in stark disagreement that Gates, the author of *Signifying Monkey,* made negative references to Crowley's mother. The exact words that Gates allegedly uttered in response to Crowley's request for Gates to step outside was: "Ya, I'll speak to your mama outside." In an African American context playing the dozens (verbal discourse involving talking negatively about another person's mother) is common, but when that sort of speech crosses the racial divide it can be extremely problematic, especially if that other person is a white police officer. Later, Gates would suggest that Crowley picked this up from watching an episode of *Good Times.* Gates's response to this allegation was: "The idea that I would, in a vulnerable position talk about the man's mother is absurd," he told Gayle King of Sirius radio. "I don't talk about people's mothers. ...You could get killed talking about somebody's mother in the barbershop, let alone with a white police officer...I think they did some historical research, and watched some episodes of *Good Times.*" For Gates to be so quick in coming up with that specific reference suggests some disingenuous aspects to Gates' account. Indeed the officer's statement "I apologize that I was not aware who Professor Gates was...I am still just amazed that somebody of his level of intelligence would stoop to such a level, berate me, accuse me of being a racist, of racial profiling." Perhaps Gates became the signifying monkey and when confronted with his own words that would demean his scholarly reputation resorted to the common trope of psychological projection, blaming his accuser. Interestingly, one of his Harvard colleagues revealed that Gates would often tell racial jokes.

In a news conference at the White House, President Barack Obama made remarks that escalated the ongoing tension. Beyond his undeniable comment that "There's a long history in this country of African Americans and Hispanics being stopped disproportionately by the police," President Obama stated that the Cambridge Police Department acted stupidly in arresting Professor Gates. With America still very divided by race and to a lesser extent class, this comment had the effect of demonizing the entire Cambridge Police Department and aligning the president with Black people especially since Obama stated: "Well, I should say at the outset that Skip Gates is a friend, so I may be a little biased here." Outrage from the Cambridge Police Department was swift although many Black people applauded the president's remarks, remarks that he clarified in a subsequent interview. The president's remarks did restart a long overdue conversation about race and community policing and perhaps will begin a conversation about the larger issue of white male privilege, which Professor Gates will never attain even if he becomes the president of Harvard University. Furthermore, many believed that the president should not have stepped into a police matter himself (especially without the facts) and placed a call to Crowley, something that one of his aides could have done. This phone call suggested that Crowley and white male police officers represent that last bastion of white male supremacy and President Obama's call reestablished white male subjectivity. Indeed, the professionalism of President Obama, Professor Gates, and Sergeant Crowley will all be diminished by their behavior in this incident. Although the highly visible, wealthy, and astute scholar Gates will never become the poster guy for police brutality or racial profiling, this incident represents the larger reality of the ongoing conflict between many Blacks and white police across America. It seems that, in Crowley's mind Gates represented the stereotypical dangerous Black man, despite Gates' advanced age, five foot six height, one hundred forty pounds, and cane (perhaps a dangerous weapon). According to the police reports, Crowley repeatedly requested police cars to keep coming to Gates' home because of the disturbance. This request is usually associated with an angry and erratic gun-toting or knife-wielding individual, and Crowley based on his police report suggests that he was in eminent fear of his life in this encounter. As argued in *Eating the Black Body: Miscegenation as Sexual Consumption in African Literature,* in America's white supremacist culture the Black male body is often criminalized regardless of the age, size, demeanor, or obvious physical limitations of the individual. Before the charges on Gates were dropped, Al Sharpton announced that he would come to the arraignment. Sharpton, one the most vocal challengers of racial profiling, has stated:

To see policing as a national issue—that all over the country people are having to renegotiate how the police and the community ought to deal—that's a direct result of our work. Three states—New Jersey, Missouri, and Maryland—now have racial profiling laws. Most people were saying that racial profiling didn't exist when we started our work on the issue. Now it is a household phrase. (248)

Al Sharpton and many other put their freedom on the line to be arrested in protest to the killing of Amadou Diallo among others and the miscarriage of justice subsequent to the killings. Tragically, young Black males' encounters with other young Black males comprise the larger issue; Black males are killing each other at a rate astronomically greater than the rate at which Black males are killed by white male police officers. This self-directed genocide must be placed in the context of a generally failed public education system where Black males are turned off by the fourth grade and gradually drop out or graduate with little or no marketable skills. Those who do go to college need years of remediation. While the enduring plagues of racial hatred and white privilege are fundamental aspects of American society, self-destructive life choices and unhealthy personal habits cannot be blamed solely on white supremacy and racism. A prime example of this can be found in the sacred halls of the United States Congress. On Friday November 13, 2009, former Representative William Jefferson, a New Orleans Democrat whose political career once seemed to hold high promise, was sentenced Friday to 13 years in prison for using his office to try to enrich himself and his relatives. Jefferson's sentence was far less than recommended by prosecutors, who had sought at least 27 years. The prosecutor's rationale for the exceptionally long sentence when compared to other Congressmen convicted for similar crimes was that had Jefferson's schemes come to full fruition, he stood to reap hundreds of millions of dollars in eleven separate bribery schemes. Mr. Jefferson, 62, who was convicted on Aug. 5 of bribery, racketeering and money laundering involving business ventures in Africa, might have to spend the rest of his life behind bars with such a sentence, since there is no parole in the federal prison system, and the only leniency is 15 percent off for good behavior. Agents investigating the case found $90,000 wrapped in foil and hidden in boxes of frozen pie crusts in his freezer. Ironically, Jefferson, a graduate from Harvard Law School, became the first Black person from Louisiana elected to Congress since Reconstruction. Jefferson's lawyer, Robert Trout, related that while his client acknowledged a level of responsibility for his conduct, he also believed that he was operating within the law. Like Jefferson in *A Lesson Before Dying*, William Jefferson's life is over unless he wins an appeal.[3]

Like Cross Damon, Charles Taylor, Easy Rawlins, Jefferson, and Grant Wiggins in *The Outsider, The Third Generation, Devil in a Blue Dress*, and *A Lesson Before Dying*, respectively, Professor Gates learned a profound and personal lesson about the problems and tragic possibilities when innocent Black men encounter white male police. Like the characters in these four novels, Gates's immediate reaction to a white male police officer was that of loathing and apprehension. However, one need only examine the official Cambridge Police Department report to obtain a clear picture of an obnoxious and confrontational Black scholar, crying racism like the proverbial Peter crying wolf; and Gates was constantly wolfing, signifying, and dising the police until the silver handcuffs brought him back to reality. Based on Lucia Whalen's statement it appears that Crowley equivocated that part of his report that he spoke to her outside of her house and that he fabricated her statement about the "two black men." Sergeant Crowley's professionalism and legacy will always be marred by this encounter. Professor Gates's legacy—scholar of African American Studies, entrepreneur of Microsoft software, op-editorial writer for *The New York Times*, contributor to a number of PBS documentaries, McArthur Fellow (the genius award), one-man intellectual and media conglomerate, co-founder of the genealogy website AfricanDNA.com, director of the W. E. B. Du Bois Institute for African and African American Research at Harvard, editor in chief of the website Oxford African American Studies Center, editor in chief of The Root, a website on African American news, culture and genealogy—is clearly extensive. Ironically, he also graciously penned an endorsement for John L. Jackson Jr.'s *Racial Paranoia: The Unintended Consequences of Political Correctness* (2008); the back cover blurb states:

> By listening to conversations about race and studying its endless iterations in popular culture, John L. Jackson, Jr. arrives at a nuanced and utterly convincing reading of how, when we talk about race, we pretend to talk about everything but race, and how all of us learn to understand what's being said. This important new book will help us decipher and make sense of our national conversation about race.

Gates' prophetic discourse is so in line with his behavior and statements to Crowley; however, pretending to "talk about everything but race" and pretending to be a victim of racial profiling, Gates did open up a national conversation on numerous nuances of race, especially an element that he did not possess—white male privilege.

All said Professor Gates will also have a significant stain on his professional and academic profile because of his behavior during and after this event. It is hard to comprehend that he would be handcuffed and arrested if he simply and respectfully identified himself to the officer who was called to the scene to protect Professor Gates' property. Simply put, Professor Gates did not act in a manner that reflected his elite status as a distinguished Black Harvard Professor; perhaps for a second he thought he had the rights and privileges associated with white males of a similar or even lower socioeconomic status. Even former Secretary of State General Colin Powell, who has held numerous high-level positions in government and who routinely comes into contact with police officers and security personnel, questioned Gates' behavior. Powell stated on Larry King's CNN program that you do not become confrontational with the police; you should cooperate and then protest your case at a later point. Powell said: "When you're faced with an officer trying to do his job and get to the bottom of something, this is not the time to get into an argument with him...I was taught as a child. You don't argue with a police officer." Perhaps this was Gates's chance to become a "speakerly text" and to engage in his own self-directed "battle royal" and throw some verbal blows for all the Black men who have been demeaned, harassed, emasculated, and physically beaten by racist white police officers across America. Having to teach about the horrors of the Middle Passage, the terrorism during Black people's enslavement, sadistic extra-legal lynchings, the legal abuse of the Scottsboro Boys, the demonic killing of Emmett Louis Till, and the on-going killing of unarmed Black men, who knows what exactly triggered Gates' verbal assault. Perhaps racial memory kicked in and the spirits of Frederick Douglass, Henry Garnett, David Walker, George Jackson, Charles Hamilton Houston, W. E. B. Du Bois, and Malcolm X took possession of Henry Louis Gates' tongue with the stunned and shocked James Crowley having no understanding of this Black man's rage. Maybe there was some deep-seated psychological transference from the Gates-controlled graduate seminar room to this unexpected encounter. There is little doubt that Professor Gates viewed this situation from his historical racial lens and that he was having a racial moment; a racial moment can be best described as a present experience that conjures up past traumatic experiences read, studied, or personally experienced. And while Sergeant James Crowley in the context of his official police duties had every legal right to arrest any individual regardless of race, class, or gender whose conduct he deemed disorderly, (especially if he was repeatedly provoked), he did as Professor Gates allegedly stated in his repeated haranguing and verbal jostling of Crowley "mess with the wrong individual." Because of all of the media attention brought to him and the Cambridge Police Department and because of the tremendous public presence and influence that Gates has in academia, in the national media and currently in the Oval Office of the White House, like the psychologically distraught gun-toting Michael Douglas' character in the film *Falling Down* (1993), the white police officer, James Crowley became a unknowing victim of Black history, caught between the dialectical discourse of a Black professor of an Ivy League institution and a Black president in the White House. And Gates engaged in the delusional process of believing he had white male privilege and status in a white supremacist culture where white police officers maintain and establish order. The public culmination of the conflict was when Crowley and Gates agreed to meet President Obama in the White House and share a beer. Here there were no apologies given, but an agreement to meet again privately. Reflecting on the situation, Gates stated: "The most important thing I learned, I learned about police officers the stresses and realities of the excellent job the police do every day," he said. "At the same time, racial profiling is a very dangerous thing with a long history, and we have to make Americans more sensitive to the realities of racial profiling." Gates not missing an opportunity to promote his 1994 memoir, *Colored People,* gave Sergeant Crowley a signed copy, he said, with the inscription, "Linked together forever in history." Sensing the larger moment in America's racial history, Gates stated: "Through an accident of fate this guy and I are linked together," he said, "and the question is how can he help end racial profiling and how can I help members of my community be sensitive to the concerns of the police? If we can do that, then James Crowley and I will have taken control of our lives and our peculiar experience together and move it out of a Tom Wolfe novel and into a positive impact." With the vehement racism that this incident produced via websites, radio talk shows, and emails it is unlikely that any serious conversations or societal change will occur. The tragic reality is that there is a justice system for white males and another justice system for Black males when you consider that according to 2008 figures there are nearly 5,000 Black males imprisoned in America for every 100,000 Black men in the population. Compare this to only 730 white male inmates per 100,000 white men. Black men are routinely stopped, searched, harassed, humiliated, emasculated, assaulted, arrested and sometimes killed by police in America; this reality represents the extreme denial around racial profiling that most whites are not interested in examining much less admitting. These disturbing statistics are rooted in the educational and economic disparities around race. As William Julius Wilson argues in *More Than Just Race: Being Black and Poor in the Inner City* (2009): "Indeed one of the legacies of historic racial subjugation in the country is the extremely high crime rates. And as long as these disturbing rates persist, people of all racial and ethnic groups will often react to black males in public and private spaces in negative ways" (2). In America's white supremacist culture white police trump any concerns Black men have over unfairness. Furthermore, in this specific encounter with its intense and enduring undertones of racial antagonism, white America represents the fifty-first state, the state of denial. As Michael Eric Dyson reminds us in *Can You Hear Me Now?*: "The paradox of our situation is that Americans are fatigued and fascinated by race" (185). White America continues to lynch with the racial disenfranchisement of Black people through social policies manifested in the everyday behavior of police officers, judges, district attorneys, and teachers.

Gates' encounter with the police echoed in the minds of many when the Florida Highway Patrol arrived at Tiger Woods' residence on November

27, 2009. Woods crashed his 2009 Cadillac Escalade into a fire hydrant and a neighbor's tree as he was pulling out of his driveway in Isleworth, an Orlando suburb. Allegations of infidelity become more certain when Woods issued a statement on his website admitting to transgressions and apologized to his family and supporters. Again the issue is that regardless of class status, Black men are constantly having interactions with legal authorities.

Without a doubt, despite the election of a Black man as President, this has been a year with a plethora of tragic tales in the lives of Black men and those who love and respect them. Michael Jackson died after an overdose of propofol; Chris Brown brutally beat his girlfriend, Rihanna; Plaxico Burress was incarcerated for accidentally shooting himself with his own gun; Henry Louis Gates Jr. was arrested for shooting off his mouth at his residence; former Congressman William Jefferson will be on lockdown for thirteen years in a federal prison for bribery; Tiger Woods hitting a tree at the end of his residence with his Cadillac reveals that he is ladies man and a real "player," and lastly we will close out the year with rumors that director Lee Daniel's film *Precious* based on Sapphire's book *Push* (1997) will garner Academy Award nominations for a film based on as dark-skinned and over-weight Black female being raped and having to twice mother children by her own Black father. All of these incidents involve legal authorities as the racist and sterotypical notions of Black male subjectivity are tragically reinforced and reinscribed on the curtain-less stage.

When we consider the numerous state laws making literacy illegal for Blacks and the current difficulties for Back males pursuing a transformative education the lives of Frederick Douglass and David Walker come to mind. Douglass was born in slavery and Walker was born a free man; however, both men became literate and used their powerful voices to challenge the American system of racial disenfranchisement. In Douglass' first autobiography he provides a synthesis between his horrific days of abuse and neglect in slavery and his current ability to write himself into existence:

> I was seldom whipped by my old master, and suffered little from anything else than hunger and cold. I suffered much from hunger, but much more from cold. In hottest summer and coldest winter, I was kept almost naked—no shoes, no stockings, no jacket, no trousers, nothing on but a coarse tow linen shirt, reaching only to my needs. I had no bed. I must have perished with cold, but that, the coldest nights, I used to steal a bag which was used for carrying corn to the mill. I would craw into this bag, and there sleep on the cold, damp, clay floor, with my head in and feet out. My feet have been so cracked with the frost, that the pen with which I am writing might be laid in the gashes. (28)

Beyond the absolute physical neglect suffered, the paradox is that slaves like Douglass had to steal in order to survive as slaves for their masters' exploitation with little hope for freedom. Douglass' body inscribed with physical and psychological abuse allows him to vividly write in a manner that is absolutely compelling for current Black male writers who are challenging America's new and improved system of racial disenfranchisement where white privilege represents the law of the land. Remarking on his own newly discovered subjectivity, in his *Narrative* Douglass states: "My long-crushed spirit rose, cowardice departed, bold defiance took its place; and I now resolved that, however long I might remain a slave in form, the day had passed forever when I could be a slave in fact" (89). As one of the numerous eulogists stated that "what the cause of freedom wanted was a man who had been in hell; in the hell of human slavery...who knew what it was to be compelled to yearn in vain for mother-love; to fight his way inch by inch, into the simple rudiments of human speech, of human knowledge, into any of the prerogatives of manhood" (Rankin 33). On the other hand, Walker's prose in his *Appeal* was equally a denouncement of the demonic aspects of Black people's enslavement and of those Blacks who failed to challenged this system. Discussing the malevolence of whites during the period of enslavement, Walker states:

> The causes, my brethren, which produce our wretchedness and miseries, are so very numerous and aggravating, that I believe the pen only of a Josephus or a Plutarch, can well enumerate and explain them. Upon subjects, then, of such incomprehensible magnitude, so impenetrable, and so notorious, I shall be obliged to omit a large class of, and content myself with giving you an exposition of a few of those, whch do indeed rage to such an alarming pitch; that they cannot but be a perpetual source of dismay to every reflecting mind. (179)

Malcolm X and George Jackson represent the more contemporary Black men who articulated their enduring rage against oppression and suffered the deadly consequences. These Black men represent the epitome of Black Outlaws, individuals who despite their circumstances challenged America to live up to its democratic ideas and wrote themselves into existence in manners that would send a call that writers such as Richard Wright, Chester Himes, Walter Mosley and Ernest J. Gaines would respond to. Their response would confirm Black people's steadfast desire for inclusion and respect. In Richard Wright's *12 Million Black Voices* (1941), Wright places the racial in America in a broad and somewhat sanguine perspective;

> We black folk, our history and our present being, are a mirror of all the manifold experiences of America. What we want, what we represent, what we endure is what America is. If we black folk perish, America will perish. If America has forgotten her past, then let her look into the mirror of our consciousness and she will see the living past living in the present, for our memories go back, through our black folk of today, through the recollections of our black parents, and through the tales of slavery told by our back grandparents, to the time when none of us black or white, lived in this fertile land. The differences between black folk and white folk are not blood or color, and the ties that bind us are deeper than those

that separate us. The common road of hope which we all travel has brought us
into a stronger kinship than any words, laws, or legal claims. (146)

Unfortunately, white America has failed the test of looking into the mirror
and in many cases is willing to break any mirror that would cause self-
reflection. This denial combined with a deep-seated nihilism in the minds
of many Black people represents the unspoken problems around race. This
deep-seated nihilism was powerfully on display in the senseless and brutal
killing of the sixteen-year-old Black male honor student Derrion Albert in
Chicago on October 1, 2009. Prosecutors said Derrion was pummeled with
wooden planks and kicked in the head after he found himself in the midst
of a large fight between two groups of Black youths a few blocks from his
school, Christian Fenger Academy High School, on the South Side. Silvanus
Shannon, 19; Eugene Riley, 18; Eugene Bailey, 17; and Eric Carson, 16, were
charged with first-degree murder on Monday and held without bail. The
police said a video of the violent incident helped them identify the suspects.
In his article "Behind the Laughter" Bob Herbert states: "Dozens of boys
and girls of school-age and younger are murdered in Chicago every year.
One hundred were killed there last year, according to the police. The blood
of the young is spattered daily on the stoops, sidewalks and streets of
American cities from coast to coast, and we won't even take notice unless,
for example, we can engage in the ghoulish delight of watching the murder
played over and over again on video" (20). As Herbert relates this incident
represents just one of the many incidents of Black youth killing each other
across the country; in Chicago there were 34 murders in high schools; this
represents the primary killing field. On the national landscape one in every
10 young male dropouts is locked up in jail or juvenile detention; however,
we find that the figure for Blacks males is one in four. Ernest Dickerson's
film *Juice* (1992) provides one disturbing answer to this intraracial issue
when one psychologically disturbed youth Black male character states that
he hates his Black peers because he hates himself. This senseless violence
must be placed in the content of the larger psychological, physical, and economic violence that Black people experience. Too many Black youth have a
clear sense of the limited opportunities for them as they look at the realities
of their parents' lives due to employment and foreclosures—two economic
factors that are extremely high in comparison to whites. White supremacy
has a long track record in producing the transgenerational transgression of
trauma that manifests itself in deep-seated self-hatred and rage among many
Blacks, especially the male youth. These youth are coming out of the womb
crippled by socioeconomic policies that make it extremely difficult to secure
the footing needed to build the foundations for their future lives. With the
current unemployment rate of Black people at a gut-wrenching 24% and

the poverty rate for Black children at a desperate 35%, there is little doubt that the quality of Black life in America is beyond desperate.

Based on the works of these four writers who document the struggles of young Black males, it is clear that literacy plays a critical factor in socioeconomic success. Douglass used numerous methods in his desire to become literate despite the legal and cultural sanctions against teaching enslaved Blacks to read. As a free man Walker with his vast knowledge of world history understood the importance of literacy. Literacy provides agency and subjectivity for black males in ways that are empowering.

The demonization of Black males continues to be a continuous factor for some whites who commit crimes and need to blame someone else. Like the now infamous cases of Charles Stuart, Susan Smith, and Christopher Pittman, who blamed Black men for their crimes of murder and manslaughter, we now have the case of Bonnie Sweeten, a white suburban mother who on May 26, 2009, placed a 911 call claiming two Black men had carjacked her and kidnapped her daughter—but instead flew to Disney World with her child to escape a looming arrest. She was sent to prison for 9 to 23 months. Bonnie Sweeten, 38, pleaded guilty in Bucks County Court to identity theft and filing a false police report, misdemeanors that typically bring probation. But a judge offended by Sweeten's performance on a 911 tape said her hoax led to a frantic national search, traumatized her daughter and, perhaps worst of all, tore open society's racial wounds. Ironically, Sweeten was a paralegal and notary public; she held a full-time job at a law firm.[4] With the nationwide demonization of black males it is not surprising that a Black male would be the target of Sweeten's racial deception.

In America white supremacy and racism remain the virulent and complex societal factors facing Black people, especially Black males who remain the main target of eradication and incarceration. As the prison industrial complex grows because the miseducational complex remains its direct feeder, the outlook for Black males remains grim, but as preeminent legal scholar and author Derrick Bell so astutely argues there is always progress:

> Even in the face of this enormous obstacle, the commitment of those who seek racial justice remains strong. Tangible progress has been made, and the pull of unfinished business is sufficient to strengthen and spur determination. But the task of equal-justice advocates has not become easier simply because neither slavery's chains, nor the lyncher's rope, nor humiliating Jim Crow signs are any longer the main means of holding black people in a subordinate status. Today, while all manner of civil rights laws and precedents are in place, the protection they provide is diluted by lax enforcement, by the establishment of difficult-to-meet standards of proof, and worse of all, by the increasing irrelevance of antidiscrimination laws to race-related disadvantages, now as likely to be a result of social class of color. (*And We Are Not Saved*[5])

Clearly the notion of a post-racial society in America since the election of President Barack Obama is a delusion because every economic indicator shows that Black people are at the lowest level and the average white person has ten times the wealth of the average Black person. It is apparent that a commitment to democracy and equality must involve the entire society, especially those at the lowest level. According to political theorist Claude Lefort the "important point" about democracy in the face of inequality is that it

> is instituted and sustained by the dissolution of the markers of certainty. It inaugurates a history in which people experience a fundamental indeterminacy as to the basis of power, law and knowledge, and as to the basis of relations between self and other, at every level of social life (at every level where division, and especially the division between those who held power and those who were subject to them, could once be articulated as a result of a belief in the nature of things or in a super principle). (19)

Based on Lefort's analysis there is the enduring hope that those in power will realize the nefarious nature of white supremacy and white male privilege.

Richard Wright, Chester Bomar Himes, Ernest J. Gaines, and Walter Mosley have given us timeless novels that illustrate the complex relationships that Black males have with the legal authorities in America and yet they remain strong in the face of adversity. For these writers issues of race and class become critical to the construction of their Black male characters' subjectivity within America's culture of white male supremacy. The enduring racial discrimination that Black men encounter has transformed from the brutal and sadistic violence associated with lynchings and other forms of violence to social and economic disenfranchisement. Like Toni Morrison's traumatized Black veteran of World War I, Shadrack in *Sula*, the Black men characterized here all represent the Bad Nigger: They challenge America's system of racial hegemony, yet their narratives conclude in tragedy. As H. Nigel Thomas argues: "Death always concludes most of the Bad Nigger tales; however, it is the Bad Nigger's life that is important" (160). The Bad Nigger conjures up the folk hero Staglee. As Julius Lester reminds us: "Folktales are stories that give people a way of communicating with each other about each other—their fears, their hopes, their dreams, their fantasies, giving their explanations of why the world is the way it is (VII). Staglee was without a doubt the "boldest nigger that ever lived," especially in his challenges to the dominant white society. The tragic and heartrending deaths of Cross Damon and Jefferson are balanced with the redemption and hope found with Charles Taylor, Easy Rawlins, and Grant Wiggins; as a teacher Grant is especially important because he has a commitment to empower Black students. Regardless of the outcomes these writers are fixated on a critical examination of the psyches of Black men in the face of oppressive conditions, especially the Black Outlaws who challenge white supremacy.

Notes

1   The consumption of the Black male body speaks to the numerous ways that Black bodies are used in America's white supremacist culture. For example, Black males involved in the Hip Hop industry have been used by major white-male-controlled music corporations that have made immense profits. Also, as pointed out in the analysis of Frank Lucas, the incarceration of Black men creates employment for whites as lawyers, police officers, correction officers, defense attorneys, prosecutors, judges, probation officers, and all the other support service industries that are necessary in the legal arena. As argued in *Eating the Black Body: Miscegenation as Sexual Consumption in African American Literature* (New York: Peter Lang Publishing, Inc., 2006): "In many cases, whites' consumption of blackness leads to an internalization of inferiority where some Black individuals seek to consume other Black individuals or offer themselves up for consumption" (167).

2   Chinua Achebe's *Things Fall Apart* challenges Joseph Conrad's *Heart of Darkness*, which depicted African civilization as primordial and cultureless. Moreover, Conrad's novel depicted African societies as being rife with disease, death, and destruction. Countering this racial essentialism, Achebe presents Nigeria as a complex of advanced social institutions and artistic traditions of Igbo culture. Okonkwo, the son of the effeminate and lazy Unoka, strives to make his way in a world that on the surface seems to value manliness. In so doing, he rejects everything which he believes his father stood. Unoka was idle, poor, profligate, cowardly, gentle, and interested in music and conversation. Okonkwo chooses to become productive, wealthy, thrifty, brave, violent, and adamantly opposed to music and anything else that he perceives to be "soft," such as conversation and emotion. He is stoic to a fault. Just as his father was at odds with the values of the community around him, so too does Okonkwo find himself unable to adapt to changing times as the white man comes to live among the Umuofians. As it becomes evident that compliance rather than violence constitutes the wisest principle for survival, Okonkwo realizes that he has become a relic, no longer able to function within his changing society. Thus Okonkwo represents a Black outlaw because he challenges the norms of his Igbo society as well as the ongoing influence of European society represented by Christianity and its value system.

3   William Jefferson's tragic situation calls to mind the problems that Adam Clayton Powell had when he was in Congress in terms of allegations that Powell had misappropriated Education and Labor Committee funds for his personal use and other charges including evading a subpoena in New York. However unlike Jefferson, Powell has no equal in terms of the amount of legislation he got passed as the first Black Congressman from New York and the first from any Northern state other than Illinois in the Post-Reconstruction Era. Like a Black outlaw, Powell challenged the informal ban on Black representatives using Capitol facilities reserved for white members only. Clashing with segregationists in his own party, Powell took Black constituents to dine with him in the "whites only" House restaurant. More importantly, Powell was instrumental in passing legislation that made lynching a federal crime as well as introducing legislation that desegregated public schools. Equally significant, he challenged the racist Southern

practice of charging Black people a poll tax to vote and stopped racist congressmen from saying the word "nigger" in sessions of Congress. For many Black people in Harlem and around the country, Powell represented a Black politician who was relentless in fighting for justice and equality, a Black outlaw. It is interesting to note that the nefarious Black outlaw John A. Muhammad, the D.C sniper who killed ten individuals in the fall of 2002, was executed at a Virginia state prison in Greensville a couple of days before Jefferson was sentenced to thirteen years in prison. Another tragic aspect to the senseless killing of innocent individuals and the execution of John A. Muhammad is that his fellow outlaw, Lee B. Malvo, who was seventeen years old at the time of the killings will spend the rest of his life in prison. Like many Black males who went to war fighting for America, Muhammad came back a traumatized individual whose killing spree can be compared to that of the equally traumatized Major Nidal Malik Hasan, who killed thirteen individuals and wounded twenty-eight others at the Fort Hood Army base in Texas on November 5, 2009. More than likely Hasan by his religion and ethnicity will be characterized as the angry Black male and will be dealt with in the very same manner as Muhammad, the death penalty by lethal injection. No active military individual has been put to death in fifty years. What becomes clear is that America is very much shaped by violence, and Black outlaws in all different forms are playing their roles on the stage revealing the shadowy side of the American body politic.

4   In 1989 in Massachusetts, Charles Stuart shot himself and killed his pregnant wife for insurance money and blamed it on a Black man. After the police arrested several Black men on suspicion of being involved in the incident, Stuart's brother admitted that he was involved in his brother's wife's killing. Charles Stuart later committed suicide. Next, in South Carolina, in 1994, Susan Smith claimed that a Black man hijacked her car with her kids in it. What was so shocking about Smith disingenuous statements was that she gave the police a very detailed description of a Black male who was 30 to 40 years old and wore a skull cap and other specific attire. She went on television and received a lot of media attention. She would later admit to rolling her car into a lake with her children in it. Why did she do this horrible crime? She wanted to start her life over by marrying a wealthy man without having the burden of her old family. In 2005 in South Carolina, Christopher Pittman killed his grandparents and burned down their house. Later, he took his grandparents' car, their guns, his dog, and $33.00 and left. He was picked up after getting stuck two counties away in the woods. Before confessing, he told a story of a large Black male who had kidnapped him after murdering his grandparents and setting fire to their house. When he ultimately confessed,he proclaimed that his grandparents deserved what they got. He later claimed that he was under the influence of an overdose of Zoloft. Two other incidents of equal significance involve Ashley Todd and Brian Wells. In 2008, in Pennsylvania, Ashley Todd, a young Republican thought it would be a good idea to carve a backwards B on her face and blame it on a Black Barack Obama supporter. The police investigated her story and found out it was disingenuous only after John McCain and Sarah Palin called her and offered her their condolences. In 2003, pizza deliveryman Brian Wells came to a bank in Erie, Pa. with a bomb locked around his neck. He told police that group of Black men had taken him hostage and put the bomb there. After receiving close to $9,000, the pizza man was blown to bits by the bomb. Police would later find out that Wells was in on the plot with a few of his white friends. These separate incidents speak to the larger phenomenon of how Black males are viewed in the society by both whites and Blacks.

Selected Bibliography

Abdul-Jabbar, Kareem, and Alan Steinberg. *Black Profiles in Courage: A Legacy of African-American Achievement*. New York: HarperCollins, 2000.

Achebe, Chinua. *Things Fall Apart*, 1959. New York: Anchor Books, 1999.

Adams, Janus. *Freedom Days: 365 Inspired Moments in Civil Rights History*. New York: John Wiley, 1998.

Allen, James, ed. *Without Sanctuary: Lynching Photography in America*. Santa Fe: Twin Palms Publishers, 2000.

Angelo, Bonnie. "The Pain of Being Black." *Time* May 22, 1989: 120–23.

Asante Jr., M. K. *It's Bigger Than Hip Hop: The Rise of the Post Hip Hop Generation*. New York: St. Martin's Press, 2008.

Asim, Jabari. ed. "Introduction: Twelve Moods for Justice." *Not Guilty: Twelve Black Men Speak Out on Law, Justice, and Life*. New York: Amistad, 2001. xiii–xxii.

———. "Black Man Standing." *Not Guilty: Twelve Black Men Speak Out on Law, Justice, and Life*. New York: Amistad, 2001. 25–40.

Babb, Valerie Melissa. *Ernest Gaines*. Boston: Twayne, 1991.

Baker Jr., Houston A. *Blues Ideology and African American Literature: A Vernacular Theory*. Chicago: University of Chicago Press, 1987.

———. *Singers of Daybreak: Studies in Black American Literature*. Washington, DC: Howard University Press, 1983.

———. "On Knowing Our Place." *Richard Wright: Critical Perspectives Past and Present*. New York: Amistad Press, 1993. 200–25.

Banner, Stuart. "Traces of Slavery: Race and the Death Penalty in Historical Perspective." *From Lynch Mobs to the Killing State: Race and the Death Penalty in America*. Edited by Charles J. Ogletree Jr. and Austin Sarat. New York: New York University Press, 2006. 96–113.

Bardolph, Richard ed. *The Civil Rights Record: Black America and the Law, 1849–1970*. New York: Thomas Y. Crowell, Co., 1970.

Barksdale, Richard and Kenneth Kinnamon. *Black Writers of America: A Comprehensive Anthology*. New York: Macmillan Company, 1972.

Barretini, Mark. "Transgression, Racialed Policing and the Limits of Identity: *Deep cover*" *Journal of Criminal Justice and Popular Culture*. 10.3. (2004) 148–60.

Batista, Judy. "Vick Finishes His Sentence; Future Is Cloudy." *New York Times* (July 21, 2009): 12.

Bell, Bernard W. *The Contemporary African American Novel: Its Folk Roots and Modern Literary Branches*. Amherst: University of Massachusetts Press, 2004.

Bell, Derrick. *Faces at the Bottom of the Well: The Permanence of Racism.* New York: Basic Books, 1992.

————. "Police Brutality Portent of Disaster and Discomforting Divergence." *Police Brutality: An Anthology.* Edited by Jill Nelson. New York: W. W. Norton & Company, 2000. 88–101.

————.*And We Are Not Saved: The Elusive Quest for Racial Justice.* New York: Basic Books, Inc., 1987.

Bennett, Juda. *The Passing Figure: Racial Confusion in Modern American Literature.* New York: Peter Lang Publishing, 1996.

Bennett, Lerone. *The Challenge of Blackness.* Chicago: Johnson Publishing Company, 1972.

Benson, Kimberly W. "Re-Weaving the 'Ulysses Scene': Enchantment, Post-Oedipal Identity, and the Buried Text of Blackness in Toni Morrison's *Song of Solomon.*" *Comparative American Identities: Race, Sex, and Nationality in the Modern Text.* Ed. Hortense J. Spillers. London: Routledge, 1991. 87–109.

Berger, Roger A. " 'Black Dick': Race, Sexuality, and Discourse in the L.A. Novels of Walter Mosley." *African American Review* 31.2 (1997): 281–94.

Berry, Mary Frances. *Black Resistance, White Law: A History of Constitutional Racism in America.* New York: Penguin Group, 1994.

Blassingame, John W. *The Slave Community: Plantation Life in the Antebellum South.* New York: Oxford University Press, 1974.

Blount, Marcellus and George Cunningham, eds. "Introduction." *Representing Black Men.* New York: Routledge, 1996.

Bogle, Donald. *Toms, Coons, Mulattos, Mammies and Bucks.* New York: Continuum Publishing Co., 1989.

Bonilla-Silva, Eduardo. *Racism without Racists: Color-Blind Racist and the Persistence of Racial Inequality in the United States.* Lanham,MD: Rowman and Littlefield, 2003.

Boothe, Demico. *Why Are So Many Black Men in Prison?* New York: Full Surface Publishing, 2007.

Bright, Stephen B. "Discrimination, Death, and Denial: The Tolerance of Racial Discrimination in Infliction of the Death Penalty." *From Lynch Mobs to the Killing State: Race and the Death Penalty in America.* Edited by Charles J. Ogletree Jr. and Austin Sarat. New York: New York University Press, 2006. 211–59.

Brooks, Peter. *Reading for the Plot: Design and Intention in Narrative.* New York: Vintage Books, 1984.

Brown, Richard Maxwell. *Strain of Violence: Historical Studies of American Violence and Vigilantism.* New York: Oxford University Press, 1975.

Browne-Marshall, Gloria J. *Race, Law, and American Society: 1607 to Present.* Foreword by Derrick Bell. New York: Routledge, 2007.

Brundage, W. Fitzhugh. *Lynching in the New South: Georgia and Virginia, 1889–1930.* Urbana: University of Illinois Press, 1993.

Bryant, Jerry H. *Victims and Heroes: Racial Violence in the African American Novel.* Amherst: University of Massachusetts Press, 1997.

Buckley, Gail. *American Patriots: The Story of Blacks in the Military from the Revolution to Desert Storm.* New York: Random House, 2001.

Butler, Judith. *The Psychic Life of Power.* Stanford: Stanford University Press, 1997.

Camper, Carol. "Into the Mix." *Miscegenation Blues: Voices of Mixed Raced Women.* Edited by Carol Camper. Toronto: Black Women and Women of Color Press, 1994. xv–xxxiii.

Carby, Hazel. *Race Men*. Cambridge: Harvard University Press, 1998.

Carruthers, Jacob H. *Intellectual Warfare*. Chicago: Third World Press, 1999.

Cash, W. J. *The Mind of the South*. New York: Alfred Knopf, 1941.

Cassuto, Leonard. *The Inhuman Race: The Racial Grotesque in American Literature and Culture*. New York: Columbia University Press, 1997.

Caweiti, John G. *Adventure, Mystery, and Romance: Formula Stories as Art and Popular Culture*. Chicago: University of Chicago Press, 1976.

Chafe, William H. Raymond Gavins and Robert Korstad, eds. *Remembering Jim Crow: African Americans Tell About Life in the Segregated South*. New York: The New Press, 2001.

Chang, Jeff. *Can't Stop Won't Stop: A History of the Hip Hop Generation*. Introduction by DJ Kool Herc. New York: St. Martin's Press, 2005.

Chodorow, Nancy. *The Reproduction of Mothering: Psychoanalysis and the Sociology of Gender*. Los Angeles: University Press of California, 1978.

Christianson, Scott. *Notorious Prisons: An Inside Look at the World's Most Feared Institutions*. London: The Lyons Press, 2004.

Coale, Samuel. *The Mystery of Mysteries: Cultural Differences and Designs*. Bowling Green: Bowling Green State University Popular Press, 2000.

Cohen, William. *At Freedom's Edge: Black Mobility and the Southern White Quest for Racial Control, 1861–1915*. Baton Rouge: Louisiana State University Press, 1991.

Coles, Robert A. "Richard Wright's *The Outsider:* A Novel in Transition." *Modern Language Studies* 13.3 (1983): 53–61.

Collier-Thomas, Bettye and V. P. Franklin. *My Soul Is a Witness: A Chronology of the Civil Rights Era 1954–1965*. New York: Holt, 2000.

Conrad, Joseph. *Heart of Darkness*. Original 1902. New York: W. W. Norton & Company, 2006.

Cooper, Christopher. "Meditation in Black and White: Unequal Distribution of Empowerment by Police." *Not Guilty: Black Men Speak Out on Law, Justice, and Life*. Edited by Jabari Asim. New York: Amistad, 2001. 125–41.

Cooper, John. *You Can Hear Them Knocking: A Study in the Policing of America*. New York: Kennikat Press, 1981.

Cose, Ellis. *The Rage of a Privileged Class*. New York: HarperCollins Publishers, 1993

Crooks, Robert. "From the Far Side of the Frontier: The Detective Fiction of Chester Himes and Walter Mosley." *College Literature* 22.3 (1994): 68–89.

Crouch, Stanley. "What's New? The Truth, As Usual." *Police Brutality: An Anthology*. Edited by Jill Nelson. New York: W. W. Norton & Company, 2000. 157–68.

Cunningham, George P. " 'Called Into Existence': Desire, Gender, and Voice in Frederick Douglass's *Narrative* of 1845." *Differences: A Journal of Feminist Cultural Studies* 1.3 (1989):108–35.

Dalton, Harlon L. *Racial Healing: Confronting the Fear Between Blacks and Whites*. New York: Doubleday, 1995.

Daniels, Cora. *Ghettonation: A Journey into the Land of Bling and the Home of the Shameless*. New York: Doubleday, 2007.

Daniels, Ron. "The Crisis of Police Brutality and Misconduct in America: The Causes and the Cure." Edited by Jill Nelson. *Police Brutality: An Anthology*. New York: W. W. Norton & Company, 2000. 240–60.

Davey, Monica and Gretchen Ruethling. "After 50 Years, Emmett Louis Till's Body Is Exhumed." *New York Times* (June 2, 2005): 20.

Davis, Allison. *Love, Leadership and Aggression: The Psychological Factors in the Making of Four Black Leaders.* San Diego: Harcourt, Brace, Jovanovich Publishers, 1983.

Davis, Angela. *Women, Race, & Class.* New York: Vintage Books, 1983.

Davis, Robert Con ed. *The Fictional Father: Lacanian Reading of the Text.* Amherst: The University of Massachusetts Press, 1981.

———. ed. *Lacan and Narration: The Psychoanalytic Difference in Narrative Theory.* Baltimore: Johns Hopkins University Press, 1983.

Dawahare, Anthony. *Nationalism, Marxism, and African American Literature Between the Wars: A New Pandora's Box.* Jackson: University Press of Mississippi, 2003.

Delgado, Richard and Jean Stefancic. *Understanding Words That Wound.* Boulder, CO: Westview, 2004.

Dickson-Carr, Darryl. *African American Satire: The Sacredly Profane Novel.* Columbia: University of Missouri Press, 2001.

Douglass, Frederick. *Narrative of the Life of Frederick Douglass.* 1845. *The Classic Slave Narratives.* Ed. Henry Louis Gates Jr. New York: NAL, 1987. 241–331.

———. *My Bondage and My Freedom.* Edited and with an Introduction by William L. Andrews. Chicago: University of Illinois Press, 1987.

Du Bois, W. E. B. *The Gift of Black Folk: The Negroes in the Making of America.* Introduction by Truman Nelson. New York: Washington Square Press, 1970.

———. *Philadelphia Negro.* 1889. New York: Cosimo Classics, 2007.

Dworkin, Andrea. *Intercourse.* New York: The Free Press, 1987.

Dyson, Michael Eric. *The Michael Dyson Reader.* New York: Basic Books, 2004.

———. *Open Mike: Reflections on Philosophy, Race, Sex, Culture, and Religion.* New York: Basic Books, 2003.

———. *Can You hear Me Now?: The Inspiration, Wisdom and Insight of Michael Eric Dyson.* New York: Basic Books, 2009.

———. *Come Hell or High Water: Hurricane Katrina and the Color of Disaster.* New York: Civitas, 2006.

———. *Is Bill Cosby Right? Or Has the Black Middle Class Lost Its Mind?* New York: Basic Civitas, 2005.

———. *Reflecting Black.* Minneapolis: University of Minneapolis Press, 1993.

Eckholm, Erik. "Plight Deepens for Black Men, Studies Warn." (*New York Times,* July 17, 2009): 18.

Eilberg-Schwartz, Howard and Wendy Doniger, eds. *Off with Her Head: The Denial of Women's Identity in Myth, Religion, and* Culture. Berkeley: University of California Press, 1995.

Ellison, Ralph. *Going to the Territory.* New York: Vintage Books, 1986.

———. *Shadow and Act.* New York: Vintage Books, 1972.

Enaharo, Khari. *Race Code War: The Power of Words, Images and Symbols on the Black Psyche.* Chicago: African American Images, 2003.

Eyerman, Ron. *Cultural Trauma: Slavery and the Formation of African American Identity.* New York: Cambridge University Press, 2001.

Fabre, Michel. *The Unfinished Quest of Richard Wright.* Translated from the French by Isabel Barzum. Chicago: University of Illinois Press, 1993.

Fanon, Frantz. *Black Skin, White Masks.* New York: Grove Press, 1967.

———. *The Wretched of the Earth.* Preface by J.-P. Sartre. Trans. Constance Farrington. New York: Grove, 1968.

Feagin, Joe R. "The Continuing Significance of Race: Anti-Black Discrimination in Public Places." *American Sociological Review* 56 (1991): 101–16.

Ferguson, Ann Arnett. *Bad Boys: Public Schools in the Making of Black Masculinity.* Ann Arbor: University of Michigan Press, 2001.

Fishkin, Shelley Fisher. "Interrogating 'Whiteness,' Complicating 'Blackness': Remapping American Culture." *Criticism and the Color Line: Desegregating American Literary Studies.* Edited by Henry B. Wonham. New Brunswick: Rutgers University Press, 1996. 251–90.

Foner, Eric. *Nothing but Freedom: Emancipation and Its Legacy.* Baton Rouge: Louisiana State University Press, 1983.

Foucault, Michel. *Discipline & Punish: The Birth of the Prison.* New York: Vintage Books, 1995.

——. "Two Lectures." *Power/Knowledge: Selected Interviews and Other Writings, 1972–1977.* Ed. Colin Gordon. Trans. Colin Gordon, et al. New York: Pantheon, 1980. 78–108.

Franklin, V. P. *Black Self-Determination: A Cultural History of African-American Resistance.* With a foreword by Mary Frances Berry. New York: Lawrence Hill Books, 1992.

Freeman, Gregory A. *Lay This Body Down: The 1921 Murders of Eleven Plantation Slaves.* Chicago: Lawrence Hill Books, 1999.

Freese, Peter. *The Ethnic Detective: Chester Himes, Harry Kemelman, Tony Hillerman.* Abeiten zur Amerikanistik 10. Essen: Blaue Eule, 1992.

Freud, Sigmund. *Beyond the Pleasure Principle.* Original 1922. New York: W. W. Norton, 1961.

——. *The Ego and the Id.* London: Hogarth, 1962.

Friedman, Lawrence M. "*Brown* in Context." *Race, Law, & Culture: Reflections on Brown v. Board of Education.* Edited by Austin Sarat. New York: Oxford University Press, 1997. 49–73.

Gaines, Ernest J. *A Lesson Before Dying.* New York: Vintage Books, 1993

——. *Mozart and Leadbelly: Stories and Essays.* New York: Alfred A. Knopf, 2005.

——. "The Sky Is Gray." 1968. *Bloodline.* New York: Norton, 1976. 83–120.

Galdwell, Malcolm. *Blink: The Power of Thinking without Thinking.* New York: Little Brown, 2005.

Garrod, Andrew, ed. *Souls Looking Back: Life Stories of Growing Up Black.* With a foreword by James Comer. New York: Routledge, 2008.

Gates Jr., Henry Louis. *Thirteen Ways of Looking at a Black Man.* New York: Vintage Books, 1998.

George, Nelson. *The Michael Jackson Story.* New York: Dell, 1984.

Gilmore, Brian. "Twisted Street Logic." *Not Guilty: Twelve Black Men Speak Out on Law, Justice, and Life.* Edited by Jabari Asim. New York: Amistad, 2001. 39–52.

Gilroy, Paul. *Against Race: Imaging Political Culture beyond the Color Line.* Cambridge: Harvard University Press, 2000.

Ginsburg, Ralph. *100 Years of Lynching.* 1962. Baltimore: Black Classics Press, 1988.

Girard, Rene. *Deceit, Desire, and the Novel: Self and Other in Literary Structure.* Baltimore: Johns Hopkins University Press, 1965.

GoldSmith, Meredith. "Shopping to Pass, Passing to Shop: Bodily Self Fashioning in the Fiction of Nella Larsen. In Recovering the Back Female Body: Self Representation by African American Women. Edited by Michael Bennett and Varessa D. Dickerson. New Brunswick: Rutgers University Press, 2000, 97–120.

Gould, Stephen J. *The Mismeasure of Man.* New York: W. W. Norton & Company, 1981.

Graham, Lawrence Otis. *Our Kind of People: Inside America's Black Upper Class.* New York: HarperPerennial, 1999.

Graham, Maryemma. "The Fusion of Ideas: An Interview with Margaret Walker Alexander." *African American Review* 27.2: 279–86.

Hacker, Andrew. *Two Nations: Black and White, Separate, Hostile, Unequal.* New York: Ballantine Books, 1993.

Halberstam, David. *The Powers That Be.* New York: Alfred A. Knopf, 1979.

Harper, Philip Brian. *Are We Not Men?: Masculine Anxiety and the Problem of African-American Identity.* New York: Oxford University Press, 1996.

Harris, Cheryl I. "Whiteness as Property." *Harvard Law Review* 106.8 (1993): 1706–91.

Harris, Trudier. *Exorcizing Blackness: Historical and Literary Lynching and Burning Rituals.* Bloomington: Indiana University Press, 1984.

Hartman, Saidiya V. *Scenes of Subjection: Terror, Slavery and Self-Making in Nineteenth-Century America.* New York: Oxford University Press, 1997.

Henn, T. R. *The Harvest of Tragedy.* London: Methuen, 1956.

Herman, Judith. *Trauma and Recovery: The Aftermath of Violence from Domestic Abuse to Political Terror.* New York: Ballantine Books, 1992.

Himes, Chester Borum. *The Third Generation.* 1954. New York: Thunder Mouth Press, 1989.

———. *The Quality of Hurt: The Early Years, The Autobiography of Chester Himes.* 1972. New York: Paragon House, 1990.

———. *My Life of Absurdity.* New York: Paragon, 1990.

———. *If He Hollers Let Him Go.* New York: Thunder's Mouth Press, 1988.

Ho, Karen and Wende Elizabeth Marshall. "Criminality and Citizenship: Implicating the White Nation." In *Race Consciousness: African American Studies for the New Century.* Eds. Judith Jackson Fossett and Jeffrey A. Tucker. New York: New York University Press, 1997. 208–27.

Holland, Sharon Patricia. *Raising the Dead: Readings of Death and (Black) Subjectivity.* Durham: Duke University Press, 2000.

Holloway, Karla F. C. *Codes of Conduct: Race, Ethics and the Color of Our Character.* New Brunswick, NJ: Rutgers University Press, 1992.

———. *Passed On: African American Mourning Stories.* Durham: Duke University Press, 2002.

Holt, Elvin and William H. Jackson. "Reconstructing Black Manhood: Message and Meaning in Spike Lee's *Get On The Bus.* *CLA Journal* 47.4 (2004): 409–25.

hooks, bell. *Black Looks: Race and Representation.* Boston: South End Press, 1992.

———. *Killing Rage: Ending Racism.* New York: Henry Holt, 1995.

———. *Outlaw Culture: Resisting Representation.* New York: Routledge, 1994.

———. *Rock My Soul: Black People and Self-Esteem.* New York: Washington Square Press, 2003.

Huggins, Nathan Irvin. *Revelations: American History, American Myths.* New York: Oxford University Press, 1995.

Hugh, Holton. *The Thin Black Line: True Stories by Black Law Enforcement Officers Policing America' Meanest Streets.* New York: Tom Doherty Associates, LLC., 2008.

Hughes, Riley. "Review of *The Third Generation* by Charles Himes." *Catholic World* (April 1954): 72.

Hutchinson, Earl Ofari. *The Assassination of the Black Male Image.* New York: Touchstone, 1994.

Hyder Sr., Donnie A. *Leave White Folks Alone: Black People Stop Blaming White Folks for Your Problems.* Atlanta: Wyndham House Publishers, Inc., 2008.

Jackson. Florence. *The Black Man in America, 1932–1954.* New York: Franklin Watts Inc., 1975.

Jackson Jr., John L. *Racial Paranoia: The Unintended Consequences of Political Correctness.* New York: Basic Books, 2008.

Jackson, Kenneth T. *The Ku Klux Klan in the City, 1915–1930.* New York: Oxford University Press, 1967.

Jackson, Michael. *Moonwalk.* New York: Doubleday, 1998.

Jacobson, Mark. *American Gangster and Other Tales of New York.* Foreword by Richard Price. New York: Black Cat, 2007.

Jameson, Fredric. *The Political Unconscious: The Narrative as a Socially Symbolic Act.* Ithaca: Cornell University Press, 1981.

Jefferson, Margo. *On Michael Jackson.* New York: Vintage Books, 2007.

Jefferson, Thomas. *Notes on the State of Virginia.* Original 1782. Reprint: New York: W. W. Norton & Co., 1987.

Johnson, James Weldon. *The Autobiography of an Ex-Colored Man.* New York: Barnes and Noble, 2007.

Johnson, Matt. *Incognegro: A Graphic Mystery.* Art by Warren Pleece. New York: DC Comics, 2008.

Joyce, Joyce Ann. *Richard Wright's Art of Tragedy.* Iowa City: University of Iowa Press, 1986.

———. *Warriors, Conjurers and Priests: Defining African-centered Literary Criticism.* Chicago: Third World Press, 1994.

Kafka, Frantz. "In the Penal Colony" *The Complete Stories.* Edited by Nathan Glazer. New York: Schocken, 1971.

Katznelson, Ira. *When Affirmative Action Was White: An Untold History of Racial Inequality in Twentieth-Century America.* New York: W. W. Norton & Company, 2005.

Kaufman, Michael. "The Construction of Masculinity and the Triad of Men's Violence." In *Men's Lives.* Edited by Michael Kimmel and Michael A. Messner. Boston: Allyn and Bacon, 1999. 4–17.

Kaufman-Osborn, Timothy V. "Capital Punishment as Legal Lynching?" *From Lynch Mobs to the Killing State: Race and the Death Penalty in America.* Edited by Charles J. Ogletree Jr. and Austin Sarat. New York: New York University Press, 2006. 21–54.

Kelly, Robin D. G. *Race Rebels: Culture. Politics, and the Black Working Class.* New York: The Free Press, 1994.

Kennedy, Randall. *Sellout: The Politics of Racial Betrayal.* New York: Vintage Books, 2009.

———. *Nigger.* New York: Pantheon, 2002.

Killens, John Oliver. *Youngblood.* Original 1954. Athens: Georgia University Press, 1982.

King, Debra Walker. *African Americans and the Culture of Pain.* Charlottesville: University of Virginia Press, 2008.

King, Joyce. *Hate Crime.* New York: Penguin Books, 2002.

Kitwana, Bakari. *The Hip Hop Generation: Young Blacks and the Crisis in African-American Culture.* New York: Basic Civitas Books, 2002.

Kluger, Richard. *Simple Justice.* New York: Alfred A. Knopf, 1976.

Kopkind, Andrew. "The Stuart Case: Race, Class and Murder in Boston" *The Nation,* February 5, 1990, 250: 153.

Larsen, Charles, ed. *An Intimation of Things Distant: The Collected Fiction of Nella Larsen.* New York: Doubleday, 1992.

Leary, Joy Degruy. *Post Traumatic Slave Syndrome: America's Legacy of Enduring Inquiry and Healing.* With a foreword by Randall Robinson. Milwaukie, Oregon: Uptone Press, 2005.

Lee, Spike. *That's My Story and I'm Sticking to It*. As told to Kaleem Attab. New York: W. W. Norton & Company, 2005.

———. *Do The Right Thing*. New York: Fireside, 1989.

Lefort, Claude. *Democracy and Political Theory*. Trans. David Macey. Cambridge: Polity, 1988.

Lemann, Nicholas. *The Promised Land: The Great Black Migration and How It Changed America*. New York: Vintage Books, 1992.

Lesser, Wendy. *Picture at an Execution: An Inquiry into the Subject of Murder*. Cambridge: Harvard University Press, 1993.

Lipsitz, George. *The Possessive Investment in Whiteness: How White People Profit from Identity Politics*. Philadelphia: Temple University Press, 1998.

Litwack, Leon F. *Trouble in Mind: Black Southerners in the Age of Jim Crow*. New York: Vintage Press, 1999.

———. *Been in the Storm So Long: The Aftermath of Slavery*. New York: Vintage Books, 1979.

Lock, Helen. "Invisible Detection: The Case of Walter Mosley." MELUS 26.1 (2001): 77–89.

Loewen, James E. *Sundown Towns: A Hidden Dimension of American Racism*. New York: The New Press, 2005.

Lopez, Ian F. Haney. *White by Law: The Legal Construction of Race*. New York: New York University Press, 1996.

Lott, Tommy L. *The Invention of Race: Black Culture and the Politics of Representation*. Malden, MA: Blackwell Publishers, 1999.

Lowe, John, ed. *Conversations with Ernest Gaines*. Jackson: University of Mississippi Press, 1995.

Lui, Meizhu, Barbara Robles, Betsy Leonard-Wright, Rose Brewer, and Rebecca Adamson, with United for a Fair Economy. *The Color of Wealth: The Story Behind the U.S. Racial Wealth Divide*. New York: The New Press, 2006.

Lynch, Michael F. "Haunted by Innocence: The Debate with Dostoevsky in Wright's 'Other Novel,' *The Outsider*." *African American Review* 30.2 (1996): 255–266.

Majors, Richard and Janet Mancini Billson. *Cool Pose: The Dilemmas of Black Manhood in America*. New York: Lexington Books, 1992.

Mann, Corame Richey and Marjorie Zatz, eds. *Images of Color/ Images of Crime*. Los Angeles: Roxbury, 2002.

Marable, Manning. *The Great Well of Democracy: The Meaning of Race in America*. Basic Civitas, 2002.

———. "The Black Male: Searching Beyond Stereotypes." In *Men's Lives*. Edited by Michael Kimmel and Michael A. Messner. Boston: Allyn and Bacon, 1999. 18–24. (indent?)

———. *Race, Reform, and Rebellion: The Second Reconstruction and Beyond in Black America, 1945–2006*. Jackson, MS: University of Mississippi, 2007.

———. *Living Black History: How Reimagining the African-American Past Can Remake America's Racial Future*. New York: Basic Civitas, 2006.

Mason Jr., Theodore O. "Walter Mosley's Easy Rawlins: The Detective and Afro-American Fiction." *Kenyon Review* 14.4 (1992): 173–83.

May, Rollo. *Power and Innocence: The Search for the Sources of Violence*. New York: Basic Books, 1973.

McCall, Nathan. *Makes Me Wanna Hollar: A Young Black Man in America*. New York: Vintage 1994.

McCollough, Bob. "PW Interviews Walter Mosley." *Publishers Weekly* 23 May 1994: 67–68.

McDowell, Deborah E. "Boundaries: Or Distant Relations and Close Kin." *Afro-American Literary Study in the 1990s.* Edited by Houston A. Baker, Jr. and Patricia Redmond. Chicago: The University of Chicago Press, 1989. 51–77.

McIntyre, Charshee C. L. *Criminalizing a Race: Free Blacks During Slavery.* New York: Kayode Publications, Ltd., 1992.

McMahon, Frank. "Rereading *The Outsider:* Double Consciousness and the Divided Self." *Mississippi Quarterly* (Fall 1997) 50.4: 288–305.

McMillen, Neil R. *The Citizen's Council: Organized Resistance to the Second Reconstruction 1954–64.* Chicago: University of Illinois Press, 1994.

Messerschmidt, James. *Masculinities and Crime: Critique and Reconceptualization of Theory.* Lanham, MD: Rowman & Littlefield Publishers, Inc., 1993.

Michaels, Walter Benn. "The Souls of White Folks." *Literature and the Body: Essays on Populations and Persons.* Edited by Elaine Scarry. Baltimore: The Johns Hopkins University Press, 1990. 185–209.

Miller, Jody. *Getting Played: African Americans Girls) Urban Inequality and Gendered Violence.* New York: New York University, 2008.

Milliken, Stephen F. *Chester Himes: A Critical Appraisal.* Columbia: University of Missouri Press, 1976.

Mizell, Linda. *Racism.* New York: Walker and Company, 1992.

Moore, Suzanne. "Here's Looking at You, Kid!" In *The Female Gaze: Women as Viewers of Popular Culture.* Edited by Lorraine Gamman and Margaret Marshment. Seattle: The Real Comet Press, 1989. 44–59.

Morgan, Edmund. *American Slavery, American Freedom: The Ordeal of Colonial America.* New York: Norton, 1975.

Morrison, Toni. "On the Backs of Blacks." *Time* Special Issue, "The New Face of America" (Fall 1993): 57. *Sula,* 1973. New York: Penguin 1992.

Mosley, Walter. *Devil in a Blue Dress.* New York: W. W. Norton & Company, Inc., 1990.

———. *Workin' on the Chain Gang: Shaking Off the Dead Hand of History.* New York: The Ballantine Publishing Group, 2000.

———. "On the Other Side of Those Mean Streets." Interview with Charles L. P. Silet. *Armchair Detective* 26.4 (1993): 8–19.

Muffler, John P. "Education and the Separate but Equal Doctrine." *Black Scholar* 17.3 (1986): 35–41.

Murray, Albert. *The Omni-Americans: Black Experience & Culture.* New York: Vantage Books, 1983.

Neal, Mark Anthony. "Just Another 'Nigga': Reflection on Black Masculinity and Middle-Class Identity." *Not Guilty: Black Men Speak Out on Law, Justice, and Life.* Edited by Jabari Asim. New York: Amistad 2001. 1–13.

Nelson, Jill, ed. "Introduction." *Police Brutality: An Anthology.* New York: W. W. Norton & Company, 2000.

Nordan, Lewis. *Wolf Whistle: A Novel.* Chapel Hill: Algonquin Books of Chapel Hill, 2003.

Nussbaum, Martha. *Poetic Justice: The Literary Imagination and the Public Life.* New York: Beacon Press, 1997.

Ogdon, Bethany. "Hard-Boiled Ideology." *Critical Quarterly* 34.1 (1992): 71–87.

Ogletree Jr., Charles J. "Making Race Matter in Death Matters." *From Lynch Mobs to the Killing State: Race and the Death Penalty in America.* Edited by Charles J. Ogletree Jr. and Austin Sarat. New York: New York University Press, 2006. 55–95.

Ogletree Jr., Charles J. and Austin Sarat. "Introduction." *From Lynch Mobs to the Killing State: Race and the Death Penalty.* New York: New York University Press, 2006.

Oliver, William. *The Violent Social World of Black Men.* New York: Lexington, 1994.

Papa, Lee. " 'His feet on your neck': The New Religion in the Works of Ernest J. Gaines." *African American Review* 27.2: 187–93.

Parenti, Christian. *Lockdown America: Police and Prisons in the Age of Crisis.* New York: Verso, 2000.

Patterson, Orlando. *Rituals of Blood: Consequences of Slavery in Two American Centuries.* New York: Basic Books, 1998.

———. *The Ordeal of Integration: Progress and Resentment in America's Racial Crisis.* Washington, DC: Counterpoint, 1998.

—. *Slavery and Social Death: A Comparative Study.* New York: Oxford University Press, 1982.

Preston, Rohan. "Police State of Mind." *Not Guilty: Black Men Speak Out on Law, Justice, and Life.* Edited by Jabari Asim. New York: Amistad, 2001. 153–164.

Rampersad, Arnold. *Ralph Ellison: A Biography.* New York: Vintage Books, 2008.

Rand, William E. "Chester Himes as a Naturalistic Writer in the Tradition of Richard Wright and Theodore Dreiser." *CLA Journal* 44.4 (2001): 442–50.

Rankin, J. E. "Tribute by the Rev. J. E. Rankin. D. D., President of Howard University." *In Memoriam, Frederick Douglass.* Philadephia:Yorston, 1987: 32–38.

Reed, Ishmael. "The Author and His Works, Chester Himes: Writer." *Black World* 22.5 (March 1972): 24–38.

———. *Airing Dirty Laundry.* New York: Addison-Wesley Publishing Company, 1994.

Ro, Ronin. *Gangsta: Merchandising Rhymes of Violence.* New York: St. Martin's Press, 1996.

Roberts, Dorothy. *Killing the Black Body: Race, Reproduction, and the Meaning of Liberty.* New York: Pantheon Books, 1997.

Robin, Corey. *Fear: The History of a Political Idea.* New York: Oxford University Press, 2004.

Robinson, Devin A. and Veron Roper. *Blacks: From the Plantations to the Prison.* Fayetteville: Going Against the Grain Publications, 2008.

Robinson, Randall. *Quitting America: The Departure of a Black Man from His Native Land.* New York: Penguin Books, 2004.

———. *The Debt: What America Owes to Blacks.* New York: Penguin Group, 2000.

Rowey, Hazel. *Richard Wright: The Life and Times.* Chicago: The University of Chicago Press, 2001.

Royster, Deirdre A. *Race and the Invisible Hand: How White Networks Exclude Black Men from Blue-Collar Jobs.* Berkeley: University of California Press, 2003.

Russell, Katheryn K. " 'What Did I Do to Be So Black and Blue?' Police Violence and the Black Community." *Police Brutality: An Anthology.* Edited by Jill Nelson. New York: W. W. Norton & Company, 2000. 135–48.

Russell, Kathy, Midge Wilson and Ronald Hall. *The Color Complex: The Politics of Skin Color Among African Americans.* New York: Harcourt Brace Jovanovich Publishers, 2000.

Sallis, James. *Chester Himes: A Life.* New York: Walker & Company, 2000.

Savran, David. *Taking It Like A Man: White Masculinity, Masochism, and Contemporary American Culture.* Princeton: Princeton University Press, 1998.

Scott, Daryl Michael. *Contempt and Pity: Social Policy and the Image of the Damaged Black Psyche, 1880–1996.* Chapel Hill: University of North Carolina Press, 1997.

Scruggs, Charles. *Sweet Home: Invisible Cities and the Afro-American Novel.* Baltimore: Johns Hopkins University Press, 1993.

Sharkey, Joe. *Deadly Greed: The Stuart Murder Case in Boston and the 1980s.* New York: Prentice Hall, 1991.

Sharpton, Reverend Al with Karen Hunter. *Al on America.* New York: Kensington Publishing Corp., 2002.

Sherman, Charlotte Watson. "Walter Mosley on the Black Male Hero." *American Visions* 10.4 (1995): 34–37.

Smith, Damu. "The Upsurge of Police Repression." *The Black Scholar* 12.1 (1985): 45.

Smith, Valerie. *Not Just Race, Not Just Gender: Black Feminist Readings.* New York: Routledge, 1998.

Sniderman, Paul M. and Thomas Piazza. *The Scar of Race.* Cambridge: The Belknap Press, 1993.

Soitos, Stephen F. "Black Detective Fiction." *Mystery and Suspense Writers: The Literature of Crime, Detection, and Espionage* II. Eds. Robin W. Winks and Maureen Corrigan. New York: Scribner's, 1998. 995–1008.

———. *The Blues Detective: A Study of African American Detective Fiction.* Amherst: University of Massachusetts Press, 1996.

Spencer, Jon Michael. *The New People: The Mixed-Race Movement in America.* With a foreword by Richard E. Van Der Ross. New York: New York University Press, 1977.

Spillers, Hortense. "Mama's Baby, Papa's Maybe: An American Grammar Book." *Black White, and in Color: Essays on American Literature and Culture by Hortense (OK TO ADD?) Spillers.* Chicago: Chicago University Press, 2003. 203–29.

Stamper, Norm. *Breaking Rank: A Top Cop's Expose of the Dark Side of American Policing.* New York: Nation Books, 2005.

Stein, Thomas Michael. "The Ethnic Vision in Walter Mosley's Crime Fiction." *Amerika Studien/American Studies* (Amsterdam) 39.2 (1994): 197–212.

Stoddard, Lothdrop. *The Rising Tide of Color.* New York: Blue Ribbon Books, 1920.

Suggs, Jon-Christian. *Whispered Consolations: Law and Narrative in African American Life.* Ann Arbor: The University of Michigan Press, 2000.

Sundquist, Eric J., ed. *Frederick Douglass: New Literary and Historical Essays.* New York: Cambridge University Press, 1990.

Takaki, Ronald. *Violence in the Black Imagination: Essays and Documents.* New York: Oxford UP, 1993.

Tal, Kali. *Worlds of Hurt: Reading the Literatures of Trauma.* Cambridge: Cambridge University Press, 1996.

Taraborrelli, J. Randy. *The Magic and the Madness.* New York: Ballantine Books, 1991.

Tate, Claudia. *Desire and the Protocols of Race: Black Novels and Psychoanalysis.* New York: Oxford University Press, 1997.

Thomas, Alexander and Samuel Sillen. *Racism and Psychiatry.* Introduction by Kenneth B. Clark. New York: Carol Publishing Group, 1993.

Thomas, H. Nigel. "The Bad Nigger Figure in Selected Works of Richard Wright, William Melvin Keey and Ernest Gaines." *CLA Journal* 39.2 (1995) 143–164.

Thompson, Carlyle Van. *Eating the Black Body: Miscegenation as Sexual Consumption in African American Literature and Culture.* New York: Peter Lang Publishing Inc., 2006.

———. *The Tragic Black Buck: Racial Masquerading in the American Literary Imagination.* New York: Peter Lang Publishing Inc., 2004.

Till-Mobley, Mamie and Christopher Benson. *Death of Innocence: The Story of the Hate Crime That Changed America*. New York: Random House, 2003.

Troutt, David Dante. "The Race Industry, Brutality, and the Law of Mothers." *Not Guilty: Black Men Speak Out on Law, Justice, and Life*. Edited by Jabari Asim. New York: Amistad, 2001. 53–67.

———. *The Monkey Suit: And Other Short Fiction on African American Justice*. New York: The New Press, 1998.

Volosinov, V. N. *Freudianism: A Critical Sketch*. Bloomington: Indiana University Press, 1987.

Voogd, Jan. *Race Riots & Resistance: The Summer of 1919*. New York: Peter Lang Publishing Inc., 2008.

Wachtel, Paul L. *Race in the Mind of America: Breaking the Vicious Circle Between Blacks and Whites*. New York: Routledge, 1999.

Walker, David. "The Appeal in Four Articles, Together with a Preamle, to the Coloured Citizens of the World. *Norton Anthology of African American Literature*. Edited by Henry Louis Gates Jr. and Nellie Y. McKay. New York: W. W. Norton & Company, 1997. 179–90.

Walker, Margaret. *Richard Wright Daemonic Genius: A Portrait of the Man, A Critical Look at His Work*. New York: Amistad, 1988.

Wallace, Michele. *Invisibility Blues: From Pop to Theory*. New York: Verso, 1990.

Washington, Booker T. *Up from Slavery*. In *Three Negro Classics*. Edited by John Hope Franklin. New York: Avon Books, 1969.

Washington, James M., ed. *A Testament of Hope: The Essential Writings and Speeches of Martin Luther King Jr*. New York: Harper Collins, 1986.

Waters, Mary C. *Black Identities: West Indian Immigrant Dreams and American Realities*. Cambridge: Harvard University Press, 1997.

Watkins, S. Craig. *Hip Hop Matters: Politics. Pop Culture and the Struggle for the Soul of a Movement*. Boston: Beacon Press, 2005.

Weiner, Mark S. *Black Trials: Citizenship from the Beginnings of Slavery to the End of Caste*. New York: Vintage Books, 2006.

Wellman, David. *Portraits of White Racism*. New York: Cambridge University Press, 1993.

Wesley, Marilyn C. "Power and Knowledge in Walter Mosley's *Devil in a Blue Dress*." *African American Review* 35.1: 103–16.

West, Cornel. *Race Matters*. Boston: Beacon Press, 1993.

White, Hayden. *Tropics of Discourse: Essays in Cultural Criticism*. Baltimore: Johns Hopkins University Press, 1978.

———. *The Content of Form: Narrative Discourse and Historical Representation*. Baltimore: Johns Hopkins University Press, 1987.

Wiegman, Robyn. *American Anatomies: Theorizing Race and Gender*. Durham: Duke University Press, 1995.

Wildman, Stephanie M. and Adrienne D. Davis. "Language and Silence: Making Systems of Privilege Visible." *Critical Race Theory: The Cutting Edge*. Edited by Richard Delgado. Philadelphia: Temple University Press, 1995. 573–79.

Williams, John A. "My Man Himes: An Interview with Chester Himes." Eds. John A. Williams and Charles F. Harris. New York: Random House, 1970.

Williams, Juan. *Enough: The Phony Leaders, Dead-End Movement, and the Culture of Failure That Are Undermining Black America—and What We Can Do about It*. New York: Crown Publishers, 2006.

Williams, Patricia. *The Rooster's Egg: On the Persistence of Prejudice*. Cambridge: Harvard University Press, 1995.

Wilson, Amos N. *The Falsification of Afrikan Consciousness: Eurocentric History, Psychiatry and the Politics of White Supremacy*. New York: Afrikan World InfoSystems, 1993.

Wilson, William Julius. *More Than Just Race: Being Black and Poor in the Inner City*. New York: W. W. Norton & Company Inc., 2000.

———. *When Work Disappears: The World of the New Urban Poor*. New York: Knopf, 1996.

Wise, Tim. *White Like Me: Reflections on Race from a Privileged Son*. Berkeley: Soft Skull Press, 2008.

———. *Between Barack and a Hard Place: Racism and White Denial in the Age of Obama*. SanFrancisco: City Lights Books, 2009.

Woods, Paula L., ed. "Introduction." *Spooks, Spies and Private Eyes: Black Mystery, Crime and Suspense Fiction of the 20th Century*. New York: Doubleday, 1995. xv–xx.

Woodson, Carter G. *Mis-Education of the Negro*. Chicago: African American Images, 2000.

Woodward, C. Vann. *The Strange Career of Jim Crow*. New York: Oxford University Press, 1966.

Wright, Bobby. *The Psychopathic Racial Personality*. Chicago: Third World Press, 1984.

Wright, Bruce. *Black Robes, White Justice: Why Our legal System Doesn't Work for Blacks*. New York: Kensington, 2002.

Wright, Richard. *Black Boy: A Record of Childhood and Youth*. New York: Harper & Row, 1937.

———. *Native Son*. New York: Harper & Brothers Publishing, 1940.

———. "The Ethics of Living Jim Crow: An Autobiographic Sketch." In *Black Writers in America: A Comprehensive Anthology*. New York: Macmillan Publishing Company, 1972. 542–48.

———. *The Outsider*. 1953. Introduction by Maryemma Graham. New York: HarperCollins Publishers, 2003.

———. "The Man Who Lived Underground." *Eight Men: Stories by Richard Wright*. With a foreword by David Bradley. New York: Thunder Mouth Press, 1987. 27–92.

.———. *12 Million Black Voices*. New York: Thunder Mouth Press, 1991.

———. "Our Strange Birth." *Black Identity*. Edited by Frances E. Kearns. New York: Holt, Rinehart and Wilson, 1970. 5–13.

———. "How 'Bigger' Was Born." *Saturday Review*, 22 (1940): 19–20.

———. *Uncle Tom's Children*. Original 1940. New York: HarperPerennial, 1993.

———. *Rite of Passage*, New York: Harper Collins Publishers 1994.

Wu, Frank H. *Yellow: Race in America Beyond Black and White*. New York: Basic Books, 2002.

X, Malcolm, and Alex Haley. *The Autobiography of Malcolm X*. Original 1964. New York: Ballantine, 1992.

Youncy, George. *Black Bodies, White Gazes: The Continuing Siginificance of Race*. Lanham, Maryland: Rowman & Littlefield Publishers Inc. 2008.

Yarborough, Richard. "Race, Violence, and Manhood: The Masculine Ideal in Frederick Douglass's 'The Heroic Slave.'" *Haunted Bodies: Gender and Southern Texts*. Ed. Anne Goodwyn Jones and Susan V. Donaldson. Charlottesville: UP of Virginia, 1997. 159–84.

Zangrando, Robert L. *The NAACP Crusade Against Lynching, 1909–1950*. Philadelphia: Temple University Press, 1980.